Using Reflection and Metacognition to Improve Student Learning

Using Reflection and Metacognition to Improve Student Learning

Across the Disciplines, Across the Academy

Edited by Matthew Kaplan, Naomi Silver, Danielle LaVaque-Manty, and Deborah Meizlish

Foreword by James Rhem

New Pedagogies and Practices for Teaching in Higher Education series

Series Editors: James Rhem and Susan Slesinger

STERLING, VIRGINIA

Sty/us

Published by Stylus Publishing, LLC
22883 Quicksilver Drive
Sterling, Virginia 20166-2102

Library of Congress Cataloging-in-Publication Data
Using reflection and metacognition to improve
student learning : across the disciplines, across the
academy / edited by Matthew Kaplan, Naomi Silver,
Danielle LaVaque-Manty, and Deborah Meizlish ;
foreword by James Rhem.—1st ed.
p.   cm. — (New pedagogies and practices for
teaching in higher education series)
Includes bibliographical references and index.
ISBN 978-1-57922-824-8 (cloth : alk. paper)
ISBN 978-1-57922-825-5 (pbk. : alk. paper)
ISBN 978-1-57922-826-2 (library e-edition)
ISBN 978-1-57922-827-9 (consumer e-edition)
1. College teaching—Psychological aspects.   2. Learning,
Psychology of.   3. Metacognition.   I. Kaplan, Matthew
(Matthew Lee), editor of compilation.   II. Silver, Naomi,
editor of compilation.   III. LaVaque-Manty, Danielle,
1968- editor of compilation.   IV. Meizlish, Deborah,
editor of compilation.
LB2331.U85 2013
378.125—dc23
                                              2012042512

13-digit ISBN: 978-1-57922-824-8 (cloth)
13-digit ISBN: 978-1-57922-825-5 (paper)
13-digit ISBN: 978-1-57922-826-2 (Library e-edition)
13-digit ISBN: 978-1-57922-827-9 (Consumer e-book)

Printed in the United States of America

All first editions printed on acid-free paper
that meets the American National Standards Institute
Z39-48 Standard.

Bulk Purchases

Quantity discounts are available
for use in workshops and for staff
development.
Call 1-800-232-0223

First Edition, 2013

10   9   8   7   6   5   4

Contents

Acknowledgments

We are grateful to the talented authors who agreed to contribute chapters to this volume. Their work represents a wide range of disciplines and insights gained from direct experience in applying the literature on metacognition and reflection to promote deeper learning for students in their courses. We appreciate their willingness to share the lessons they've learned.

We also wish to thank the Teagle and Spencer foundations for support of the research program that gave rise to this book. Ours was one of thirteen projects funded under an initiative titled "Systematic Improvement of Undergraduate Education in Research Universities," headed by Robert Thompson of Duke University. We focused on the potential of metacognition to improve disciplinary thinking and writing. After James Rhem saw us present on our research at the annual meeting of the Professional and Organizational Development Network (POD), he approached us about the need for a volume that would make the fields of metacognition and reflection accessible to college teachers from across the academy and suggested we compile a volume on that topic for the series on New Pedagogies and Practices for Teaching in Higher Education, which he edits. We are grateful for his initial encouragement as well as his ongoing insight, which helped us shape the book.

Finally, this project would not have been possible without the support of our home departments, the University of Michigan's Center for Research on Learning and Teaching and Sweetland Center for Writing. Both gave us the time to pursue the research and the book project. We appreciate being part of two organizations that value scholarly inquiry and the dissemination of new ideas.

Foreword

Not that long ago, the word *pedagogy* didn't occur that often in faculty conversations about teaching. Today, one hears it frequently. Without putting too much weight on the prominence of a single word, subtle shifts in discourse, in vocabulary, often do mark significant shifts in thinking, and faculty thinking about teaching has changed over the last several decades. Faculty have always wanted to teach well, wanted their students to learn and succeed, but for a very long time faculty have taught as they were taught, and for the students who were like them in temperament and intelligence, the approach worked well enough. When only a highly filtered population of students sought higher education, the need to look beyond those approaches to teaching lay dormant. When a much larger and more diverse population began enrolling, the limits of traditional teaching emerged more sharply.

At the same time, intelligence itself became a more deeply understood phenomenon. Recognition of multiple kinds of intelligence—visual, auditory, kinesthetic, and so on (Gardner, 1983)—found wide acceptance, as did different styles of learning even within those different kinds of intelligence (e.g., Myers-Briggs et al.). Efforts to build ever more effective "thinking machines," that is to say, computers, through artificial intelligence sharpened understanding of how information needed to be processed in order for it to be assembled and utilized effectively. The seminal article "Cognitive Apprenticeship: Teaching the Craft of Reading, Writing, and Mathematics" by Alan Collins, John Seely Brown, and Susan E. Newman (1989) was one by-product of this research, and one instructive aspect of this work lay in how it looked back to accumulated wisdom to lay its foundations for moving forward. Public schools had long dealt with large, diverse populations rather than highly filtered ones. Teachers there understood *scaffolding, wait time,* and *chunking* in conscious ways that were new to teachers at more advanced levels in education. Now, many of these terms, and more importantly these conscious and deliberate ways of thinking about teaching, have become commonplace in higher education.

Even more recently all this work has found support and expansion in the findings of neurobiological research into the human brain and how it operates, and in the study of groups and how they operate.

If renewed attention to teaching in higher education began as something of a "fix-it" shop approach aimed at helping individual faculty having problems with their teaching, it didn't stay that way very long. As Gaff and Simpson (1994) detail in their history of faculty development in the United States, pressure from the burgeoning "baby boom" population brought the whole business of university teaching up for reconsideration. What was relevant? What were appropriate educational goals and what were the most effective means of meeting them? Traditionally, the primary expectation of faculty was that they remain current in their fields of expertise. Now, a whole new set of still forming expectations began to spring up on campuses all over the country.

Change often fails to come easily and smoothly. Generational and social conflicts, together with passionate political conflicts centering on the unpopular war in Vietnam, may have fueled the pressure for changes in teaching while making them more conflict-ridden than they needed to be. It is important to repeat: faculty have always wanted to teach well and have their students succeed. As the clouds of conflict from those decades have passed, the intellectual fruits have remained and grown. Some ascribe credit for change in faculty attitudes toward teaching to the social pressures of those decades. Whatever truth lies in that ascription, it seems equally clear that faculty's innate intellectual curiosity and eagerness to succeed in their life's work deserve as much credit, certainly in today's faculty interest in improved teaching.

Faculty face a challenge in embracing new understandings of effective teaching not unlike the challenge of any population of diverse intelligences in learning and applying new information. Some understanding emerging in the 1980s (when much of the new thinking on teaching and learning began to appear) has cross-disciplinary, universal applicability, the "Seven Principles of Good Practice in Higher Education" by Arthur Chickering and Zelda Gamson (1987) for example. But just as diverse people learn in diverse ways, diverse faculty will apply even universal principles in different ways since both personalities and disciplinary cultures vary. Perhaps that is why many pedagogical insights into effective teaching have not aggregated into one universal, best way to teach. Instead the forward-moving inquiry into effective teaching has spawned a variety of pedagogical approaches, each with strengths appropriate to particular teaching styles and situations.

While faculty today have greater curiosity about new understandings of effective ways to teach, they remain as cautious as anyone else about change. If they teach biology, they wonder how a particular approach might play out in teaching biology rather than how it works in teaching English literature. If they teach English literature, they may wonder if problem-based teaching (an approach highly effective in the sciences) has anything to offer their teaching and if anyone in their discipline has tried it. Every new idea requires translation and receives it in the hands of the next person to take it up and apply it in his or her work. And this is as it should be. Thus, this series of books strives to give faculty examples of new approaches to teaching as they are being applied in a representative sample of academic disciplines. From the start, the central goal has been to offer faculty ideas in contexts; that is to say, to present them enough theory so that whatever idea about teaching and learning being discussed makes sense intellectually, but then to present that idea in an applied context. From this combination faculty can see how an approach might fit in their own practice. Faculty do not need formulae; they need only to see ideas in contexts. They'll take it from there. And so our series of books offers faculty a multipaned window into a variety of nontraditional pedagogical approaches now being applied with success in different disciplines in higher education. Faculty will look in and find something of value for their own teaching. As I've said and believe with all my heart, faculty have always wanted to teach well and see their students succeed.

This addition to the series pushes active understanding of the teaching and learning dynamic one important step further. Metacognition, or thinking about thinking, opens the door to learning in new, unexpected, and profoundly encouraging ways for students. As a fellow who's always felt math anxiety and guilt about not being better in math, one small research study highlights the encouragement (Ramirez & Beilock, 2011) I'm talking about. In this study one group of students with math anxiety wrote about it before taking a math exam; the control group (also with math anxiety) did not. The group who'd consciously surveyed their inner learning landscape by writing about it did better on the exam than the group who had not. So "going meta" (to borrow the phrase coined by Lee Schulman in speaking of the scholarship of teaching and learning) can help students learn. Seeing one's self as a learner with certain strengths and characteristics, certain proclivities and talents, empowers students and when all is said and done, surely that remains the fundamental aim of teaching today. The work of Matt Kaplan and his colleagues in this volume attests to the power of metacognition and makes a strong argument for including such approaches in college teaching.

—James Rhem
Executive Editor
The National Teaching & Learning Forum

REFERENCES

Chickering, A., & Gamson, Z. (1987, March). Seven Principles of Good Practice in Higher Education. *AAHE Bulletin*, 3–7.

Collins, A., Brown, J. S., & Newman, S. E. (1989). Cognitive apprenticeship: Teaching the craft of reading, writing, and mathematics. In L. B. Resnick (Ed.), *Knowing, learning, and instruction: Essays in honor of Robert Glaser* (pp. 453–494). Hillsdale, NJ: Erlbaum.

Gaff, J. G., & Simpson, R. D. (1994, Spring). Faculty development in the United States. *Innovative Higher Education, 18*(3), 167–176.

Gardner, H. (1983). *Frames of mind: The theory of multiple intelligences.* New York: Basic Books.

Ramirez, G., & Beilock, L. (2011). Writing about testing worries boosts exam performance in the classroom. *Science, 331*(6014), 211–213.

Reflective Pedagogies and the Metacognitive Turn in College Teaching

Naomi Silver

*R*eflection and *metacognition*, the key terms of this book, have deeply inter-twined histories in discourse on teaching and learning. In a general sense, interest in the two terms arises from the recognition that, in learning and in professional practice, content and procedural knowledge alone are insufficient for persistent and self-directed growth in a learner's or practitioner's understanding and expertise. Additionally, knowledge about *how* one learns content or practices a procedure is required. It is this attention to *how* that gives rise to the moment of *reflexivity* in reflection and the moment of *meta* in metacognition—that is, the moment of standing above or apart from oneself, so to speak, in order to turn one's attention back upon one's own mental work. In broad terms, then, *reflection* is often defined as a conscious exploration of one's own experiences (see, for example, Boud, Keogh, & Walker, 1985), and *metacognition* as the act of thinking about one's own thought processes (see Flavell, 1979). In the course of this chapter, I will aim to elaborate these initial definitions by placing them within the context of the educational trends and research out of which they developed, outline their connections to other important educational concepts, and overview the specific reflective and metacognitive pedagogical practices offered by the volume's contributors.

WHY METACOGNITION AND REFLECTION, AND WHY NOW?

The idea for this book grows out of a three-year research project at the University of Michigan (U-M), undertaken by the editors as part of a multi-university collaborative funded by the Teagle and Spencer foundations tasked

Many thanks are due to Zak Lancaster (graduate student research assistant on "The Impact of Metacognitive Strategies Within Writing in the Disciplines" project, and now assistant professor at Wake Forest University) for his tremendous help in compiling elements of the literature review that appears in this chapter.

with "chang[ing] the nature of the conversation [about U.S. higher education] from critiques to a focus on efforts at systematic improvement in undergraduate education" (Thompson, forthcoming). Titled "The Impact of Metacognitive Strategies Within Writing in the Disciplines," the U-M project aimed to develop targeted, exportable classroom strategies to help bridge the gap between students' and faculty's (or novices' and experts') understandings of disciplinary writing and thinking (Pace, 2004; Shulman, 2000).

Research in education has identified the importance of helping students develop the ability to monitor their own comprehension and to make their thinking processes explicit to teachers; and indeed, interest in the role of reflection and metacognition in fostering these abilities has exploded in the past few decades. Some landmarks in metacognition are the publication of the 1998 textbook *Metacognition in Educational Theory and Practice* (Hacker, Dunlosky, & Graesser) and its 2009 companion volume by the same editors, *Handbook of Metacognition in Education*, and the 2006 founding of the journal *Metacognition and Learning*. In studies of reflection, development in the field may be charted via such titles as Boud et al.'s (1985) *Reflection: Turning Experience Into Learning*, Yancey's (1998) *Reflection in the Writing Classroom*, Moon's (1999) *Reflection and Learning in Professional Development: Theory and Practice*, and Lyons's (2010) edited *Handbook of Reflection and Reflective Inquiry: Mapping a Way of Knowing for Professional Reflective Inquiry*. As these titles suggest, research on metacognition has had its widest impact in the fields of cognitive and educational psychology, while research on reflection has been largely taken up by professional practitioners and in experiential learning pedagogies.

As early as 1990, student metacognition was identified in a comprehensive metareview of research on learning variables as being primary among the elements deemed "most important to good learning outcomes" (Wang, Haertel, & Walberg, 1990, p. 37). In this connection, the authors note:

> We were surprised and encouraged that in this synthesis the metacognitive items emerged as most important, including comprehension monitoring, use of self-regulatory, self-control strategies, and use of strategies to facilitate generalization of concepts. Metacognitive variables are heavily cited in the current literature, in contrast to an earlier focus on relatively stable general mental abilities. A better understanding of those alterable variables may ultimately help the great majority of students to reach higher achievement levels through appropriate training in metacognition. (p. 37)

As one attempt to move this research agenda forward, our project at U-M applied metacognitive theory to questions of disciplinary understanding, asking if students would become better disciplinary thinkers if they understood the nature and components of thinking and writing entailed by that discipline, and if explicit instructor focus on disciplinary metacognition would help students better connect diverse disciplinary writing tasks and develop more versatile identities as disciplinary writers. Our results offer a provisional *yes* to both questions (Meizlish, LaVaque-Manty, Silver, & Kaplan, forthcoming). Further, they suggest that student and faculty engagement with course material and writing tasks is resoundingly improved by the introduction of metacognitive teaching strategies (see chapter 6).

The Importance of Engagement

This second finding of our project, regarding *engagement*, may in fact offer one of the primary rationales for reading this book, because, indeed, while we all want to improve our students' learning, fewer of us may feel prepared to investigate our students' reflective and metacognitive strategies as educational researchers do, and we may feel put off by the technical vocabulary employed by much of the research. As it turns out, more familiar concepts like engagement, motivation, self-efficacy, and agency all connect positively to the key terms of this volume, *reflection* and *metacognition* (see, for example, Bandura, 1989; Schunk, 1991). The National Survey of Student Engagement (NSSE), which began in 2000, has brought the importance of engagement to student learning in college and beyond to the attention of college educators at a wide range of institutions, and higher education research has documented that college outcomes are tightly linked to student educational effort; that is, they "depend largely on students' engagement in educationally purposeful activities" (Hu & McCormick, 2012, para. 3). As George Kuh, the founding director of NSSE, has noted, "Student engagement is generally considered to be among the better predictors of learning and personal development. . . . The very act of being engaged also adds to the foundation of skills and dispositions that is essential to live a productive and satisfying life after college" (Carini, Kuh, & Klein, 2006, p. 2). Consequently, "engagement in this sense is not just a proxy for learning but a fundamental purpose of education" (Shulman, 2002, p. 40).

One way to engage students is to help them become involved in and responsible for their own learning, making decisions about how they go about learning in addition to deciding what they want to learn and how they want to use that learning. Metacognition allows students to make decisions about how they learn best by helping them become aware of what they are doing when they are learning. For instance, if when writing a paper a student always gets stuck trying to move from one idea to another, he might just get frustrated and give up, gloss over the problem by making an artificial or overly facile transition, or use any number of other hedging strategies. But, if he has

been taught to "monitor" his writing process by inserting self-reflective comments into the margins of his papers, noting when he is having trouble (or
when he finds something that works for him), then he is prompted at those
moments to name what the problem is, and this act of naming and describing
may help him better understand why he is running into trouble. In the best
case scenario, this self-reflective naming and describing may even help him to
solve the problem and make a revision in the paper rather than need to insert
a comment to request feedback from his instructor. This discovery of his own
problem-solving ability, in turn, may help this student enjoy writing more
and find more engagement in the act of writing.

The student who can monitor her progress and make adjustments in
this way is referred to as a self-directed or self-regulated learner, and indeed
the literature on self-regulated learning provides a useful connector between
metacognition and motivation or engagement. To repeat a frequently cited
formulation, self-regulated learners are

> metacognitively, motivationally, and behaviorally active participants in their own
> learning process. Metacognitively, self-regulated learners are persons who plan,
> organize, self-instruct, self-monitor, and self-evaluate at various stages during the
> learning process. Motivationally, self-regulated learners perceive themselves as
> competent, self-efficacious, and autonomous. Behaviorally, self-regulated learners
> select, structure, and create environments that optimize learning. (Zimmerman,
> 1986, p. 308; see also Zimmerman & Moylan, 2009)

Many of us may recognize in these descriptions the highly successful students we have encountered—students who are motivated to excel, but whose
motivation is linked to a deeper engagement with and excitement about
learning that extends beyond a particular task or class, and who are poised to
exploit this learning in the service of personal and professional goals as well.

The Importance of Instruction

How, then, do we engage students by helping them become self-regulated
learners who actively employ metacognitive and reflective strategies in their
learning? What are the next steps for college educators in their own classrooms? One key element is the clear importance of explicitly teaching students to develop metacognitive awareness and strategies and to apply them
in a range of situations. In their review of the literature on metacognition in
learning, Veenman, Van Hout-Wolters, and Afflerbach (2006, p. 9) highlight
three "fundamental principles . . . for successful metacognitive instruction."
Instructors who are most effective in teaching reflection and metacognition:

> (a) embed . . . metacognitive instruction in the content matter to ensure connec-
> tivity, (b) inform . . . learners about the usefulness of metacognitive activities to
> make them exert the initial extra effort, and (c) [incorporate] prolonged training
> to guarantee the smooth and maintained application of metacognitive activity.

Readers will find examples of these three principles put into practice throughout the chapters of this book.

Nonetheless, qualitative research presented in the literature, as well as our
own experiences in presentations and consultations with faculty at U-M and
elsewhere, suggests that many teachers lack a rich understanding of metacognition and how it functions, and even those familiar with the concept
have not necessarily developed methods for integrating it into their curriculum (Veenman et al., 2006). Reasons for this absence range from a lack of
knowledge of the research to a sense that it does not apply to a wide range of
disciplines or to a concern that employing such strategies will be too time-
intensive. Compounding these reasons is the relative absence in the literature
of hands-on, user-friendly guides for college-level teachers to implement
metacognitive and reflective pedagogy in a range of disciplines.

Using Reflection and Metacognition to Improve Student Learning aims to
provide such a framework for college educators. In seven practitioner examples
from the science, technology, engineering, and mathematics (STEM) fields, the
social sciences, and the humanities, along with sample syllabi, course materials, and student examples, this volume offers a range of strategies for incorporating reflective and metacognitive instruction into college classrooms, as well
as theoretical rationales for the strategies presented. By providing successful
models from courses in a broad spectrum of disciplines, we hope to reassure
readers that they need not reinvent the wheel or fear the unknown, but can
instead adapt tested interventions that aid learning and have been shown to
improve both instructor and student satisfaction and engagement.

WHAT IS REFLECTION? WHAT IS METACOGNITION? HISTORIES AND DEFINITIONS

Although both concepts have been traced back to classical philosophy and
rhetorical practices—particularly Plato's report of Socrates's call to the self-
examined life and Cicero's report of Simonides's creation of the technique
of "memory places" (see, for example, Dunlosky & Metcalfe, 2009)—the
contemporary history of both *reflection* and *metacognition* dates to the early
twentieth century and the work of William James, John Dewey, Lev Vygotsky,
and Jean Piaget (see Fox & Riconscente, 2008; Tarricone, 2011).

Not surprisingly, in a field that has seen so much growth and interest over the past century, the definitions of *reflection* and *metacognition* are both varied and contested in the research literature (Boud et al., 1985; Moon, 1999; Tarricone, 2011; Weinert, 1987). In a nontechnical sense, the two terms are relatively synonymous and are often used interchangeably by educators. As Duffy, Miller, Parsons, and Meloth's "Nomenclature Problems in Describing Metacognitive Aspects of Teaching" puts it, "Given that metacognition is 'thinking of one's thinking,' it is a short step to associating metacognition with 'reflecting' on one's thinking" (2009, p. 242). In classroom activities, for instance, a "reflection" may be an assignment about a particular lesson meant to promote student metacognition, so students may be asked to complete a "metacognitive reflection" exercise (see, for example, Fogarty, 1994; White, Frederiksen, & Collins, 2009).

In a more technical sense, these terms have developed relatively independently in research and practice. Until quite recently, researchers and educators who work on reflection have not often referred to *metacognition*, while for those in the field of metacognition, *reflection* sometimes constitutes a particular moment or stage in a metacognitive schema. In their "Cyclical Phase Model of Self-Regulatory Feedback," for instance, Zimmerman and Moylan (2009) define a "Forethought Phase," a "Performance Phase," and a "*Self-Reflection* Phase" of student activity (emphasis added). In the latter, students make a "self-judgment" in which they compare their own performance against a standard (a typical metacognitive move), and they also describe a "self-reaction" that assesses their affect in relation to their self-judgment. These moments of self-reflection then feed back into student forethought for the next iteration of the activity (p. 300). In this example, as in those mentioned in the previous paragraph, *reflection* appears to become an occasion for taking stock of one's cognitive processes.

Reflection

The definition mentioned previously is not out of line with more researched notions of reflection, certainly, but the construct as theorized by John Dewey is broader in its scope, and also more rigorous. In his landmark book *How We Think*, Dewey defines *reflective thought* as "*Active, persistent, and careful consideration of any belief or supposed form of knowledge in light of the grounds that support it, and the further conclusions to which it tends*" (1910, p. 6, emphasis in original). Deweyan reflection is more sustained than a general stock-taking, then, and perhaps closer to the much broader concept of *critical thought* itself. Reflection, for him, constitutes a meticulous process of evidence- and implication-seeking, with the aim not only of fuller understanding by means of creating connections and relationships within experiences but of transforming experience and one's environment as a result (Dewey, 1910, 1916). Reflective activity, then, is fundamentally constructive as well as ethical; it implies responsibility for and identification with the outcomes of an action (Dewey, 1916, pp. 172–173). Significant for Dewey is the claim that a reflective operation must begin with a genuine problem, something that causes the thinker to feel discomfort or uncertainty, what Dewey calls "a *forked-road situation*, a situation which is ambiguous, which presents a dilemma, which proposes alternatives" (1916, p. 11, emphasis in original). In attempting to seek the basis for this dilemma and to restore equilibrium, the reflective learner or practitioner considers each possibility in turn before arriving at a provisional understanding. As Dewey asserts, "To maintain the state of doubt and to carry on systematic and protracted inquiry—these are the essentials of thinking" (1910, p. 13).

Following Dewey's early focus on reflective thought, the role of reflection in education began receiving serious scholarly attention in the 1980s. An early book-length collection is the multiauthored examination of reflection in experience-based learning by Boud et al. (1985). Indicating the scope of interest in this topic, the editors make a point of noting that the book's "contributors have been chosen from very diverse areas" (p. 15), ranging from management and medical education to professional and spiritual development to teacher and technical training, and more. While these contributors identify and describe reflective practice within the contexts of their particular areas, the editors offer a more general framework for reflective pedagogy that defines *reflection* initially as "a form of response of the learner to experience" (p. 18), and they develop this definition with a model of the reflective process that includes "returning to the experience, attending to feelings, and re-evaluating the experience" (p. 21). As in the literature on self-regulated learning considered earlier, Boud et al. propose to join the affective and cognitive dimensions of reflective practice to address the full range of learner experience.

Donald Schön's (1983, 1987) work on the idea of the reflective practitioner is another widely significant influence coming out of the 1980s. He, too, examines the role of reflection in a range of professional settings—engineering, management, architecture, psychotherapy, town planning, among others—in order to define a framework that describes how professionals' tacit knowledge of their work may be more deliberately mobilized and taught to learners in the field, ultimately resulting in a curriculum for a "reflective practicum" to form the core of professional training (1987). Indeed, Schön's work has been so inspirational for professional fields that, as one author puts it, when he "published *The Reflective Practitioner: How Professionals Think in Action* [in 1983], he set off a near cottage industry in the professions, making 'reflection' and 'reflective practice' almost household words" (Craig, 2010, p. 198).

Schön claims an additional goal for his work as outlining an "epistemology of practice" (1983, p. viii) that may help to bridge divisions between so-called theory and practice, universities and professional settings. One approach to this work of bridging is to describe the process by which practitioners in the field define an object of study. He writes:

> In real-world practice. . . problems do not present themselves to the practitioner as givens. They must be constructed from the materials of problematic situations which are puzzling, troubling, and uncertain. In order to convert a problematic situation to a problem, a practitioner must do a certain kind of work. He must make sense of an uncertain situation that initially makes no sense. . . . Problem setting is a process in which, interactively, we *name* the things to which we will attend and *frame* the context in which we will attend to them. (1983, p. 40, emphasis in original)

Like Dewey (who was the subject of Schön's dissertation), Schön sees the act of thinking or theorizing ("problem setting") as arising from uncertainty, from the confrontation with confusion or ambiguity. It is in these moments that a professional practitioner's tacit knowledge is challenged, and metacognition—the act of stepping back from the situation to "name" and "frame"—begins. In this process, "artistic, intuitive" (1983, p. 49) practical knowledge can become available to research and inquiry as a defined object of study and can be transferred to new situations (pp. 138–139), thus continuing a recursive relationship between theory and practice. Schön's much-cited terms to describe this process of performing "research . . . in the practice context" (p. 68) are *reflection-in-action* and *reflection-on-action*. These terms make explicit the temporal dimension of reflection, the "time frames" within which reflective thought and action occur (Hatton & Smith, 1995, p. 34). While Schön defines a two-part temporal process (during and after action), other researchers aver the importance of a three-part cycle that also includes a planning or anticipation stage prior to action (see Schraw, 1998, for a much-cited example). Indeed, Schön's construct has received some criticism for its neglect of reflection before action, although others suggest it is implicit in the iterative process he describes (see Moon, 1999, p. 49, for an overview).

Metacognition

William James ("introspective observation"), Jean Piaget ("directed thought" and "decentration"), and Lev Vygotsky ("inner speech" and "reflective consciousness") are frequently cited as early thinkers of metacognition (see Fox & Riconscente, 2008, for an overview of their conceptual contributions). John H. Flavell, however, is most often named as the originator of the term *metacognition*. In the 1970s and 1980s, he wrote a number of studies and position pieces establishing the importance of the construct for cognitive psychology and education, particularly in the area of memory studies. In a brief 1976 article on the "Metacognitive Aspects of Problem Solving," Flavell offers the following initial definition of the construct: "'Metacognition' refers to one's knowledge concerning one's own cognitive processes and products or anything related to them, e.g., the learning-relevant properties of information or data" (1976, p. 232). This definition is popularly paraphrased as the act of "thinking about one's thinking" (see chapter 7 for one example). But in this same article, Flavell immediately complicates this definition with the following elaboration:

> Metacognition refers, among other things, to the active monitoring and consequent regulation and orchestration of these processes in relation to the cognitive objects or data on which they bear, usually in the service of some concrete goal or objective. (1976, p. 232)

In this article we find the bases for all of the major metacognitive schemas in circulation: metacognition depends on *knowledge* of cognition, and it involves the *monitoring* and *regulation* or control of this knowledge.

Lest these definitions seem too abstract, Flavell quickly offers the following concrete instances of metacognition in action:

> For example, I am engaging in metacognition ... if I notice that I am having more trouble learning A than B; if it strikes me that I should double-check C before accepting it as a fact; if it occurs to me that I had better scrutinize each and every alternative in any multiple-choice type task situation before deciding which is the best one; if I become aware that I am not sure what the experimenter really wants me to do; if I sense that I had better make a note of D because I may forget it; if I think to ask someone about E to see if I have it right. Such examples could be multiplied endlessly. (1976, p. 232)

As these examples demonstrate, far from constituting an arcane topic of educational psychology, *metacognition* appears to describe a basic set of processes for navigating information in a range of contexts.

In later work, Flavell teases out the various dimensions of metacognition these examples represent to define "four classes of phenomena: (a) *metacognitive knowledge*, (b) *metacognitive experience*, (c) *goals* (or *tasks*), and (d) *actions* (or *strategies*)" (1979, p. 906, emphasis in original). We might, then, understand the first scenario offered, in which "I notice that I am having more trouble learning A than B" (1976, p. 232), as demonstrating both metacognitive knowledge and metacognitive experience, the former being demonstrated in the recognition of ease or difficulty with the material to be learned and the latter in the affect of "trouble" that accompanies this recognition. Likewise, the third scenario, in which "it occurs to me that I had better scrutinize each and every alternative in any multiple-choice type task situation before deciding which is the best one" (1976, p. 232), may be understood to display metacognitive knowledge, goals, and strategies; here knowledge of the task type ("multiple choice") is used to devise a strategy ("scrutinizing alternatives") to achieve a goal ("choosing the best answer").

Flavell's construct, however, does not indicate whether the metacognitive knowledge achieved in this process is accurate or whether the strategy selected is the most apt, suggesting a challenge for educators. Indeed, research on the metacognitive constructs of "metamemory" and "judgments of learning" suggests that learners often misjudge how well they will remember something or how well they have learned it (see Dunlosky & Metcalfe, 2009, for a helpful overview of the research in these areas). Luckily, there are metacognitive schemas available that point to strategies for assessing one's cognitive knowledge. Gregory Schraw, for example, identifies "three essential skills" for improving metacognitive regulation: "planning, monitoring, and evaluating" (1998, p. 115). As might be expected, planning involves processes prior to beginning a learning task, such as selecting a strategy, making predictions, allocating time, and so on; monitoring denotes "one's on-line awareness of comprehension and task performance" (1998, p. 115), such as self-testing over the course of a learning task; and evaluating is a post-task activity, wherein one assesses outcomes and performance in light of goals and strategy choices. The most successful learners, then, employ metacognitive interventions at every stage of activity, and ideally, their evaluative work post task makes possible the transfer both of cognitive and metacognitive knowledge to be employed in new contexts.

This issue of transfer, however, remains one of the important open questions in the research, namely, whether metacognition is domain specific or domain general. In the same article, Schraw makes the argument that "cognitive skills tend to be encapsulated within domains or subject areas, whereas metacognitive skills span multiple domains, even when those domains have little in common" (1998, p. 116), a position supported by additional studies. Nonetheless, other researchers argue the opposite position, claiming that metacognitive activity varies widely in relation to different cognitive tasks.

In their review of this literature, Veenman et al. (2006) suggest that the "grain" of analysis may play a role in the findings on one side or the other, but in any case, more research here is needed. For our purposes, one way to think about the issue could be to say that the broader functions of metacognition are domain general (as Flavell's many examples would attest), but that individual students may not use those functions in every area where it might benefit them without explicit instruction and practice in their use and transfer. Metacognition, then, is an area of self-regulated learning that needs development like all others.

OVERVIEW OF THE BOOK

The chapters in this volume address many of the current questions in the literature on reflection and metacognition and engage with several of the authors mentioned previously, while remaining focused on hands-on strategies for teaching and improving metacognitive knowledge and reflective practice. Some key themes include the transfer of metacognitive knowledge across disciplinary contexts, the importance of explicit instruction in metacognition and reflection, the increase of student and instructor engagement in classes that incorporate metacognitive and reflective pedagogies, and a corollary growth in instructors' own pedagogical metacognition and reflection. The chapters are grouped roughly by discipline, with chapters 2 through 4 describing approaches used in STEM-field courses in calculus, physics, chemistry, biology, and engineering; chapters 5 and 6 representing social science settings in political science and psychology, as well as a humanities course in English; and chapters 7 and 8 addressing the humanities fields of English, writing studies, and communication studies.

In chapter 2, Marsha C. Lovett describes the implementation of "exam wrappers" in calculus, physics, chemistry, and biology courses at her university, an intervention designed to shift student focus from a sole concern with exam grades to an understanding of exams as "a tool for learning." This intervention takes place at the "evaluation" stage of Schraw's three-part schema, in that students respond to a "structured reflection activity" when their graded exams are returned to them, but this reflection is designed to mobilize students' planning and monitoring capacities as well. The activity prompts students to reflect on what they did to study for the exam, compare that work to their performance on the exam, and plan for ways to adjust their strategies as they prepare for subsequent exams. Lovett approaches metacognition as a skill that can be learned like any other, and, important for instructors, one that can be taught like a content area, using familiar instructional techniques. She concurs with research on the domain generality of metacognition, but also suggests that it is most effectively taught in connection to domain-specific content, and not as a general study skill. Consequently, while she affirms that exam wrappers "can be applied to almost any course—as long as it has exams," she offers examples of how to tailor the strategy to the content area of a variety of courses.

Paula P. Lemons, Julie A. Reynolds, Amanda J. Curtin-Soydan, and Ahrash N. Bissell take as their focus in chapter 3 the role of metacognition in teaching and promoting critical thinking, arguing that ability in the former is fundamental for achievement of the latter. The curriculum described in this chapter is primarily interested in helping students understand that the practice of biology requires both content knowledge and critical thinking, that is, that memorization of biological facts is insufficient to obtain biological understanding. Consequently, their intervention—a lab-based instructional module called "Critical Thinking in Biology"—is geared toward separating these elements of disciplinary thinking so that students can recognize when each element is in play and see how they might improve at both, a process of achieving metacognitive knowledge, applying metacognitive awareness or monitoring to their own performance, and eventually executing metacognitive control to alter their own learning choices. These authors emphasize the importance of training students in the use of metacognitive strategies and of incorporating these strategies and this pedagogy throughout the course. They also implicitly reflect on their own pedagogical metacognition when they discuss revising instructional materials to better align with their goals for the course.

Chapter 4 takes up Donald Schön's call for reflective practice in professional schools and describes the "Integrated Design Engineering Assessment and Learning System" (IDEALS) as a means for building reflective and metacognitive skills into an engineering curriculum, which has tended to neglect areas that are not an explicit part of program accreditation. The authors, Denny Davis, Michael Trevisan, Paul Leiffer, Jay McCormack, Steven Beyerlein, M. Javed Khan, and Patricia Brackin, propose that this curriculum be incorporated into the capstone design course typical in most engineering schools, as it most closely mimics "an authentic professional environment for developing skills transferable to professional practice and for assessing real professional skills," goals the authors suggest are enhanced by strategies of reflection and metacognition such as planning, reflection-in-action, reflection-on-action, and evaluation. The IDEALS curriculum is carried out via a series of online modules, complete with instructor guides, that address specific professional skills taken up by the capstone course, including teamwork, professional development, and professional responsibility. This curriculum is most highly effective when instructors align their selection of class modules with course goals and student interests, and when they identify and reinforce the metacognitive and reflective dimensions of assignments and learning. The chapter concludes by reporting evidence of the intervention's role in promoting transfer of professional skills in engineering into the workplace and other professional environments.

Mary C. Wright, Jeffrey L. Bernstein, and Ralph Williams continue the focus on reflective pedagogies in chapter 5 in their presentation of *hevruta*, a dialogue-based learning strategy implemented in courses in political science and English at two different institutions. This chapter uses a five-stage model of reflection developed by Jennifer Moon (1999) to describe the progress of students in these classes from more basic acts of noticing and sense-making in regard to disciplinary material to a complex engagement in "transformative learning" by the end of the course, which impacted students' motivation as well as content knowledge. In the *hevruta* model, student pairs work together in discussion of a particular text in order to produce a careful analysis of it, work that may entail both free-flowing conversation and line-by-line analysis of particularly difficult or interesting passages. In both the humanities and social science courses, the instructors lead students to reflect further on the ideas and processes generated in the dialogue via written work and full group postdiscussion, but tailor the *hevruta* methodology to address the particular needs of their setting.

In chapter 6, Mika LaVaque-Manty and E. Margaret Evans employ the three phases of Schraw's (1998) metacognitive model—planning, monitoring, and evaluation activities—in relation to essay assignments in upper-level writing-intensive courses in political theory and developmental psychology, in order to achieve two related metacognitive goals: to help students become aware of what it means to "think like" a disciplinary practitioner and to become more fully aware and in control of their own writing processes. Indeed, they claim that the latter precisely enables the former, in that students' attention to and reflection on their writing within the domain-specific context of the course gives them direct insight into the material practices of the discipline. This chapter draws some similar conclusions to Lovett's in chapter 2, namely, that effective student metacognition requires instruction; that the pedagogical interventions described here are portable to a range of instructional contexts, even beyond academic subjects; but that, nonetheless, a domain-specific context is essential for seeding valuable metacognitive insights. LaVaque-Manty and Evans make the further point that attending to their students' metacognitive instruction achieved the unanticipated benefit of increasing their own metacognition around student learning, course planning, and execution (an insight, as we saw, that is implicit in chapter 3 as well).

Like LaVaque-Manty and Evans, in chapter 7, E. Ashley Hall, Jane Danielewicz, and Jennifer Ware investigate metacognition in regard to student writing, but they use a different tool, *design plans*, which encompasses the full composing process. They wish to promote a "reciprocal flow between monitoring and control" in their students' experiences of composing with the aim of helping students deepen their understanding of the writing process and the complexity of the texts they produce. Describing the intervention as it was implemented in honors English, first-year composition, and upper-level communication studies courses, the authors emphasize the importance of sustained attention to the intervention, including explicit discussion and modeling of metacognitive and reflective processes in order to aid their students in becoming more self-sufficient in employing the strategies. Both like and unlike the work of outlining a project's content, a design plan, in response to a series of categories, organizes a writer's thoughts about the project. Iterative work with this plan throughout the semester fosters students' metacognition by confronting them with the evidence of their own thinking at various points in the process, thinking that is able to be revised and made more complex as students' thoughts develop. The authors assert this process results in "concrete and transferable knowledge that students can draw from in future composing situations."

Chapter 8 offers yet a third approach to promoting reflection and metacognition in writing, through the use of electronic portfolios (see Cambridge, Cambridge, & Yancey, 2009; and Rath, 2010, for discussions of this growing field). Kathleen Blake Yancey, Leigh Graziano, Rory Lee, and Jennifer O'Malley describe an electronic portfolio pedagogy implemented in three courses within the new Editing, Writing, and Media program at their institution. As in the interventions described in chapters 4 on engineering and 6 on political theory and psychology, electronic portfolios are examined here for their role in promoting "expert" or "professional" processes for achieving metacognitive and cognitive knowledge and transfer of knowledge, as grounded in Schön's concept of reflection-in-action and Yancey's (1998) extension of it as "reflection-in-presentation." The authors address the ways in which portfolio pedagogy sustains students' reflection as "ongoing and cumulative," at the same time that they introduce several questions about the explicit role theories of reflection might play in their courses. In so doing, they themselves enact a reflective practice and sound a call for widespread instructor engagement in "examining the *effects* of our curricula and our pedagogy on our students," thus transforming us all into reflective practitioners.

As this overview demonstrates, the chapters in this book bring together a wide range of strategies for developing reflective and metacognitive pedagogies. Of course, the emphasis in most of these chapters on the necessity of teaching students to recognize and utilize reflective and metacognitive tools and strategies and then integrating this instruction at several moments throughout a course suggests that reflective and metacognitive teaching is not a no-cost proposition. It can, however, be low cost; once these strategies have been tailored to meet the goals and objectives of a new course, they tend to suggest a logical structure in their frequent focus around the before, during, and after stages of a given activity. The payoff, of course, comes in the clear evidence of better student performance and greater student engagement as a result of their implementation. The chapters that follow provide ample instances of student work as well as interview and survey responses that exhibit students' appreciation of these strategies and tools for their own learning and development. That instructor engagement with a course, with students, and with pedagogical reflection and metacognition also increases is merely a bonus. We hope that readers will find these examples of reflection and metacognition in college teaching to be engaging, and that in implementing them, they might heed the call to become reflective educational practitioners.

REFERENCES

Bandura, A. (1989). Regulation of cognitive processes through perceived self-efficacy. *Developmental Psychology, 25*(5), 729–735.

Boud, D., Keogh, R., & Walker, D. (Eds.). (1985). *Reflection: Turning experience into learning.* New York: Nichols.

Cambridge, D., Cambridge, B., & Yancey, K. B. (2009). *Electronic portfolios 2.0: Emergent research on implementation and impact.* Sterling, VA: Stylus.

Carini, R. M., Kuh, G. D., & Klein, S. P. (2006). Student engagement and student learning: Testing the linkages. *Research in Higher Education, 47*(1), 1–32.

Craig, C. J. (2010). Reflective practice in the professions: Teaching. In N. Lyons (Ed.), *Handbook of reflection and reflective inquiry: Mapping a way of knowing for professional reflective inquiry* (pp. 189–214). London: Springer.

Dewey, J. (1910). *How we think.* Boston: Heath.

Dewey, J. (1916). *Democracy and education: An introduction to the philosophy of education.* New York: Macmillan.

Duffy, G. G., Miller, S., Parsons, S., & Meloth, M. (2009). Teachers as metacognitive professionals. In D. J. Hacker, J. Dunlosky, & A. C. Graesser (Eds.), *Handbook of metacognition in education* (pp. 240–256). New York: Routledge.

Dunlosky, J., & Metcalfe, J. (2009). *Metacognition.* Los Angeles: Sage.

Flavell, J. H. (1976). Metacognitive aspects of problem solving. In L. B. Resnick (Ed.), *The nature of intelligence* (pp. 213–235). Hillsdale, NJ: Erlbaum.

Flavell, J. H. (1979). Metacognition and cognitive monitoring: A new area of cognitive-developmental inquiry. *American Psychologist, 34*(10), 906–911.

Fogarty, R. J. (1994). *The mindful school: How to teach for metacognitive reflection.* Glenview, IL: Skylight.

Fox, E., & Riconscente, M. (2008). Metacognition and self-regulation in James, Piaget, and Vygotsky. *Educational Psychology Review, 20,* 373–389.

Hacker, D. J., Dunlosky, J., & Graesser, A. C. (Eds.). (1998). *Metacognition in educational theory and practice.* Mahwah, NJ: Erlbaum.

Hacker, D. J., Dunlosky, J., & Graesser, A. C. (Eds.). (2009). *Handbook of metacognition in education.* New York: Routledge.

Hatton, N., & Smith, D. (1995). Reflection in teacher education: Towards definition and implementation. *Teaching and Teacher Education, 11*(1), 33–49.

Hu, S., & McCormick, A. C. (2012). An engagement-based student typology and its relationship to college outcomes. *Research in Higher Education, 53*(7), 738–754.

Lyons, N. (Ed.). (2010). *Handbook of reflection and reflective inquiry: Mapping a way of knowing for professional reflective inquiry.* London: Springer.

Meizlish, D., LaVaque-Manty, D., Silver, N., & Kaplan, M. (Forthcoming). Think like/write like: Metacognitive strategies to foster students' development as disciplinary thinkers and writers. In R. J. Thompson (Ed.), *Changing the conversation about higher education.* New York: Rowman & Littlefield.

Moon, J. A. (1999). *Reflection and learning in professional development: Theory and practice.* London: Kogan Page.

Pace, D. (2004). Decoding the reading of history: An example of the process. In D. Pace & J. Middendorf (Eds.), *Decoding the disciplines: Helping students learn disciplinary ways of thinking* (pp. 13–21). New Directions for Teaching and Learning, No. 98. San Francisco: Jossey-Bass.

Rath, A. (2010). Reflective practice as conscious geometry: Portfolios as a tool for sponsoring, scaffolding and assessing reflective inquiry in learning to teach. In N. Lyons (Ed.), *Handbook of reflection and reflective inquiry: Mapping a way of knowing for professional reflective inquiry* (pp. 498–515). London: Springer.

Schön, D. A. (1987). *Educating the reflective practitioner: Toward a new design for teaching and learning in the professions.* San Francisco: Jossey-Bass.

Schön, D. A. (1983). *The reflective practitioner: How professionals think in action.* New York: Basic.

Schraw, G. (1998). Promoting general metacognitive awareness. *Instructional Science, 26*(1–2), 113–125.

Schunk, D. H. (1991). Self-efficacy and academic motivation. *Educational Psychologist, 26,* 207–232.

Shulman, L. S. (2000). Teacher development: Roles of domain expertise and pedagogical knowledge. *Journal of Applied Developmental Psychology, 21*(1), 129–135.

Shulman, L. S. (2002). Making differences: A table of learning. *Change: The Magazine of Higher Learning, 34*(6), 36–44.

Tarricone, P. (2011). *The taxonomy of metacognition*. Hove, East Sussex, England: Psychology Press.

Thompson, R. J. (Ed.). (Forthcoming). *Changing the conversation about higher education*. New York: Rowman & Littlefield.

Veenman, M. V. J., Van Hout-Wolters, V. H. A. M., & Afflerbach, P. (2006). Metacognition and learning: Conceptual and methodological considerations. *Metacognition and Learning, 1*(1), 3–14.

Wang, M. C., Haertel, G. D., & Walberg, H. J. (1990). What influences learning? A content analysis of review literature. *Journal of Educational Research, 84*(1), 30–43.

Weinert, F. E. (1987). Introduction and overview: Metacognition and motivation as determinants of effective learning and understanding. In F. E. Weinert & R. J. Kluwe (Eds.), *Metacognition, motivation, and understanding* (pp. 1–16). Hillsdale, NJ: Erlbaum.

White, B., Frederiksen, J., & Collins, A. (2009). The interplay of scientific inquiry and metacognition. In D. J. Hacker, J. Dunlosky, & A. C. Graesser (Eds.), *Handbook of metacognition in education* (pp. 175–205). New York: Routledge.

Yancey, K. B. (1998). *Reflection in the writing classroom*. Logan, UT: Utah State University Press.

Zimmerman, B. J. (1986). Becoming a self-regulated learner: Which are the key subprocesses? *Contemporary Educational Psychology, 11*, 307–313.

Zimmerman, B. J., & Moylan, A. R. (2009). Self-regulation: Where metacognition and motivation intersect. In D. J. Hacker, J. Dunlosky, & A. C. Graesser (Eds.), *Handbook of metacognition in education* (pp. 299–315). New York: Routledge.

2

Make Exams Worth More Than the Grade

Using Exam Wrappers to Promote Metacognition

Marsha C. Lovett

All too often, when students get back a graded exam, they focus on a single feature—the score they earned. Although this focus on the grade is understandable, it can lead students to miss out on several valuable learning opportunities. Of particular—and often unrecognized—importance is the opportunity to discover how their study strategies and learning processes went awry. This is the domain of metacognition: learning about one's own learning.

Inspired by research on how students learn and after working within the constraints of typical college courses, I developed, with several Carnegie Mellon professors, what I have called *exam wrappers*—structured reflection activities that prompt students to practice key metacognitive skills after they get back their graded exams. Exam wrappers ask students three kinds of questions: (a) how they prepared for the exam, (b) what kinds of errors they made on the exam, and (c) what they might do differently to prepare for the next exam. Appendices A1 and A2 present two sample exam wrappers. The main goal of exam wrappers is not to collect students' responses to these questions per se but rather to promote students' engagement in reflection and self-monitoring and hence foster their metacognitive development.

This chapter puts exam wrappers in the context of current research on metacognition, explains what exam wrappers are and how to use them, and describes our results from incorporating exam wrappers in four introductory math and science courses at Carnegie Mellon University. The chapter is organized as follows: the first section explains why exams offer a useful (and often unexploited) platform for promoting metacognition. The next

I would like to thank my colleagues from CMU's Mellon College of Science—the professors (past and present)—who spent their time and effort to promote metacognitive skills. Without them, this work would not have been possible.

section provides background information on metacognitive skills and how they develop. This is followed by more detail on what exam wrappers are, why they work, and how to use them. The next section presents a case study to explain how we have used exam wrappers across several introductory math and science courses and then summarizes empirical results demonstrating exam wrappers' value. The chapter concludes by explaining how other wrappers can extend the notion to other instructional instruments.

EXAMS AS A PLATFORM FOR METACOGNITIVE INSTRUCTION

With exam wrappers, we hope to transform how students and instructors use exams as a tool for learning. Currently, most students seem to think of exams as the "end" of learning. ("After the test, I'm done with this material.") The following alternatives are tantalizing:

1. When students get back their graded exams, they reflect on their learning processes ("What did I do to study for this exam?"), compare that to the outcome ("Where did I have difficulties on the exam?"), and make adjustments as necessary ("Next time, I should solve more practice problems so I know better how to set things up").
2. When instructors review the graded exams, they reflect on how students performed, compare that to the learning objectives for the course, and then adjust their subsequent teaching to address any unmet needs.

These steps—reflect, compare, adjust—promote a view of exams as part of a learning cycle in which refined understanding informs changed behavior and in turn produces improved performance. For students, this *self-regulated learning cycle* exercises key components of metacognition, components that can serve to reinforce and enhance exams. For instructors, the cycle not only leads to adaptive teaching, but it also facilitates instructors' support of their students' metacognitive development. In other words, we want to use exams to jump-start the self-regulated learning cycle.

Those who stand to gain particular benefits from this goal are students transitioning to college. These students comprise an arguably high-risk group because they are expected to show greater independence and self-management in their learning, at the same time they are encountering new difficulties associated with college life and college-level material (Pascarella & Terenzini, 2005). These students can also be especially sensitive to exam results, leading them to develop counterproductive habits as a response to adverse outcomes. Yet, if instructors enable these students to use exams to foster their metacognition, they can establish a culture of self-regulated learning that will carry forward throughout their time in college.

BACKGROUND ON METACOGNITION
AND ITS DEVELOPMENT

Metacognition is knowledge about one's own knowledge, thinking about one's own thinking, and learning about one's own learning (cf. Flavell, 1976). Students benefit from metacognition because it enables them to reflect on their own thinking and learning processes, to accurately assess what they know and don't know, and then to make good choices for self-regulated learning. These are critical skills in any domain and are particularly valuable for students making the transition from high school to college, given the increased responsibility that such students have for their own learning.

Fortunately, metacognition need not be mysterious or intimidating. Research on how students learn has revealed the basic mechanisms by which students acquire, develop, and apply metacognitive skills (cf. Ambrose, Bridges, DiPietro, Lovett, & Norman, 2010). This research can be distilled down to four key points that are especially relevant to instructional practice:

1. Metacognition is *not* a monolithic skill that students have or lack entirely, but rather a complex of many different skills, including but not limited to (a) knowing one's own strengths and weaknesses in cognition, (b) identifying appropriate learning goals, (c) planning one's approach to a learning task, (d) monitoring progress, (e) evaluating performance, and (f) reflecting on what did and did not work in order to adjust for the next exam (Butler & Winne, 1995; Zimmerman, 2001). Because these are all distinct skills, students may be stronger in some areas than in others (Ertmer & Newby, 1996; Winne & Hadwin, 1998). Moreover, different learning situations may make greater demands on some of these skills compared to others.

2. Metacognitive skills are *not* learned through a distinct mechanism. Although some frameworks distinguish metacognition from other types of knowledge (Anderson & Krathwohl, 2001), this does not imply that students learn metacognitive skills in a fundamentally distinct way. Research shows that students develop their metacognitive skills through practice and feedback, just as they would for any other skill (Azevedo & Cromley, 2004; Palinscar & Brown, 1984).

3. Metacognitive skills are *not* automatically transferred across contexts. Although it is true that metacognitive skills are widely applicable and thus are considered "domain general," instructors cannot assume that students will automatically apply them appropriately outside the domain, task, or context in which they were learned.

Rather, metacognitive skills follow the standard pattern: the more dissimilar the learning and application contexts (e.g., in time, topic, format), the more difficult it is for students to apply what they learned (Barnett & Ceci, 2002; Carr, Kurtz, Schneider, Turner, & Borkowski, 1989; Halpern, 1998).

4. Metacognitive skills are *not* best learned as generic "study skills." Given the domain generality of metacognitive skills, attempts have been made to teach metacognition as a set of high-level strategies, without any specific disciplinary context. Unfortunately, students who are taught metacognitive skills in the abstract are not better at transferring them and instead often show difficulty implementing the skills in specific situations (Lizarraga, Baquedano, Mangado, & Cardelle-Elawar, 2009; Meyers & Nulty, 2009; Schraw, Crippen, & Hartley, 2006).

Keeping these points in mind can demystify metacognition and can help instructors think more productively about how to foster it. In essence, these points lead to the conclusion that metacognitive skills are skills *just like any other*. Hence, for instructors to develop and promote their students' metacognition, they can look to the kinds of instructional strategies they are already using for teaching disciplinary content. The practical implications are fairly straightforward and likely quite familiar too:

1. When designing metacognitive instruction, be sure to identify and articulate the specific metacognitive skills you want students to learn. This will guide your design decisions and inform students about where to focus their efforts.

2. Create (multiple) opportunities for students to practice the targeted metacognitive skills, and find ways to provide feedback so students can refine their skills. Keep in mind that multiple, small assignments are often preferable to a single, large assignment. Also, while individualized feedback is ideal, aggregate (e.g., class or group-level) feedback is often a reasonable substitute.

3. Make sure that students are exposed to metacognitive skills across a diverse range of situations, so they learn these skills with greater generality and robustness. Diversity here means that the situations exhibit different surface features such as topic, format, solution method, and so forth. The needed degree of variation corresponds to the distance you want students to be able to transfer their metacognitive skills. Although it may seem difficult to achieve the necessary diversity, note that students' exposure to metacognition can be through their own

practice or by other means, such as the instructor modeling metacognitive skills across different contexts or explicitly highlighting the deep features that should trigger metacognition.

4. Ground the metacognitive processes you want students to learn in the content of your course. With concrete material to reflect on and reason about, students get several benefits. Metacognitive skills are easier to engage, and therefore students are more likely to use them. The value of metacognition is more salient to students because they can see its effect on outcomes they care about, namely, improved learning and performance in the course. And the metacognitive practice that students receive is authentic to the discipline (e.g., in a writing course, students learn to self-assess and adjust in the particular ways that writers need to).

EXAM WRAPPERS

Design Considerations for Exam Wrappers

To devise a practical and effective intervention that helps students develop metacognitive skills, we need to consider several realities of teaching and learning. First, however much instructors may value metacognition, they still face great pressure to cover the course content (especially in introductory courses) and hence must allocate their class time sparingly. So any practical intervention must impinge minimally on class time. Second, today's college students are busy and as such tend to be highly sensitive to the time they spend on course-related activities, especially if they do not see a connection to their grade or the course content. So students must be able to complete any practical intervention within the (likely small) amount of time they are willing to invest. Third, courses vary widely in many different ways, including the disciplinary content (e.g., biology versus physics), format of the course (e.g., lecture versus small-group discussion), and types of activities (e.g., problem set versus essay), and instructors do not want to have to design a distinct instrument for every course. So any practical intervention must be easily adaptable across diverse course features. Fourth, in order to produce significant learning gains, instructors need to give students repeated practice opportunities. Moreover, the repetitions need to allow enough variety, to avoid seeming dull and predictable, and to support transfer. So any effective intervention must be repeatable and yet flexible enough to accommodate variation in format. Finally, and most importantly, metacognition will not improve unless students are actively engaging in metacognitive practice of the sort discussed earlier. In other words, to be most effective, the intervention must be (a) targeted on the metacognitive skills that instructors want their students to learn, (b) repeatable for multiple practice opportunities, (c) exemplified in diverse contexts, and (d) grounded in the content of students' disciplinary learning.

For the reasons identified in the beginning of this chapter, exams offer an ideal platform for achieving metacognitive gains. My approach was to build metacognitive practice *around* exams and in so doing satisfy the previously listed constraints. As the name suggests, this is what exam wrappers are all about.

What Are Exam Wrappers?

Exam wrappers are short activities that direct students to review their performance (and the instructor's feedback) on an exam with an eye toward adapting their future learning (again, see Appendices A1 and A2 for two samples). Exam wrappers ask students three kinds of questions: How did they prepare for the exam? What kinds of errors did they make on the exam? What could they do differently next time? Each of the question types is discussed next.

1. *How students prepared for the exam.* Asking students to reflect on how they prepared for the exam forces them to confront the choices, explicit or implicit, they made about their studying. This prompts students to consider issues such as whether they studied enough or sufficiently in advance. Similarly, asking students which of various study strategies they employed (e.g., reviewing notes, solving practice problems, rereading the textbook) highlights that there are many options they *could* have taken. It also presents various study strategies that students might not have even considered and thus suggests some new possibilities for how they might prepare differently next time.

2. *What kinds of errors students made.* Once they have received a grade, students do not always think carefully about their performance on an exam. If they did well, they might mark it as a success without much further thought; if they did poorly, there's a strong temptation to leave the painful event behind. Thus, the second set of questions posed in exam wrappers is designed to encourage students to analyze their performance in greater depth, giving students something constructive to do with the feedback a graded exam offers. One way to do this is to identify the critical components or stages of the tasks on the exam and have students estimate their degree of difficulty (e.g., how

many points they lost) with each component. For example, did they read the question carefully, did they have trouble "setting up" the problem, did they fail to understand the concepts involved, or did they make mistakes on the required arithmetic or algebra? Focusing students' reflection at this level informs their analysis of their own performance. Moreover, the labels for the different possibilities provide a concrete language for students to use when assessing their own performance. Note that this part of the exam wrapper is a natural place for instructors to tailor the questions to their own needs. For example, the exam wrappers in Appendices A1 and A2 use different labels to fit the needs of two disciplines: physics and calculus. Instructors may also want to adapt these labels to include specific misconceptions or difficulties that have been revealed in their course by past students. Or, they may want to include more general issues that affect students' exam performance. For instance, an instructor I worked with recently was concerned about test anxiety adversely affecting her students' exam performance, so she incorporated this issue into her exam wrapper.

3. *How students should study for the next exam.* Students can use their responses to the first and second types of exam-wrapper questions to think about how they should approach the next exam. A key goal of the third type of exam-wrapper question is to help students see the association between their study choices and their exam performance so they can better predict what study strategies will be effective in the future. One way to do this is to ask students to look back at their responses to the first two parts of the wrapper and then to list specific ways they might prepare differently for the next exam to improve their performance. Another option is to prompt students to attribute their various difficulties (from part two of the wrapper) to specific study strategies (from part one) they did or did not employ. Rather than merely *telling* students to "study harder" or "do more practice problems before the exam," this third type of exam-wrapper question helps students discover effective study strategies on their own. In effect, exam wrappers are asking students to give their future selves advice.

Why Exam Wrappers Work

The earlier section on design considerations described five constraints that a metacognitive intervention should satisfy to be practical and effective.

Understanding the ways in which exam wrappers satisfy these constraints helps explain why they work.

1. *Impinge minimally on class time.* Exam wrappers require only a few minutes and are completed at a time when students arguably are somewhat distracted anyway. Moreover, instructors can eliminate even this minimal impact on class time by giving exam wrappers as part of homework.

2. *Be easily completed by students within the time they are willing to invest.* With typically only one page of questions, none of which requires much writing, exam wrappers take relatively little student time.

3. *Be easily adaptable.* As we have seen, exam wrappers include three main question types, and these question types can be applied to almost any course—as long as it has exams. (See the following section, How to Use Exam Wrappers, for different ways of implementing exam wrappers.) In addition, this general approach can be applied to any type of graded assignment. (See the section titled Other Kinds of Wrappers for a brief discussion of other ways to employ this type of tool.)

4. *Be repeatable yet flexible.* The core questions being asked in an exam wrapper do not diminish in value when asked repeatedly. At the same time, it is easy to adjust the details of exam wrappers so as to keep the exercise fresh. Instructors can easily vary the specific content of exam wrapper questions, add new questions, and tailor the questions to their particular instructional situation. (See Appendix B for two additional exam wrappers beyond those presented in Appendices A1 and A2.)

5. *Exercise the skills instructors want their students to learn.* The reflection required to complete an exam wrapper leads students to assess their own strengths and weaknesses, evaluate their performance, identify which strategies work for them, and generate appropriate adjustments. These are key metacognitive skills that many instructors want to promote.

How to Use Exam Wrappers

Here I describe a basic recipe for how to use exam wrappers, along with variations and options instructors may find useful.

Step 1: Students prepare for and take the first exam using their typical study strategies. No special intervention is needed for this first exam.

Step 2: The instructor gives students the exam wrapper instrument when the graded exams are returned and asks students to complete the exam wrapper as soon as possible upon seeing their exam performance. Ideally, this is done right then in class and need only take 10 minutes of class time. But there are other possibilities. Students can complete the exam wrappers as homework, submitting their responses by a specified deadline. Or students can complete the exam wrappers online as a nongraded assignment (e.g., within a course management system or online instructional environment or with an online survey system).

Step 3: The instructor collects the exam wrappers. Although exam wrappers are not graded activities, it is important to collect them because (a) the exam wrappers will need to be returned to students at a later point (see Step 4) and this prevents them from getting lost, and (b) the instructional team may want to review students' responses to gain insight into their students' learning that they otherwise might not be able to obtain. In particular, the instructor or teaching assistants can skim students' responses to see whether there are patterns in how students analyzed their strengths and weaknesses or in how students described their approach to studying for the exam. For example, instructors may be surprised to learn the amount of time students spent studying (either how much or how little), when students chose to start their studying (e.g., 2 a.m. the night before), or how students spent their study time (e.g., memorizing formulae rather than solving practice problems). The instructional team can also consider the additional instructional support students said they would like to receive and possibly provide something along these lines. A wide variety of adjustments may be suggested based on what the instructional team learns from the exam wrappers about students' strengths, weaknesses, and study strategies.

Step 4: At the time when students should begin studying for the next exam, the instructor returns the completed exam wrappers (from the previous exam) to students. The idea here is that students review their own recommendations for how to study more effectively, given their own past experiences, strengths, and weaknesses. Depending on the class format and the time available, there are many variations on this step that instructors can use. For example, Figure 2.1 shows a set of follow-up questions that can accompany the completed exam wrapper sheet. These questions prompt students to review their exam wrapper responses and recommit to implement their own suggestions. Another option (not mutually exclusive) that works well with smaller classes is to give students a few minutes to reread their exam wrappers and then take a few minutes for students to share effective study strategies. Regardless of which approach instructors take for this step, the key aspect involves reminding students of their own advice and encouraging them to take it.

Step 5 (optional, but desirable): Repeat steps 2 through 4 for subsequent exams.

When an instructor provides exam wrappers regularly across multiple exams, students get repeated practice in applying the skills of self-regulated learning. This helps students build a habit of mind to monitor their own learning, reflect on their study strategies, and make appropriate adjustments. For reasons mentioned earlier, it can be useful to include nontrivial variation in the structure of subsequent wrappers while still prompting the desired metacognitive processes. For example, an exam wrapper used for exams later in the semester can be streamlined compared to the first exam wrapper. Having the wrapper still gets students to engage in reflection and analysis, but fading the scaffolding encourages students to take on more of the responsibility for this process.

These five steps are easy to implement, take relatively little time, and are very flexible. The metacognitive practice from using wrappers in a course offers substantial benefits. And when multiple instructors do this across different courses, students can learn metacognitive skills in multiple contexts, thereby increasing their likelihood of transferring the skills to new learning situations in the future. This is exactly what we did at Carnegie Mellon University, implementing wrappers in several introductory math and science courses, as described in the next section.

Figure 2.1 Exam wrapper add-on: Additional questions for when completed wrapper is returned

---

Physics Pre-Exam Reflection   **Name:** _____

You will soon be taking Exam #2. This sheet poses a few questions to help you reflect on your experience with Exam #1 so that you can prepare effectively for Exam #2.

1. Read through your responses on the Post-Exam Reflection sheet from the last exam. (Your TAs will hand back your sheet.) Jot down anything you read that you think will be helpful as you study for the next exam.
2. Self-assessment involves analyzing your own strengths and weaknesses. This can be helpful in deciding what you should study more or less. Given your responses on the Exam #1 reflection sheet along with your experiences learning new topics for Exam #2, what do you think you should study most as you prepare for Exam #2?
3. Read your response to question #4 on your Post-Exam Reflection sheet. Write down how you plan to implement your own suggestions to study effectively for Exam #2.

CASE STUDY: INTRODUCTORY MATH AND SCIENCE COURSES AT CARNEGIE MELLON UNIVERSITY

Where Exam Wrappers Came From

In my role at Carnegie Mellon's Eberly Center for Teaching Excellence, I often work with instructors who wish to improve their own teaching and their students' learning. The impetus for exam wrappers came in the mid-2000s, when several faculty members who were teaching introductory math and science courses came to me, reporting the same problem: "My class is full of bright, knowledgeable first-year students, but their performance on in-class activities and on exams is decidedly worse than in previous years!" These were all experienced instructors who had seen their fair share of first-year students' difficulties yet they were frustrated because their tried-and-true approaches were not working with this group of students. What was particularly striking to me was that I was hearing the same lament independently from multiple instructors across different departments. There was a mystery to solve. Why were students suddenly having such trouble and what was the source of their difficulty?

In general, my approach to helping instructors is to analyze each teaching or learning situation in terms of relevant cognitive and motivational aspects of how students learn and then to translate this "diagnosis" into practical strategies that instructors can apply. Based on what is known about how students learn, there were many possible explanations for the mystery that these instructors had brought to me—from prior knowledge gaps to dorm-life difficulties. So I began to collect data to better understand what was going on. I talked more with these instructors about their perceptions of the problem. I looked for changes or trends over the past several years in how these courses had been taught and in how students were selected for admission. Perhaps most importantly, I gathered data from the students themselves, asking them open-ended questions about their learning experiences in these courses and administering pre- and postsemester questionnaires about their motivation, beliefs about learning, study strategies, and metacognitive skills. The questionnaires I used included the Motivated Strategies for Learning Questionnaire (MSLQ; Pintrich, Smith, Garcia, & McKeachie, 1991) and the Beliefs About Knowledge and Learning Questionnaire (Schommer, 1990, 1993).

By analyzing these data, I was able to eliminate some potential hypotheses. For example, the format of instruction in most of these courses was rather stable over the preceding years and included various interactive components: two courses used "clickers" to engage students in answering conceptual questions during class, and another incorporated computer-based activities where students solved problems with the support of hints and feedback. So, the source of the problem did not appear to be that dry lectures were simply not working for this group of students. Similarly, the academic profile of students admitted in the preceding years did not indicate any significant changes. If anything, these students' Scholastic Aptitude Test scores and high school grades would have predicted increases in their first-year math and science performance.

My analyses also revealed three noteworthy clues. First, from the instructors' observations, more students than usual were failing to exhibit good habits (e.g., attending lectures, submitting homework on time, visiting office hours), a pattern that did not change even after they performed poorly on multiple exams. This suggested that students were not effectively calibrating their efforts to the demands of college-level courses. Second, when asked about their approaches to learning in math and science, students identified a fairly small repertoire of rather limited study strategies (e.g., rereading the textbook to study for an exam), and this repertoire did not grow or change much by the semester's end. Finally, the pre- and postquestionnaires on students' study strategies and beliefs about learning showed, on average:

- Students reported very little use of specific study strategies, including time management or focusing strategies. This was true throughout the semester.
- Students' beliefs about learning shifted across the semester. The strength of their belief in productive or "incremental" views of learning (e.g., learning takes time and effort; people can become better learners with practice) decreased slightly, and the strength of their belief in "innate" views of learning (e.g., learning is quick and easy; some people are born better learners than others) increased slightly.
- Students had very high expectations for their performance in college math and science courses. For example, when asked what they expected to earn as final grade, more than 90% responded in the A or B category, and this was true across all four courses: biology, chemistry, physics, and calculus.

Together, these results led to a picture of the first-year math and science students as having been successful in high school without having developed effective strategies for learning. Unfortunately, these students continued to use their ineffective strategies even after poor performance. In other words, the current students' metacognitive skills were less well developed than in years past.

This explanation resonated with the instructors, and they were eager to find a way to intervene. Yet, as mentioned earlier, these instructors did not feel comfortable taking too much time away from the disciplinary content of their courses. So we had to focus our effort where students needed it most. What students seemed to lack, even more than specific study strategies appropriate for these courses, was an *awareness* that they were not learning or performing well with their current strategies. In other words, students needed to learn to recognize when their learning was not working before they would be likely to try—let alone refine and transfer—new approaches. Thus, our intervention needed to help students (a) self-assess their own learning and (b) make changes to their study strategies accordingly. If students could improve in the skills of self-assessment and adjustment as first-year students, they could benefit not only in the four math and science courses we were focused on, but hopefully throughout the rest of their years in college (and beyond).

How could an intervention fit equally well into the four courses we were targeting? Whereas these courses differed quite a bit in their assignments and activities (e.g., whether or not they included recitation sessions, assigned weekly problem sets, gave quizzes, had labs), all four of the courses had fairly similarly structured exams, so exams offered a common platform for a metacognitive intervention across all four courses. Moreover, poor performance on exams was a key part of these instructors' initial concerns, so targeting exams seemed appropriate. And finally, for the reasons described in the first part of this chapter, exams represented a largely untapped resource for learning. In sum, this thought process led to the development of exam wrappers.

Exam Wrappers in Action

Rather than focusing on a single course to introduce exam wrappers, the idea was to get exam wrappers incorporated throughout the introductory math and science curriculum. So, with help from the introductory biology, calculus, chemistry, and physics instructors, I created exam wrappers specifically for each of these four courses (see Appendices A1, A2, and B). Our goal was to explore the practical viability of exam wrappers across several courses and to obtain an initial formative assessment.

The four courses' exam wrappers were intentionally made to be different because I did not want to impose a single form on the instructors and because differences across disciplines and teaching styles would warrant variation. Yet all the courses' exam wrappers had the same focus on the three core question types identified in the section describing what exam wrappers are. In addition, all the exam wrappers used a common language for the metacognitive skills of *self-assessment, monitoring,* and *adjustment.* Indeed, the instructors agreed to use these terms when referring to the processes embedded in exam wrappers or when they referred to these skills in their lectures, syllabi, and other conversations with students.

Each of the instructors chose how to administer the exam wrappers so they would work within their course format, classroom routines, and time constraints. For example, in one course, exams were handed back in small recitation sections, so it worked well for exam wrappers to be distributed as paper handouts to these small groups. In another course with approximately 150 students in a lecture format, the instructor included the exam wrappers with the returned exams (so there was no added time in distributing papers) and then asked students to spend the next 10 minutes writing their exam wrapper responses. And, in yet another course, where there were more than 200 students in a large lecture format, the instructor assigned students to complete an online version of the exam wrapper within a day of receiving their graded exams. Note that in two of the courses the instructors introduced additional types of metacognitive wrappers, as is described later in the chapter.

Assessing Exam Wrappers

The data we used to evaluate exam wrappers' effectiveness include (a) students' responses on the exam wrappers themselves (i.e., both the numerical and open-ended responses), (b) students' open-ended responses to an end-of-semester survey asking about their learning experiences, and (c) students' ratings of various strategies for learning taken from a questionnaire we administered at the beginning and end of the semester. Each of these measures was collected separately across the four courses. For example, students in the biology course completed an end-of-semester survey with questions focused on their learning experiences that semester *in biology.* Similarly, the questionnaire on students' beliefs about learning and strategies for learning was administered in four versions, with each version's questions making reference to the corresponding course (e.g., students in biology would be asked to rate "When studying for biology, I often try to explain the material to myself").

Students' Exam Wrapper Responses

By analyzing students' actual wrapper responses, we can get a sense of what the information wrappers can reveal and see how seriously students treated the exam wrappers, even though they were not graded assignments. Here I will focus on the calculus course, while summarizing the results from the other courses, which were similar.

On the first exam in calculus, the average score was 83%, rather high compared with the other courses' first exam scores. So, one might expect that these students—who performed quite well on average—would complete the exam wrapper somewhat hastily or superficially. However, looking at the open-ended responses to the third type of exam wrapper question—which asks what students might do differently for the next exam—we see that students articulated a variety of productive study strategies. The most common responses were "spend more time reviewing along the way" (25%) and "practice more problems" (24%), two approaches to learning and studying that any instructor would want to promote. The next most common response was "be more careful/check work" (17%), which is consistent with students' earlier responses in the exam wrapper where they analyzed their errors on the exam: on average, students estimated that 38% of the points they lost were from careless mistakes, 18% from not knowing how to approach the problem, and 8% from not understanding a concept. Less than 8% said they would do "nothing" differently. The calculus instructor was encouraged by the productive responses that students gave to the exam wrapper. The other courses showed similar patterns, as exemplified in Table 2.1.

Although the main goal of wrappers is to get students to think about what their current strategies and performance suggest they should do differently for the next exam, instructors can also get value from students' responses to the exam wrapper questions. For example, the calculus instructor was glad to learn (from the first section of the exam wrapper) that 94% of his students found the exam to be fair and 79% of students reported they received sufficient feedback on the graded exam. This reassured him that the exam he created

Table 2.1   Student responses (across biology, chemistry, and physics) to the third type of exam wrapper question

I will study more next time and start a few days earlier.
I'm happy with the grade I got and I will continue to study in the same way to get it again.
I will do more practice problems to cut back on mistakes.
Reread the textbook more, solve more practice problems, and go to course center with more questions.
Do more problems and think carefully about the concepts.
My [study] methods were not effective, but I had a good enough grasp on [the material] to do decently enough. I will study more prior to the exam and do more practice problems next time.
I could utilize the homework better because I usually did not exert much effort on the homework.
I will do more conceptual problems instead of math problems and follow the problem-solving guideline to figure out the approach.

and the grading process around it were both reasonably effective. He also was interested to learn that, on average, students reported spending 5 or more hours studying for the exam, more than half of which was working through problems of some sort. This encouraged the instructor to continue sharing old exam problems as a resource for students' study. Indeed, "study old tests" was a new strategy that some students mentioned in their exam wrapper responses.

End-of-Semester Surveys

At the end of the semester, we administered an open-ended survey asking students what they learned about their learning during the semester and what they changed as a result. Questions included the following:

> "What, if any, new strategies did you begin using in [course] this semester compared to the past?"
>
> "What, if any, old strategies did you stop using in [course] this semester compared to the past?"
>
> "What do you think is good about how you study in [course]?"
>
> "What advice do you have from your experience learning [course] this semester that you think would be useful for future students, especially in the first year?"

Across the four courses, more than half of the students articulated specific changes they had made in their approach to learning and studying. Of these, the vast majority mentioned adopting new strategies (89% in biology, 90% in chemistry, 85% in physics, and 96% in calculus). Appendix C shows a sample of responses that are representative of common themes recurring across the entire set of students' newly adopted strategies: solving more problems; focusing on key issues; being more deliberate in the timing, amount, and location of one's studying; and taking advantage of available help.

When students answered the question about offering advice to other students, they emphasized the same themes as just mentioned. An additional theme that appeared for this question was a focus on assessing one's own understanding. Although students did not use the term *self-assess,* their remarks suggested that this message from the exam wrappers got through. A few verbatim responses are worth sharing: "Try not to move on without a good understanding." "As you read the material and learn concepts, make sure you know how to apply them to problems." "Try to absorb bits of everything and figure out whether you understand the concept." "Doing old exams . . . is usually a pretty accurate assessment of if you are ready [for the test] or need to go back and study." In sum, students' end-of-semester responses show that they made important changes in their approaches to learning and that they recognized the value of those changes.

Pre- and Postsemester Changes in Students' Beliefs About Learning

At the beginning and end of the semester, I administered a questionnaire asking students about their strategies for studying and self-regulated learning. All of the questions were asked so as to elicit a numerical rating from students on a 5-point scale. Thus, the following results are reported in terms of change in students' ratings from beginning to end of the semester. For example, students would rate the degree to which a strategy (e.g., "When studying for biology, I often try to explain the material to myself") was effective for them, at the beginning and end of the semester, and we would calculate their change in rating.

Because exam wrappers were not implemented in the four math and science courses according to randomized experimental design, we cannot compare the degree of change between treatment and control groups of students. However, because of natural variation in the number of these four courses that first-year students took in their first semester, we have students getting different numbers of exam wrappers. In other words, the more of our four courses that students were taking, the more exam wrappers students were experiencing, and hence the greater their "dose" of our treatment. In the figures that follow, I present dose–response analyses, where dose is the number of courses (of these four) taken and response is the students' average change in rating. (Note: no student took all four of these courses at once.)

Figure 2.2 shows the change in students' ratings for metacognitive strategies (e.g., self-assessing, choosing the best strategies that work for them,

Figure 2.2 Change in rating for metacognitive strategies, as a function of exam wrapper "dose"

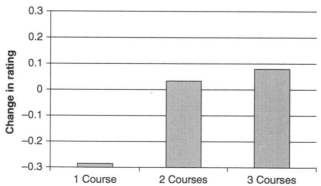

adjusting as needed) across students who were taking one, two, or three of the courses in our project. The first thing to notice in this graph is that, as predicted, students showed more positive change in their ratings of meta-cognitive skills the more courses they were taking that used wrappers. In particular, there was a large jump in students' change in rating when they were taking two or more of the courses (i.e., when they were seeing exam wrappers in multiple disciplines). This is consistent with the idea that when students experience exam wrappers in multiple contexts, they are more likely to see the value of the metacognitive skills promoted through exam wrappers. One other point worth mentioning is the direction of change for students taking one course. This change in rating score being less than zero does not necessarily imply that those students were valuing metacognitive strategies less at the end compared to the beginning of the semester; it could simply be an artifact of students making these two ratings months apart. So one should be cautious about interpreting these "change-in-rating" measures in absolute terms and instead focus on the nature of the effect across the three dose levels.

Besides asking about the metacognitive skills that exam wrappers were designed to foster, this questionnaire also asked about specific study strategies students might have tried, adopted, or abandoned as a result of more effective self-regulated learning. The questionnaire included questions on eight such strategies, and we had different predictions for the different strategies. Table 2.2 lists these strategies.

Given prior educational research (cf. Ambrose et al., 2010; Chi, Bassok, Lewis, Reimann, & Glaser, 1989) and knowing the nature of the four math and science courses (i.e., focused on problem solving and conceptual

Table 2.2 Strategies that students evaluated and our predictions

Strategy	Effective?	Dose–Response Effect
Connecting new ideas to what one already knows	Yes	Positive
Reviewing solution sets	Yes	Positive
Explaining material to oneself	Yes	Positive
Solving new problems	Yes	Positive
Rereading the text/notes	No	Negative
Memorizing facts	No	Negative
Explaining material to a friend	?	Unknown
Studying in groups	?	Unknown

Note: "Effective?" is the expectation of how effective this strategy would be for students learning in our target math and science courses. All of the dose–response predictions are consistent with students being more accurate in evaluating strategies the more exam wrappers they experience.

Figure 2.3   Students' change in rating of "effective" strategies as a function of exam wrapper dose

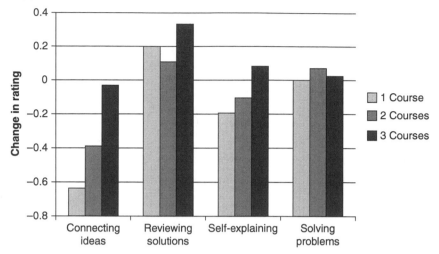

understanding), we grouped these strategies into three categories: strategies that should be effective and hence more likely to be used by students with strong metacognitive skills, strategies that are not effective and hence less likely to be used by students with strong metacognitive skills, and unknown. Our predictions for students' evaluations of these strategies are based on the idea that students who are getting more exam wrappers should be more accurately assessing the effectiveness of different study strategies.

For the first four strategies, we predicted a positive dose–response effect based on the logic that students who are engaged in more effective self-regulated learning (i.e., getting a larger "dose") should be more likely to accurately assess these strategies as effective and use them more across the semester. Figure 2.3 shows the results. Note that in all but one case this prediction is met: there is a positive trend across the three levels of one course, two courses, and three courses. Not seeing this trend for "solving new problems" is surprising but may be a result of many students recognizing the value of this strategy even at the beginning of the semester (and hence not showing an increase).

For the next two strategies in Table 2.2—rereading the text/notes and memorizing facts (neither of which would be very useful for learning in our target math and science courses)—we predicted a negative dose–response effect. Students who are engaged in more effective self-regulated learning should accurately see these strategies as less effective and hence use them less over time. Figure 2.4 shows the corresponding results. Although rereading did show the predicted negative trend, memorization showed the opposite. This

Figure 2.4 Students' change in rating of "less effective" strategies as a function of exam wrapper dose

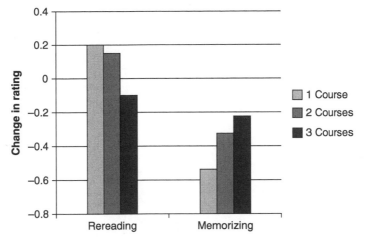

Figure 2.5 Students' change in rating for peer-based strategies as a function of exam wrapper dose

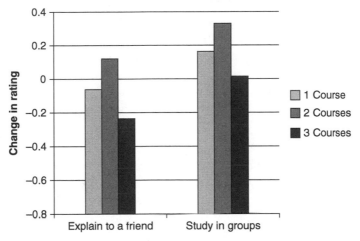

could be for the simple reason that memorization is actually more helpful in these introductory math and science courses than one would have thought.

Finally, two of the study strategies involved working with peers (explaining material to a friend and studying in groups), and for these strategies we did not have a specific prediction for the dose–response effect. Figure 2.5 presents the corresponding results. For both of these strategies, the change in rating measure shows neither a positive nor negative overall trend.

In sum, students' change in rating measures for different study strategies accorded with our prediction in four of the six cases. This is generally consistent with the idea that the more students were experiencing exam wrappers, the more likely they were to learn the value of various study strategies and accurately rate the strategies' effectiveness. Of course, it would be even better to show that students' evaluations of the different strategies match the strategies' *actual* effectiveness. Although that would be an ideal analysis, getting a measure of each strategy's effectiveness for each student would be very tricky because it would require measuring student performance on specific tasks after the student had—versus had not—engaged in a particular strategy. Nevertheless, in future work to assess the effectiveness of exam wrappers, the plan is to incorporate measures of students' actual grades on exams and other direct performance measures in order to get at this issue.

OTHER KINDS OF WRAPPERS

Exam wrappers fold metacognitive reflection around an existing instructional component. The same approach can be applied to other instructional components. At the time students are engaging in an instructional activity, simply add a scaffolding for reflection before and after. The design considerations remain the same; only the format and scope need to change. Homework wrappers and lecture wrappers are natural choices, but there are many more options, for example, small-group discussion wrappers, project wrappers, and widget wrappers around an instructional component from an online learning environment (see chapter 6 for an approach to "wrapping" papers).

We have created and used homework wrappers and lecture wrappers in several of the science courses mentioned in this chapter. Appendix D shows a sample homework wrapper used in a physics course. Notice that it first clearly articulates the goals of the assignment and then asks students to self-assess their skill level relative to those goals—all before students begin the assignment. Then, after students have finished the physics work, the homework wrapper prompts them to reassess their skills, based on what they just experienced, and to make a plan for what they should do next to further develop those skills. For lecture wrappers, we have used variations on several classroom assessment techniques (Angelo & Cross, 1993), such as minute papers, muddiest point write-ups, and clickers. In each case, the approach was to prompt students to do some reflective self-assessment about what they just learned (or did not learn) during a lecture and then to encourage students to identify some concrete next steps for learning.

I hope these examples convey how easy it is to create and use a new wrapper. The website www.learningwrappers.org is a community repository for finding and sharing wrapper ideas. Readers are invited to visit this site to learn more about wrappers, download relevant resources, and contribute their own ideas for wrapper activities.

CONCLUSION

Metacognitive skills are critical, and they are more likely to be learned when they are integral to our instructional strategy. In designing metacognitive instruction, a core principle is to think of metacognitive skills—and to teach them—as we would any other skills. And in essence, what this boils down to is giving students effective practice. As with any practice, we want to make sure that (a) metacognitive practice is well aligned with the skills we want students to learn, (b) students get repeated opportunities with feedback to make those skills into effective habits of mind, and (c) students get diverse experiences to support transfer of their metacognitive skills.

The wrappers introduced in this chapter are a simple idea with powerful consequences. They offer explicit, repeated practice at key metacognitive skills in a context (e.g., getting back graded exams) in which students are paying close attention. They are designed to be practical, portable, and easy to use. We have used wrappers successfully for exams, homework, and lectures in a variety of courses at Carnegie Mellon University, and instructors at other universities have been adopting them as well (Greco, 2012; Weimer, 2010). The scope for wrappers is quite broad and, with the advent of online, interactive educational tools, their scope will only increase.

REFERENCES

Ambrose, S. A., Bridges, M. W., DiPietro, M., Lovett, M. C., & Norman, M. K. (2010). *How learning works: Seven research-based principles for smart teaching.* San Francisco: Jossey-Bass.

Anderson, L. W., & Krathwohl, D. R. (Eds.). (2001). *A taxonomy for learning, teaching, and assessing: A revision of Bloom's Taxonomy of Educational Objectives.* New York: Longman.

Angelo, T. A., & Cross, K. P. (1993). *Classroom assessment techniques: A handbook for college teachers.* San Francisco: Jossey-Bass.

Azevedo, R., & Cromley, J. G. (2004). Does training on self-regulated learning facilitate students' learning with hypermedia? *Journal of Educational Psychology, 96*(3), 523–535.

Barnett, S. M., & Ceci, S. J. (2002). When and where do we apply what we learn? A taxonomy for far transfer. *Psychological Bulletin, 128*(4), 612–637.

Butler, D. L., & Winne, P. H. (1995). Feedback and self-regulated learning: A theoretical synthesis. *Review of Educational Research, 65*, 245–281.

Carr, M., Kurtz, B. E., Schneider, W., Turner, L. A., & Borkowski, J. G. (1989). Strategy acquisition and transfer among American and German children: Environmental influences on metacognitive development. *Developmental Psychology, 25*(5), 765–771.

Chi, M. T., Bassok, M., Lewis, M. W., Reimann, P., & Glaser, R. (1989). Self-explanations: How students study and use examples in learning to solve problems. *Cognitive Science, 13*, 145–182.

Ertmer, P. A., & Newby, T. J. (1996). The expert learner: Strategic, self-regulated, and reflective. *Instructional Science, 24*(1), 1–24.

Flavell, J. H. (1976). Metacognitive aspects of problem solving. In L. B. Resnick (Ed.), *The nature of intelligence* (pp. 231–236). Hillsdale, NJ: Erlbaum.

Greco, E. (2012). *Developing, deploying, and analyzing exam wrappers in a large introductory physics class.* American Physical Society, APS April meeting, Atlanta, GA. Abstract 15.001.

Halpern, D. F. (1998). Teaching critical thinking for transfer across domains: Disposition, skills, structure training, and metacognitive monitoring. *American Psychologist, 53*(4), 449–455.

Lizarraga, M. L. S. D., Baquedano, M. T. S. D., Mangado, T. G., & Cardelle-Elawar, M. (2009). Enhancement of thinking skills: Effects of two intervention methods. *Thinking Skills and Creativity, 4*(1), 30–43.

Meyers, N. M., & Nulty, D. D. (2009). How to use (five) curriculum design principles to align authentic learning environments, assessment, students' approaches to thinking and learning outcomes. *Assessment & Evaluation in Higher Education, 34*(5), 565–577.

Palinscar, A. S., & Brown, A. L. (1984). Reciprocal teaching of comprehension-fostering and comprehension-monitoring activities. *Cognition & Instruction, 1*, 117–175.

Pascarella, E. T., & Terenzini, P. T. (2005). *How college affects students: A third decade of research.* San Francisco: Jossey-Bass.

Pintrich, P. R., Smith, D. A., Garcia, T., & McKeachie, W. J. (1991). *A manual for the use of the Motivated Strategies for Learning Questionnaire (MSLQ).* Ann Arbor, MI: National Center for Research to Improve Postsecondary Teaching and Learning, University of Michigan.

Schommer, M. (1990). The effects of beliefs about the nature of knowledge on comprehension. *Journal of Educational Psychology, 82*, 498–504.

Schommer, M. (1993). Epistemological development and academic performance among secondary students. *Journal of Educational Psychology, 85*, 406–411.

Schraw, G., Crippen, K. J., & Hartley, K. (2006). Promoting self-regulation in science education: Metacognition as part of a broader perspective on learning. *Research in Science Education, 36*(1–2), 111–139.

Weimer, M. (2010). Exam wrappers. *Faculty Focus.* Retrieved from www.facultyfocus.com/articles/teaching-and-learning/exam-wrappers/.

Winne, P. H., & Hadwin, A. F. (1998). Studying as self-regulated learning. In D. Hacker, J. Dunlosky, & A. Graesser (Eds.), *Metacognition in educational theory and practice* (pp. 277–304). Mahwah, NJ: Erlbaum.

Zimmerman, B. J. (2001). Theories of self-regulated learning and academic achievement: An overview and analysis. In B. J. Zimmerman & D. H. Schunk (Eds.), *Self-regulated learning and academic achievement* (2nd ed., pp. 1–38). Hillsdale, NJ: Erlbaum.

Appendix A1
Sample Exam Wrapper, Physics

Physics Post-Exam Reflection   Name: _____

This activity is designed to give you a chance to reflect on your exam performance and, more important, on the effectiveness of your exam preparation. Please answer the questions sincerely. Your responses will be collected to inform the instructional team regarding students' experiences surrounding this exam and how we can best support your learning. We will hand back your completed sheet in advance of the next exam to inform and guide your preparation for that exam.

1. Approximately how much time did you spend preparing for this exam? _____

2. What percentage of your test-preparation time was spent in each of these activities?
   a. Reading textbook section(s) for the first time _____
   b. Rereading textbook section(s) _____
   c. Reviewing homework solutions _____
   d. Solving problems for practice _____
   e. Reviewing your own notes _____
   f. Reviewing materials from course website _____
      (What materials? _____)
   g. Other _____
      (Please specify: _____)

3. Now that you have looked over your graded exam, estimate the percentage of points you lost due to each of the following (make sure the percentages add up to 100):

   a. Trouble with vectors and vector notation ＿＿＿＿＿＿

   b. Algebra or arithmetic errors ＿＿＿＿＿＿

   c. Lack of understanding of the concept ＿＿＿＿＿＿

   d. Not knowing how to approach the problem ＿＿＿＿＿＿

   e. Careless mistakes ＿＿＿＿＿＿

   f. Other ＿＿＿＿＿

      (Please specify: ＿＿＿＿＿＿)

4. Based on your responses to the previous questions, name at least three things you plan to do differently in preparing for the next exam. For instance, will you just spend more time studying, change a specific study habit or try a new one (if so, name it), make math more automatic so it does not get in the way of the physics, try to sharpen some other skill (if so, name it), solve more practice problems, or something else?

5. What can we do to help support your learning and your preparation for the next exam?

Appendix A2
Sample Exam Wrapper, Calculus

Name: _____

DEPARTMENT OF MATHEMATICAL SCIENCES

Calculus Test Reflection

How much time did you spend reviewing with each of the following:

Reading class notes _____

Reworking old homework problems _____

Working additional problems _____

Reading the book _____

What percentage of your preparation for the test was done alone, and what percentage with one or more persons?

_____ % alone   _____ % with other(s)

Do you think that the problems on the exam fairly reflected the topics covered in class and recitation? Yes _____   No _____

Now that you have looked over your exam, estimate the percentage of points you lost due to each of the following:

_____ % from not understanding a concept

_____ % from not being careful (i.e., careless mistakes)

_____ % from not being able to formulate an approach to a problem

_____ % from other reasons (please specify: _____)

Did the grader's comments, together with the solutions, provide you with adequate feedback? Yes _____   No _____

Based on the previous estimates and on your approach to studying for this exam, what will you do differently in preparing for the next exam? For instance, will you change your study habits or try to sharpen particular skills? Please be specific. Also, what can we do to help?

Appendix B
Additional Sample Exam Wrappers (Biology and Chemistry)

Biology Self-Assessment & Reflection: Exam #1   Name: _____

DUE: At the next class meeting, hand in this completed form at the beginning of lecture.

This form will help you to analyze your exam performance and find strategies that work best for you in learning the material for this course. Self-assessing your progress and adjusting your study strategies accordingly is what effective learners tend to do. Please answer the following questions sincerely. Your responses will have no impact on your grade, but they will inform the instructional team about how we can best support your learning. We will return your completed form before the second exam so that you can use your own responses to guide your approach to studying next time.

1. Approximately how much time did you spend preparing for this exam?

   _____

2. What percentage of your test-preparation time was spent in each of these activities?

   a. Skimming textbook chapters _____

   b. Reading textbook chapters thoroughly _____

   c. Reviewing your own notes _____

   d. Working on practice exam questions _____

   e. Reviewing materials from Blackboard _____

   f. Other _____

      (Please specify: _____)

3. As you look over your graded exam, analyze where/how you lost points. Fill in the blanks with the number of points you lost due to each of the following:

   a. Trouble applying definitions   _____

   b. Trouble remembering structures   _____

   c. Lack of understanding of a concept   _____

   d. Not knowing how to begin a problem   _____

   e. Careless mistakes   _____

   f. Other   _____

      (Please specify: _____)

4. Based on your responses to the questions, name three things you plan to do differently in preparing for the next exam. For instance, will you just spend more time, change a specific study habit (if so, name it), try to sharpen some other skill (if so, name it), use other resources more, or something else?

5. What can we do to help support your learning and your preparation for the next exam?

Chemistry Self-Assessment & Reflection: Exam #1   Name: _____

DUE: At your next recitation session, hand in this completed form to your TA.

This form will help you analyze your exam performance and find strategies that work best for you to learn the material in this course. Self-assessing your progress and adjusting your study strategies accordingly is what effective learners tend to do. Please answer the following questions sincerely. Your responses will have no impact on your grade, but they will inform the instructional team about how we can best support your learning. We will return your completed form before the second exam so you can use your own responses to guide your approach to studying next time.

1. Approximately how much time did you spend preparing for this exam? _____

2. What percentage of your test-preparation time was spent in each of these activities?

   a. Skimming textbook chapters   _____

   b. Reading textbook chapters thoroughly   _____

   c. Reviewing homework solutions   _____

   d. Solving problems for practice   _____

   e. Reviewing your own notes   _____

   f. Tracking your time while solving problems   _____

   g. Other   _____

      (Please specify: _____)

3. As you look over your graded exam, analyze where/how you lost points. Fill in the blanks with the number of points you lost due to each of the following:

   a. Not understanding a concept or term   _____

   b. Not knowing how to begin a problem   _____

   c. Not knowing how to apply the right formula   _____

   d. Not keeping track of units   _____

   e. Careless mistakes   _____

   f. Other   _____

      (Please specify: _____)

4. Based on your responses to the questions, name three things you plan to do differently in preparing for the next exam. For instance, will you just spend more time, change a specific study habit (if so, name it), try to sharpen some other skill (if so, name it), do your homework differently, use other resources more, or something else?

5. What can we do to support your learning and preparation for the next exam?

Appendix C
Student Responses (Across Biology, Chemistry, Physics, and Calculus) Regarding Their Changed Strategies for Learning

Solving More Problems

- "I would work through more practice problems." [Biology student]
- "A new strategy I used was practicing with old exams, to better identify how to begin certain types of problems." [Chemistry student]
- "I found it very helpful to review the old/practice tests—try and do them, check the answers, figure out where I went wrong, etc." [Chemistry student]
- "Before a test I would go back to the textbook and do extra problems on the areas which I thought I need most help in." [Calculus student]
- "I began to practice questions, both from our old assignments and our homework, in order to gain a better understanding of how to properly solve the problems given out in this course." [Physics student]

Focusing on Key Aspects

- "I began using review sheets more to study for tests. . . . The review sheets were helpful and cut out busy work." [Calculus student]
- "Just skimming reading and referring to it [the textbook] while doing LOTS of practice problems." [Physics student]
- "I had to think of main concepts and theory a lot more than I was used to." [Physics student]
- "In high school I used to read the text over and over again, but that didn't always help me learn the information [in college]." [Chemistry student]

Being More Deliberate About One's Studying

- "Practicing problems right after lecture." [Calculus student]
- "Going [over] again immediately after lecture on what has been covered that day." [Physics student]
- "For this class I started preparing for exams about a week before the exam date. Previously, this was something I never had to do." [Physics student]
- "Spend more time studying." [Biology student]
- "Study earlier." [Chemistry student]

Taking Advantage of Available Help

- "I went to office hours, asked friends for help, and went to SI more often." [Chemistry student; SI refers to supplemental instruction, a weekly review session.]
- "In my previous calculus there was not the opportunity to go to review sessions for tests. I have gone to the review sessions my TA has provided and I have found them to be very useful." [Calculus student]
- "I took the help of course center." [Physics student; course center is a kind of group office hours offered by the physics department.]
- "I would go to SI and review sessions." [Biology student]

Appendix D
First Physics Homework With "Wrapper"

This homework is designed to give you practice working with vectors so that it becomes second nature to you. We want you to become very comfortable with vector addition and subtraction, so that when you are faced with a physics problem, you can focus on the science without getting bogged down in the math.

Before you begin the rest of this assignment, rate how true each of the following statements is for you now. Use a scale from 1 to 7, where 1 is "not at all true of me" and 7 is "very true of me."

a. I can add and subtract vectors using the vector diagram method.
b. I can *automatically and without much effort* add and subtract vectors using the vector diagram method.
c. I know what the difference is between a scalar and a vector.
d. I can *easily and effortlessly* recognize scalars as distinct from vectors when I'm working on a physics problem.
e. I know what the difference is between a vector's magnitude and its direction.
f. I can *easily and effortlessly* recognize and work with the difference between a vector's magnitude and its direction when I'm working on a physics problem.

[Vector addition/subtraction problems appear here]

Now that you have completed the assignment, rate how true each of the following statements is for you. Again, use a scale from 1 to 7, where 1 is "not at all true of me" and 7 is "very true of me."

a. I can add and subtract vectors using the vector diagram method.
b. I can *automatically and without much effort* add and subtract vectors using the vector diagram method.

c. I know what the difference is between a scalar and a vector.

d. I can *easily and effortlessly* recognize scalars as distinct from vectors when I'm working on a physics problem.

e. I know what the difference is between a vector's magnitude and its direction.

f. I can *easily and effortlessly* recognize and work with the difference between a vector's magnitude and its direction when I'm working on a physics problem.

It can be revealing to compare your ratings at the beginning and end of this assignment. If you feel you have made the progress you wanted, great; please write one sentence to describe your progress. If you feel you have not quite achieved the progress you wanted from this assignment, that is okay, too; please write a sentence about what action(s) you might take that could help you achieve that level of progress.

3

Improving Critical-Thinking Skills in Introductory Biology Through Quality Practice and Metacognition

Paula P. Lemons, Julie A. Reynolds, Amanda J. Curtin-Soydan, and Ahrash N. Bissell

Critical thinking has long been a desired outcome of science instruction. Numerous national reports call for college science instructors to teach in ways that promote the application of concepts to solve problems, not just the recollection and comprehension of basic facts (American Association for the Advancement of Science [AAAS], 1989, 2011; National Research Council, 2003). Most recently, the AAAS (2011) issued a call to action, setting the standard that undergraduates develop critical-thinking skills, such as the ability to apply the process of science, use quantitative reasoning, and use modeling and simulation. Many faculty also agree that students' development of critical-thinking skills is a primary objective of college (Paul, Elder, & Bartell, 1997), but data show that few college science courses actually teach or assess these skills (Ebert-May et al., 2011; Momsen, Long, Wyse, & Ebert-May, 2010; Zheng, Lawhorn, Lumley, & Freeman, 2008).

One of the most fundamental ways to teach critical thinking is to give students practice solving problems, synthesizing data, and evaluating evidence as a regular part of their coursework, because students' approaches to studying are strongly influenced by the types of questions their instructors use. For example, one study showed that students who were expecting a multiple-choice exam focused their note-taking efforts on facts and details, while those who were expecting essay tests concentrated on main ideas (Nolen & Haladyna, 1990). Another study documented that students are discouraged from seeking to deeply understand the material when exams only ask for memorization of large volumes of facts (Entwistle & Entwistle, 1992). Other researchers have shown that students tend to use deeper, more active approaches to studying when they are preparing for exams that include essays or critical-thinking

53

questions (Stanger-Hall, 2012; Traub & MacRury, 1990). Clearly, including critical-thinking questions on exams and other assignments is an important strategy for teaching critical thinking.

But are appropriate assignments sufficient to promote the desired development of students' critical-thinking skills? Probably not. For example, Tsai stated:

> Students who are not skilled in self-reflection during learning and who lack well-organized knowledge structures may deem all new information to be of equal importance and each conception to be unique and individually significant. This . . . may lead to a strategy of rote memorization and commitment of each part to detailed encoding in memory, but largely as isolated units. (2001, p. 971)

We should not assume that including critical-thinking questions in a course will automatically overcome students' tendencies toward rote learning. Prior research has shown that students must explicitly attend to the mechanics of critical thinking if they intend for those skills to transfer from one domain to another (van Gelder, 2005). We have noted in our own classrooms that students sometimes misunderstand the purpose of critical-thinking assignments. For example, some students do not recognize that critical-thinking questions are meant to measure their ability to convey deep understanding of a concept and to apply that understanding. Rather, they view the questions as tricky in the sense that they suspect we are literally attempting to mislead them in order to expose what they do not know. Some students do not recognize that critical-thinking questions require study strategies that enhance learning, retention, and domain transfer. Rather, they think the amount of study and preparation needed to succeed on the questions is excessive for an introductory course. For these reasons, we have come to believe that for students to fully benefit from critical-thinking assignments, they must integrate critical thinking as a habit of mind, recognizing the cognitive processes that constitute critical thinking and routinely practicing those processes. In other words, students must think about their critical thinking. Thus, we also include components in our assignments that require them to engage in metacognition.

Metacognition can generally be summarized as the knowledge, awareness, and control of one's own learning (White, 1998). Scholars have provided both theoretical frameworks and empirical evidence for a connection between critical thinking and metacognition (Cooper & Sandi-Urena, 2009; Halpern, 1998; Tsai, 2001; Veenman, Van Hout-Wolters, & Afflerbach, 2006).

Generally speaking, scholars see the relationship between critical thinking and metacognition in one of three ways:

1. Metacognition and critical thinking are separate constructs because it is technically possible to think of your own thoughts without critically analyzing or reflecting on those thoughts (Lipman, 1988).
2. Critical thinking is part of the construct of metacognition because practicing the cognitive steps of critical thinking may be necessary for monitoring and controlling one's thinking (Flavell, 1979; Kuhn, 1999).
3. Metacognition is part of the construct of critical thinking because a component skill of critical thinking is the ability to recognize the appropriate strategy among a range of possible strategies (Facione, 1990; Schraw, Crippen, & Hartley, 2006; van Gelder, 2005; Willingham, 2007).

After having developed and tested a variety of classroom activities and assessments that promote critical thinking and metacognition, we support the view that metacognition is part of the construct of critical thinking. More specifically, we think metacognition may be *necessary* for the development of higher-order critical-thinking skills. Biologists must explicitly teach critical-thinking skills in a way that develops self-regulated thinkers, not just more sophisticated products (e.g., solutions to more complex problems). Pedagogies, technologies, and other interventions that purport to enhance critical thinking will fail unless they are coupled with metacognitive enhancements and strategies. This task presents a number of challenges—logistical, semantic, and curricular.

We have looked for ways to overcome these challenges and develop critical thinkers in introductory biology classrooms. To start, we needed to operationalize the concept of critical thinking. Like many biology educators, we found that Bloom's *Taxonomy of Educational Objectives* (Bloom, 1956; see also Anderson & Krathwohl, 2001) is well suited to this purpose (Armstrong, Chang, & Brickman, 2007; Bissell & Lemons, 2006; Freeman et al., 2007; Hoste, 1982; Stanger-Hall, Shockley, & Wilson, 2011). Bloom's taxonomy delineates six categories of learning: basic knowledge, secondary comprehension, application, analysis, synthesis, and evaluation. Although basic knowledge and secondary comprehension do not require critical-thinking skills, application, analysis, synthesis, and evaluation all require the higher-order thinking that characterizes critical thinking. The definitions for these categories provide a smooth transition from educational theory to practice by suggesting specific assessment designs that we can use to evaluate student skills in any given category.

Once we started using Bloom's taxonomy, we needed to align our assessments with it. We did this by writing exam questions, as we had always done, but we added special attention to make sure that at least some of the exam questions explicitly required the skills of application, analysis, evaluation, or synthesis. After gaining some experience with using such higher-order assessments, we quickly discovered that many students were at a loss to understand what we were trying to accomplish and that more explicit metacognitive instruction was needed.

To simultaneously teach students critical-thinking skills and metacognition, we designed a classroom module called "Critical Thinking in Biology." The module consists of:

1. Questions that biologists consider worthwhile and that require critical thinking; the module questions mimic the questions we ask students on exams.
2. Rubrics that show students how these questions require both domain-specific knowledge and skill in critical thinking.
3. Guiding questions that encourage self-reflection and critique (metacognition).

We implemented "Critical Thinking in Biology" in the lab portion of an introductory biology course at Duke University, a private research university in the Southeast. The course enrolled about 200 students per semester. Students attended a 50-minute lecture three times per week and a 2.5-hour lab one time per week. In lab, students met in groups of 12, facilitated by a graduate teaching assistant. Students completed graded work in both lab and lecture. Exams were administered during lecture time and included questions covering both lecture and lab content.

Here we present our "Critical Thinking in Biology" module, with commentary based on our experience. We also present some preliminary data that suggest our exercise made a positive impact on students. As is too frequently the case in teaching and learning scholarship, we do not have conclusive evidence that our exercise is better than other approaches to teaching critical thinking or metacognition, but our experience has convinced us that metacognition is a supporting condition for higher-order skills, such as application, analysis, and evaluation, in that monitoring and responding to the quality of the products that arise from these skills is necessary for being a critical thinker.

"CRITICAL THINKING IN BIOLOGY" WITH COMMENTARY

For the "Critical Thinking in Biology" module, we presented the learning goals shown in Figure 3.1 to students.

Figure 3.1   Student learning goals

By the end of this exercise, you should be able to:

- Describe a strategy for tackling scientific questions.
- Describe the structure of answers to exam questions that assess critical thinking, considering the relative quality of different sample answers. This goal includes detailed analysis of the components of a complete answer, including content knowledge and critical thinking.
- Apply your improved understanding by answering another scientific problem on your own and with less guidance.
- Analyze your own answer, as well as those of your peers, in order to determine the strengths and weaknesses in your critical-thinking skills.

Part A: Tackling Scientific Questions

In advance of the lab exercise, we asked students to attempt to solve a scientific question about inheritance of traits involving pedigree analysis (Figure 3.2). Specifically, the question required students to (a) correctly read a pedigree; (b) understand key genetics terms: *autosomal, sex-linked, dominant, recessive, simple,* and *codominant*; (c) determine the mode of inheritance shown by the pedigree; (d) construct an argument for the mode of inheritance shown in the pedigree, including why the mode of inheritance selected is more likely than other possible modes of inheritance; and (e) describe evidence that would refute their proposed mode of inheritance.

Note that we gave quite a bit of guiding information to the students regarding the best methods for answering the questions (parts A and B). Instructors can be forgiven for thinking that college students should already have a good understanding of how to properly answer questions like these, but in fact we found this not to be the case. A certain amount of redundancy and reinforcement is required—not just for the material itself, but for the recommended strategies for both mastering the material and demonstrating that mastery in writing and other exercises.

This overt instruction about *how* to answer questions is crucial for setting the stage for students to approach problems more critically. Too many students believe that the design and underlying motivations for any given problem are opaque and impossible to understand. Problems requiring critical thinking are particularly challenging in this case because students perceive that there is no "correct" answer or believe that the problem is specifically designed to trick them. By revealing the connection among the content, critical-thinking skills, and written forms of both questions and answers, instructors may help students develop an improved capacity to evaluate their own understanding in new situations.

Figure 3.2   An example question

When a genetic disorder is diagnosed in a family, family members often want to know the likelihood that they or their children will develop the condition. One important factor that influences a person's chances of developing a genetic condition is how the condition is inherited (i.e., whether it is autosomal or sex-linked, dominant or recessive, simple or codominant).

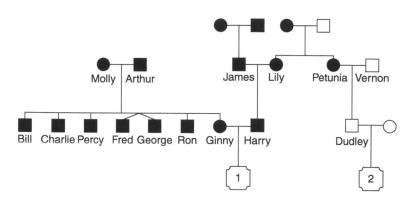

A. In examining the pedigree, what mode of inheritance best describes the trait indicated by the dark symbols? For full credit, you must name a mode of inheritance, explain what you think the most likely phenotype (affected or unaffected) and genotype of individual #1 would be, and explain why. (*Hint*: to make an argument that one mode of inheritance is more likely than others, you will need to discuss the other modes of inheritance and explain why they are less likely.)

B. Currently, we know neither the phenotype nor the genotype for individual #1 or #2. What additional information about either individual would refute the mode of inheritance you propose in Part A? Explain how this information would refute your analysis, and propose an alternative mode of inheritance that would explain the new information.

Part B: Analyzing the Structure of Answers to Scientific Questions

One of the most critical aspects of this classroom exercise was that we repeatedly and explicitly informed students of the expectation that they develop both content knowledge *and* critical-thinking skills. When students started working on the classroom exercise, we explained our expectations regarding what constitutes a complete answer (Figure 3.3).

With these expectations stated, we gave students the chance to evaluate sample responses to the pedigree question (Figure 3.2). Here we made a critical distinction between traditional forms of evaluation, in which one is looking for a "right" answer, and the form of evaluation we intended to use (Figure 3.4).

We gave students three sample essays to evaluate. All sample essays showed good understanding of content, because most students struggle less with explaining content than with constructing logical arguments. Of the three sample essays, essay 1 (Figure 3.5) was of high quality, including correct and complete content knowledge and good logical reasoning, leading to proper conclusions; essay 2 (Figure 3.6) was of moderate quality, including

Figure 3.3   Explanation of expectations regarding complete answers

Many of the questions you will be asked to complete this semester in introductory biology require you to demonstrate both (a) knowledge and understanding of the content covered in class and lab and (b) skill with thinking critically about the material. In order to help you understand how we expect you to respond to these questions, we are giving you three sample responses to this week's prelab question.

Figure 3.4   Advice for identifying and evaluating critical thinking

Please evaluate each answer. Keep in mind that a *complete* answer to this question contains two components: *content knowledge* and *critical thinking*. If an answer states the facts or knowledge correctly, but does not draw these facts together with a logical rationale and conclusion, the question has not been fully answered. Similarly, a conclusion to the question only makes sense when the answer also includes a set of pertinent facts on which the conclusion is based. With these ideas in mind, evaluate the following three sample answers using the guiding questions provided.

Figure 3.5   Sample essay 1—high quality

Part A: The mode of inheritance is autosomal recessive for the following reasons. First, there is no evidence that the trait is sex-linked because both males and females are affected. Thus, it must be autosomal. Second, the trait is most likely to be recessive because if it is, Molly and Arthur are both "bb" (where "b" denotes the recessive allele). If you cross bb × bb, the only possible genotype is "bb" and the only possible phenotype is "affected." This is consistent with the results shown in the pedigree. If the trait is dominant, there is a chance that Molly and Arthur are heterozygous for the trait. If they are both heterozygous, then it is expected that 25% of individuals would be unaffected ("bb"). Given the results of the pedigree, dominance of the trait is less likely, but not impossible. Finally, incomplete dominance is not likely, because to be affected, as they are, Molly and Arthur would have to be "BR" (where "B" and "R" represent two different versions of the trait), and thus we would expect only 50% of the individuals to be "BR" and have the affected phenotype. Again, given the results of the pedigree, this is not impossible but unlikely. If the trait is autosomal recessive, then Ginny and Harry would both be "bb" and we could conclude that individual #1 should be "bb" and "affected" too.

Part B: If we found out that individual #1 is "unaffected," this would refute the idea that the trait is autosomal recessive, because if the trait is autosomal recessive, there would be no way that two individuals (in this case Ginny and Harry) who are affected could have a child who is "unaffected." If individual #1 was found to be "unaffected," an alternative hypothesis that could explain the mode of inheritance is autosomal dominant or autosomal incomplete dominance (assuming the trait is only expressed with both alleles present).

correct and complete content knowledge, but making a mistake in reasoning, leading to a flawed conclusion; and essay 3 was also of moderate quality, including correct and complete content knowledge but failing to provide logical reasoning for the conclusions (Figure 3.7).

To evaluate the sample essays, we gave students a series of guiding questions, with each question focusing on particular aspects of explaining content knowledge or constructing arguments. Appendix A details the guiding questions pertaining to sample essay 3 (Figure 3.7) and our idealized responses

Figure 3.6 Sample essay 2—moderate quality

Part A: The mode of inheritance that is most likely is autosomal dominant because 75% of individuals in this pedigree are affected. If Molly
and Arthur are both "BB" (where "B" denotes the dominant allele), and if
you cross BB × BB, the only possible genotype is "BB" and the only possible phenotype is "affected." If Molly or Arthur (or both) were carriers
("Bb"), then it is possible that all their kids could be affected (i.e., have
genotypes Bb or BB), although statistically speaking, we would expect
one-fourth of their children to be unaffected. So Ginny's genotype is
either BB or Bb. The same argument holds for James's parents—they are
either carriers or homozygous dominant. Lily's parents must both be
carriers since Lily is affected. So Harry's genotype must also be either BB
or Bb. Therefore, individual #1 would be either BB, Bb, or bb, depending
on the genotype of Ginny and Harry. I don't think the trait is sex-linked
because both males and females are affected.

Part B: If we found out that individual #2 is "affected," this would refute
the idea that the trait is autosomal dominant, because if the trait is autosomal dominant, there would be no way that two individuals (in this
case Dudley and his wife) who are unaffected could have a child who is
"affected."

Figure 3.7 Sample essay 3—moderate quality

Part A: The most likely mode of inheritance is autosomal recessive
because that mode best describes the pedigree. Lily's parents would both
have to be carriers (heterozygous, i.e., Bb), so Lily would be homozygous recessive (bb). If all afflicted individuals are homozygous recessive,
then the only possible genotype for their offspring would be homozygous recessive. Therefore, Ginny and Harry would both be "bb" and we
could conclude that individual #1 should be "bb" and "affected" too.

Part B: If individual #1 was not affected, this would refute my proposed
mode of inheritance since the genotype for individual #1 would have
to be something other than bb. An alternative mode of inheritance is
incomplete dominance.

to those questions. For many students, this sort of detailed analysis of one response comes as something of a revelation. Many students presume that the best response strategy is to relate everything they know about a subject, figuring that the odds of getting the right answer will improve with increasing amounts of text. But the guiding questions reveal that extraneous information is likely to confuse their answers and result in lower scores. Another key insight for students is the structure of a good argument. Students often fail to show the steps in their reasoning and make errors such as contradicting themselves. The guiding questions reveal the importance of step-by-step argument construction and internal consistency within an answer. Students are surprised to learn that they do not get the benefit of the doubt when their answers are unclear—if an answer is difficult to understand, it is easier for instructors to grade consistently by presuming the student lacked the necessary knowledge or skill and lowering the grade accordingly.

Once students evaluated each of the sample essays, we asked them to evaluate their own essays using the same guiding questions. This act of reflection becomes their metacognitive moment and is an illuminating exercise for students. They often realize that they made some of the same mistakes (and did some of the same things well) that they discovered in the sample answers.

Part C: Applying Their Improved Understanding by Answering Another Scientific Problem on Their Own and With Less Guidance

Once students completed the evaluation of sample essays and had some idea of how they should approach scientific questions, they got a chance to try answering a second question (Figure 3.8).

As with the initial question, we gave students explicit advice regarding the ideal format of an answer (see notes 1–3 in Figure 3.8). This repetition helps students to recognize that these questions share certain key structural characteristics and thus probably demand similarly constructed answers, even though the content differs considerably.

Once students answered this new question, we had them exchange their answers with one another and evaluate one another's work using a rubric like the ones we use to grade exam questions. The rubric includes an outline of a complete answer (Figure 3.9) and a graphical representation of the flow of both correct and partially correct answers (Figure 3.10). The expectations communicated in the outline are valid when students get the correct and complete answer. However, it is possible to apply the correct critical-thinking skills to these problems while getting some aspect of the content wrong. The graphical representation clarifies the intersection of the content and the skills.

Figure 3.8   Another example question

There are three species of Scrub Jays in the United States; their distribution is shown on the following map. One hypothesis proposed to explain this distribution suggests that Scrub Jays were once found in a continuous range from Florida to California. Now, the Western Scrub Jay is confined to deserts in the west, and the Eastern Scrub Jay is found in eastern forests. The Island Scrub Jay is found on Santa Cruz Island, off the coast of California.

In which of these species is it most likely that genetic drift played a role in the population diverging from the ancestral state? Your answer should (1) explain your understanding of genetic drift, (2) logically link that understanding to an analysis of the populations described in text and depicted on the map, and (3) draw a conclusion about the population most likely to be affected by genetic drift.

Figure 3.9   Grading rubric for genetic drift question in Figure 3.8

Knowledge needed to answer question:

- Definition of *genetic drift*
- The relationship between population size and the likelihood of random genetic drift
- The possible relationship between range sizes and population sizes (reading the map)

Critical-thinking skills needed to answer the question:

Application and Analysis: Students must correctly define *genetic drift* and state its relationship to population size, and then apply that knowledge to an analysis of likely population sizes based on the map.

Figure 3.9 (Continued)

Complete answers will include each of the following:

I   Genetic drift refers to the occurrence of random genetic changes in a population.

IIA   Random genetic changes are most likely to occur in smaller populations.

IIB   Species I has the smallest overall range, suggesting that it also has the smallest effective population size.

III   Therefore, species I is most likely to be affected by genetic drift.

Note: There are some plausible reasons why the species with larger ranges might actually have smaller effective population sizes, but the burden of fully rationalizing this conclusion falls to the student.

Figure 3.10   Graphical grading rubric for genetic drift question in Figure 3.8

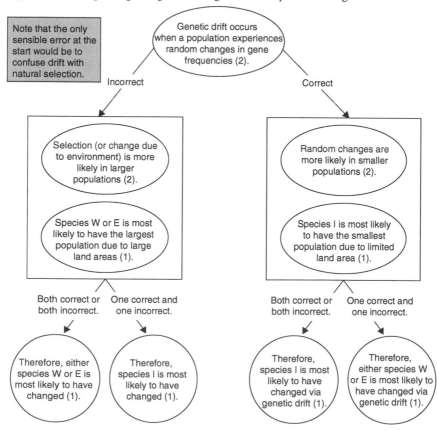

For example, one area of confusion tested by this question (Figure 3.8) is the distinction between natural selection and genetic drift and the fact that environmental conditions impact these two evolutionary processes differently. Assuming the student defines *genetic drift* properly, a series of logical deductions about the action of genetic drift as it pertains to the map should lead to the conclusion that the Island (I) population is the correct choice. However, as the graphical representation (Figure 3.10) illustrates, there are many opportunities for erroneous understanding that can nonetheless be rationalized appropriately. Students may incorrectly define genetic drift (confusing it with natural selection) but then also incorrectly state that smaller populations are more likely to evolve via selection, which leads to the conclusion that species I is most likely to change. Each part of the answer can be viewed as a decision point, and whichever decision the student makes is then carried over to the next step. Students can be rewarded for internally consistent logic, even if they err somewhere early on. Equally if not more importantly, students are *not* rewarded for internally inconsistent answers even if they happen to choose the "best" answer.

One of the main benefits of this exercise is that it promotes metacognitive awareness of the differences between correct content knowledge and correct reasoning. The point of all of this practice was to clearly draw the distinction between these differences and to illustrate for students that most questions they would see in our introductory biology course (and many other science courses) require proficiency with both parts.

Part D: Helping Students Reflect on the Classroom Exercise

Following the second question and peer-review exercise, we reconvened the class to discuss the classroom exercise. The emphasis here was not on the actual performance of the students but rather on the challenges associated with determining the most effective ways of answering questions and, on self-evaluation, to determine whether they were on the right track. We used questions to promote discussion about some of the issues the classroom exercise was meant to address (Figure 3.11).

We hoped to address some specific issues with the reflective discussion. First, students tend to be very surprised by the first exam in our introductory biology courses. They are surprised by what they were asked to do, but also surprised by the rigorous expectations of their answers (i.e., once they got their grades back). Second, as illustrated in Figures 3.6 and 3.7, there are typically two types of answers that receive only partial credit on exams: (a) answers that state conclusions correctly but fail to ground them in the

Figure 3.11   Discussion starters to help students reflect on the classroom exercise

- What do you think of the questions and answers you've seen today? Are they what you expected? How different? How similar?
- In the answers you looked at today, were there different ways to arrive at a moderate-quality answer? A high-quality answer?
- How did you approach answering the questions you were given in class today? Could you have found the answers in your textbook? What are some of the thinking skills you had to use while you were answering the questions? Did you need to recall info, explain, apply, analyze, or evaluate?
- What are some study strategies you could use to prepare for these types of questions?

appropriate facts, and (b) answers that state facts—correctly or incorrectly—but do not logically connect these facts to answer the question. Third, students tend to think they should know the correct answers to questions *in advance of* the exam. But our expectation is for students to use their basic understanding, acquired in advance of the exam, to reason through questions *during* the exam. Fourth, students usually don't realize that thinking skills can be practiced, just like skills of other kinds (e.g., playing the piano). Thus, they approach studying to gain a set of facts and explanations, not to improve their critical-thinking skills. Students often need help identifying how to practice critical thinking, so we ask them to brainstorm study strategies and then provide them with some direct advice. Some of our ideas include answering lots of critical-thinking questions from sources such as old exams, conceptual questions from the textbook, or questions they make up for themselves; manipulating questions and answering them again (Parker Siburt, Bissell, & MacPhail, 2011); critiquing their answers to questions (as they've done in this exercise); and thinking about the "big picture" of biology and trying to see how one set of lecture notes or lab exercises pertains to another.

After the discussion, we distributed a handout reiterating a couple of pieces of our metacognitive advice (Figure 3.12).

Ideally, following this classroom exercise, students should go on to develop sufficient metacognitive skills to evaluate their own performance in real time. Students should eventually reach the point where they are not surprised by their performance on problems, either while they are studying or during exams.

Figure 3.12 Additional metacognitive advice

There are a couple of important points to remember:

- Most biological questions require both content knowledge and the application of critical-thinking skills. Just as content can be learned, critical thinking can be practiced and improved.
- Exam questions in this course are intended to require you to reason through them during the exam. Thus, you need to study the material in such a way that you can reason your way to the correct answer of a problem you may never have seen before. There are many excellent ways to do this.

EVIDENCE OF STUDENT LEARNING

This exercise was tested with 125 students enrolled in an introductory biology course at Duke University in Durham, North Carolina. A sample of 35 students consented to have their work analyzed for this study (Duke University Institutional Review Board [IRB] protocol 2036). To evaluate the effectiveness of this exercise at teaching students to make explicit which critical-thinking skills they used to solve problems, we compared students' scores on their homework assignment (a pretest; Figure 3.2) to scores on a similar question given on a midterm (a posttest; Figure 3.13). To determine if learning occurred *during* the exercise, we also analyzed students' self-assessments to see if they correctly identified their own content and critical-thinking errors on their pretests.

All student responses in our sample were independently assessed by two raters who underwent experiential training prior to the assessment. To determine the inter-rater reliability, an indication of the consistency with which different raters assess the same assignment in the same way, we calculated the Pearsons correlation coefficient (Salvia & Ysseldyke, 1998). Raters assessed two components of each assignment—the accuracy of the content and the logic of the reasoning (i.e., the critical-thinking skills)—using the same rubrics given to students with the assignment. We used a student's t-test to compare the mean scores for content and critical-thinking skills between the pre- and the posttests. Finally, we calculated the percentage of accurate self-assessments by comparing students' self-assessment scores with the raters' scores. In our assessment of inter-rater reliability, the Pearson correlation coefficient (r) was 0.85 for the pretest and 0.80 for the posttest; both were statistically significant ($p < .01$) and r-values above 0.8 are considered highly reliable (Franzblau, 1958; Salvia & Ysseldyke, 1998).

Figure 3.13   Midterm exam question

You observe two distinct and geographically distant populations of but-
terflies. They have similar morphologies (body shapes) and similar life-
styles (they both drink nectar), but their color patterns are different; one
is bright green and one is dark green. You further observe that the dark
green one prefers shady, cool forest interiors, while the bright green one
is found in sunny meadows. Finally, you have seen them both be preyed
upon by birds.

A. Based on your understanding of natural selection, propose a
hypothesis for why the color patterns of the two butterfly populations are different. Your answer should include an explanation that
demonstrates your understanding of natural selection and should
logically link this explanation to a testable hypothesis.
B. Propose an experiment or set of observations you would make to
test the hypothesis you have constructed in Part A.

Table 3.1   A one-tailed, t-test comparison of 35 paired pre- and posttests

	Mean pretest score (%)	Mean posttest score (%)	t statistic	p value
Content	86	81	0.90	.19
Critical thinking	75	86	−2.15	.01

Although there was no significant difference in mean content scores
between the pre- and posttests, there was a significant improvement in the
mean critical-thinking score (Table 3.1). This suggests that this exercise helps
students understand how to make their reasoning explicit. It did not surprise
us that the average content score decreased slightly, because the pretest was
an open-book assignment whereas the posttest was administered during
a closed-book midterm exam. Although the content score may not be very
informative in this context, it does provide us with a frame of reference from
which to consider the increase in critical-thinking scores.

Additional support for the value of this assignment is the fact that 80% of
students in our sample correctly identified their own critical-thinking errors
during the self-assessment portion of our exercise. For example, students frequently acknowledged that although they got the answer correct, they understood that they did not fully explain why their answer was the most logical
conclusion given the evidence. Self-assessments included statements such as:

- "I did not provide an argument for why my answer was correct."
- "I gave an answer but not an explanation."
- "Although I explained why one genotype was possible, I did not explain why the alternative genotypes were not possible."

These self-assessments are strong evidence that prior to the exercise, students were confused about the logical reasoning they needed to answer the questions completely, but after they assessed the sample responses, they were able to return to their own writing and correctly identify where their reasoning was lacking.

Our study suggests that critical-thinking skills like application and analysis can be improved with quality practice (van Gelder, 2000). These skills are a fundamental part of the practice of science, and using these skills forces students to deeply probe their understanding of content, potentially confronting their lack of understanding or misconceptions. Our exercise provides students with deliberate and guided practice and raises their knowledge and awareness of the type of skills and reasoning needed to solve scientific problems. As such, this exercise provides a model for instructors who want to promote metacognition as a means of explicitly teaching students to think more critically.

LESSONS LEARNED

There are at least two novel elements to our classroom exercise. First, our exercise uses questions that provide a way to give credit for demonstrated critical thinking independently from demonstrated content knowledge. In our experience, most faculty would prefer to assess a student's depth of understanding by seeing whether the student can apply his or her knowledge to novel situations, not by seeing if he or she can regurgitate memorized content. However, just because a question is designed to demand critical thought does not mean that students will develop, let alone apply, such skills. Faculty can more clearly convey this challenge by explicitly breaking apart the content and critical-thinking components of the answers.

Second, our exercise provides clear guidance regarding our critical-thinking expectations together with an avenue for continual feedback and self-assessment, thereby emphasizing the importance of metacognition in achieving answers worth full credit. This exercise helps faculty incorporate metacognitive development as one of the key desired outcomes for their classes. For students, our exercise reveals new ways of thinking about scientific problems and achieving mastery, especially for courses that require the use of critical-thinking skills.

Despite these novelties, many introductory students tend to resist the invitation to think critically about biology, probably because it is new to them and is a difficult skill to master. Students who earned high marks in previous courses probably feel threatened when they do not immediately experience success on questions prompting for critical thinking. Similarly, students who earned average marks in previous courses might resent being asked to put forth a lot of effort, especially if they are not majoring in biology.

We found that some students also resist explicit instruction in metacognition. We have heard students argue, "This is not biology. Your job is to teach me biology." Some students compartmentalize their academic lives so much that even though they find metacognition interesting, they don't see how it is relevant outside of the class period where it was taught, in other courses, or in their future professional lives (personal observation from Academic Resource Center staff, Duke University).

For these reasons, we believe metacognitive instruction must be part of the fabric of a course, not just a onetime classroom exercise. We have tried a number of incorporation strategies, and most of them require just 5 or 10 minutes of a class period. For example, we frequently ask students to respond to critical-thinking questions in class, then collect student responses for review. In the next class period, we display sample student responses to the question, pointing out the high-quality and low-quality features of each response. We also sometimes ask students to document their solutions to critical-thinking questions (see Angelo & Cross, 1993, on documented problem solving), instructing them to not only record the solution to the question but also to record their thinking steps (e.g., "First I read the graph, then I remembered how insects thermoregulate, then I decided if the data shown in the graph are from an insect or a mammal"). We suggest a model in which instructors (a) regularly use critical-thinking questions to assess student learning, (b) dedicate one entire class period to a classroom exercise like "Critical Thinking in Biology," and (c) provide weekly opportunities for metacognitive instruction (e.g., through feedback on critical-thinking questions).

These preliminary data suggest that our technique has promise for helping students develop critical-thinking and metacognitive skills, and we encourage readers to experiment with the technique for use in various classroom settings. We believe the key features are robust to different implementations.

The three steps in constructing an exercise like ours are (a) writing questions that explicitly require both content and critical-thinking skills (e.g., Bissell & Lemons, 2006; Crowe, Dirks, & Wenderoth, 2008), (b) generating sample responses, and (c) modifying the rubric presented here to suit the new question. The easiest of these three is the final piece—our rubric can be easily modified for most questions. To create effective critical-thinking questions, we discovered that there were two key features that simplified the exercise. First, the question must present students with a novel scenario; otherwise, students will simply have to recall the details of a scenario they have already seen (a lower-level cognitive activity). Second, the question must ask the student to analyze data, synthesize information from multiple sources, or evaluate evidence or competing hypotheses. Generating new, suitable questions is not particularly difficult or time-consuming if these features are kept in mind.

The most time-consuming aspect of creating this exercise is generating the writing samples. Ideally, the samples should illustrate three types of answers: one with correct content and logical reasoning, one with incorrect content but logical reasoning, and one with correct content but missing or weak reasoning. We found that examples containing both incorrect content and weak reasoning were fairly trivial and not helpful as learning models. When we wrote the writing samples, we often used actual student writing as a starting point to make the responses sound more authentic and then simply edited the writing to suit our needs.

It is worth noting that we occasionally had to revise or entirely re-create the original question when we discovered that we could not generate sufficiently distinct and instructive sample answers. For example, we developed a question about photosynthesis that presented students with a novel chemical as a possible herbicide. The question read:

> Atrazine is a chemical that blocks the transfer of electrons in the electron transport chain of Photosystem II in chloroplasts. Would this chemical be an effective herbicide (i.e., a chemical that kills plants)? Your answer should include a description of how atrazine's mechanism of action would impact plants and should logically explain how that information supports your conclusion.

In attempting to create sample answers, we realized that the question didn't really require critical thinking. Rather, a correct and complete answer would include about four statements of fact that students had been told in class: (a) electron transport, as part of the light-dependent reactions, is required to power the Calvin cycle; (b) the Calvin cycle produces glucose; (c) glucose is the plant's metabolic fuel; and (d) without glucose, a plant's metabolism would shut down. The atrazine question was challenging, not because it required critical thinking, but because electron transport tends to be challenging for students to understand. We threw out this question and created a different one in its place. In this way, our process for creating questions and sample answers contains a built-in mechanism for ensuring that the questions we are asking students actually encourage the type of critical analysis we intend.

CONCLUSION

Our experience with the use of the "Critical Thinking in Biology" module suggests that this classroom exercise can help students improve their critical-thinking and metacognition skills. These skills are a fundamental part of the practice of science, and using these skills forces students to deeply probe their understanding of content, potentially confronting their lack of understanding or misconceptions. Our exercise provides students with deliberate and guided practice and raises their knowledge and awareness of the types of skills and reasoning needed to solve scientific problems. As such, this exercise provides a model for instructors who want to find ways to explicitly teach their students to think more critically.

REFERENCES

American Association for the Advancement of Science. (1989). *Science for all Americans.* Washington, DC: Author.

American Association for the Advancement of Science. (2011). *Vision and change in undergraduate biology education: A call to action.* Washington, DC: Author.

Anderson, L. W., & Krathwohl, D. (Eds.). (2001). *A taxonomy for learning, teaching, and assessing: A revision of Bloom's taxonomy of educational objectives.* New York: Longman.

Angelo, T. A., & Cross, P. K. (1993). *Classroom assessment techniques* (2nd ed.). San Francisco: Jossey-Bass.

Armstrong, N., Chang, S., & Brickman, M. (2007). Cooperative learning in industrial-sized biology classes. *CBE Life Sciences Education, 6,* 163–171.

Bissell, A., & Lemons, P. P. (2006). A new method for assessing critical thinking in the classroom. *BioScience, 56,* 66–72.

Bloom, B. S. (Ed.). (1956). *Taxonomy of educational objectives: The classification of educational goals.* New York: McKay.

Cooper, M. M., & Sandi-Urena, S. (2009). Design and validation of an instrument to assess metacognitive skillfulness in chemistry problem solving. *Journal of Chemical Education, 86*(2), 240.

Crowe, A., Dirks, C., & Wenderoth, M. P. (2008). Biology in Bloom: Implementing Bloom's taxonomy to enhance student learning in biology. *CBE Life Sciences Education, 7,* 366–381.

Ebert-May, D., Derting, T. L., Hodder, J., Momsen, J. L., Long, T. M., & Jardeleza, S. E. (2011). What we say is not what we do: Effective evaluation of faculty professional development programs. *BioScience, 61,* 550–558.

Entwistle, A., & Entwistle, N. (1992). Experiences of understanding in revising for degree examinations. *Learning and Instruction, 2,* 1–22.

Facione, P. A. (1990). *Critical thinking: A statement of expert consensus for purposes of educational assessment and instruction.* Millbrae, CA: California Academic Press.

Flavell, J. H. (1979). Metacognition and cognitive monitoring: A new area of cognitive developmental inquiry. *American Psychologist, 34*(10), 906–911.

Franzblau, A. (1958). *A primer of statistics for non-statisticians.* New York: Harcourt, Brace & World.

Freeman, S., O'Connor, E., Parks, J. W., Cunningham, M., Hurley, D., Haak, D., et al., (2007). Prescribed active learning increases performance in introductory biology. *CBE Life Sciences Education, 6*, 132–139.

Halpern, D. F. (1998). Teaching critical thinking for transfer across domains: Disposition, skills, structure training, and metacognitive monitoring. *American Psychologist, 53*(4), 449–455.

Hoste, R. (1982). What do examination items test? An investigation of construct validity in a biology examination. *Journal of Biological Education, 16*, 51–58.

Kuhn, D. (1999). A developmental model of critical thinking. *Educational Researcher, 28*(2), 16–26.

Lipman, M. (1988). Critical thinking: What can it be? *Educational Leadership, 46*, 38–43.

Momsen, J. L., Long, T. M., Wyse, S., & Ebert-May, D. (2010). Just the facts? Introductory undergraduate biology courses focus on low-level cognitive skills. *CBE Life Sciences Education, 9*, 435–440.

National Research Council. (2003). *BIO2010: Transforming undergraduate education for future research biologists.* Washington, DC: National Academies Press.

Nolen, S. B., & Haladyna, T. (1990). Personal and environmental influences on students' beliefs about effective study strategies. *Contemporary Educational Psychology, 15*, 116–130.

Parker Siburt, C. J., Bissell, A. N., & MacPhail, R. A. (2011). Developing metacognitive and problem-solving skills through problem manipulation. *Journal of Chemical Education, 88*, 1489–1495.

Paul, R. W., Elder, L., & Bartell, T. (1997). *California teacher preparation for instruction in critical thinking: Research findings and policy recommendations.* Sacramento, CA: California Commission on Teacher Credentialing.

Salvia, J., & Ysseldyke J. (1998). *Assessment.* Boston: Houghton Mifflin.

Schraw, G., Crippen, K. J., & Hartley, K. (2006). Promoting self-regulation in science education: Metacognition as part of a broader perspective on learning. *Research in Science Education, 36*(1–2), 111–139.

Stanger-Hall, K. F. (2012). Multiple-choice exams: An obstacle for higher-level thinking in introductory science classes. *CBE Life Sciences Education, 11*, 294–306.

Stanger-Hall, K. F., Shockley, F. W., & Wilson, R. E. (2011). Teaching students how to study: A workshop on information processing and self-testing helps students learn. *CBE Life Sciences Education, 10*, 187–198.

Traub, R. E., & MacRury, K. (1990). Multiple-choice vs. free response in the testing of scholastic achievement. In K. Ingenkamp & R. S. Jager (Eds.), *Test und tends 8: Jahrbuch der pädagogischen diagnostik* (pp. 128–159). Weinheim and Basel, Germany: Beltz Verlag.

Tsai, C. C. (2001). A review and discussion of epistemological commitments, metacognition, and critical thinking with suggestions on their enhancement in Internet-assisted chemistry classrooms. *Journal of Chemical Education, 78*(7), 970–974.

van Gelder, T. J. (2000). Learning to reason: A reason!-able approach. In C. Davis, T. J. van Gelder, & R. Wales (Eds.), *Cognitive science in Australia, 2000: Proceedings of the Fifth Australasian Cognitive Science Society Conference.* Adelaide, Australia: Causal.

van Gelder, T. J. (2005). Teaching critical thinking: Some lessons from cognitive science. *College Teaching, 53*(1), 41–48.

Veenman, M. V. J., Van Hout-Wolters, B. H. A. M., & Afflerbach, P. (2006). Metacognition and learning: Conceptual and methodological considerations. *Metacognition and Learning, 1*, 3–14.

White, R. T. (1998). Decisions and problems in research on metacognition. In K. G. Tobin (Ed.), *International handbook of science education* (pp. 1207–1213). Dordrecht, The Netherlands: Kluwer.

Willingham, D. T. (2007). Critical thinking: Why is it so hard to teach? *American Educator, 2*(31), 8–19.

Zheng, A. Y., Lawhorn, J. K., Lumley, T., & Freeman, S. (2008). Application of Bloom's taxonomy debunks the "MCAT Myth." *Science, 319*, 414–415.

Appendix A
Guiding Questions
(with idealized responses to sample essay 3, Figure 3.7)

What is the pertinent content knowledge that should be included in the answer?

> *Correctly reading a pedigree.*
> *Understanding the following terms as they are used in genetics:* autosomal, sex-linked, dominant, recessive, simple, *and* codominant.

Is all the pertinent content knowledge included and stated correctly? (*Note:* No definitions are required. But a reader should be able to infer from the students' written analysis of the pedigree that the student understands the symbols used in a pedigree and that he or she understands the terms indicated in question 1.)

> *Yes.*

Is there extraneous content knowledge that makes the answer less clear?

> *No.*

Does the answer in part A include a statement about which mode of inheritance is most likely?

> *Yes. It is stated as "autosomal recessive."*

Does the answer include a reasonable argument that the mode of inheritance selected is *more likely* than other modes? (*Hint:* A complete analysis would include a comparison of the following three scenarios: autosomal versus sex-linked, dominant versus recessive, simple versus codominant). Is the given conclusion consistent with the analysis?

> *No. There is no reasoning; the writer simply states, "The most likely mode of inheritance is autosomal recessive because that mode best describes the pedigree." The answer does not explain why this mode is more likely than others.*

Does the answer include a genotype and phenotype for individual #1 that is consistent with conclusions drawn in this essay?

> *Yes. Individual #1 is identified as being "bb," and there is some reasoning given to explain this conclusion.*
>
> *Reasoning: "If all afflicted individuals are homozygous recessive, then the only possible genotype for their offspring would be homozygous recessive."*

For part B, does the answer include information that successfully refutes the mode of inheritance proposed in part A?

> *Yes. The answer states that if individual #1 were unaffected, that would refute the proposed mode of inheritance.*

Does the answer explain *how* this information would refute the original analysis? (*Note to students*: Here is where you must use your critical-thinking skills to analyze the sample responses.)

> *Somewhat. The answer offers limited reasoning by saying "since the genotype for individual #1 would have to be something other than 'bb,'" but the answer does not say why it would have to be something else.*

Does the answer propose an alternative mode of inheritance that would explain the new information?

> *An alternative is offered (i.e., "incomplete dominance") but not explained.*

Assuming for the moment that the content knowledge presented is correct (and in some cases, this will be true), is the reasoning given a logical extension of those facts?

N/A for this essay.

Grade the sample answers on the following scale and be prepared to explain each of your scores to your group members:

1 = low quality (i.e., both the content knowledge and the critical-thinking components were weak)

2 = moderate quality (i.e., either the content knowledge or the critical-thinking component was strong, but the other was weak). *For this example, the content was correct, but the reasoning was weak or absent.*

3 = high quality (i.e., both the content knowledge and the critical-thinking components were strong)

Bonus: You may add a plus or a minus to your scores (1+, 3–, etc.) if the sample answer did not clearly fit into one of the three categories.

4

Reflection and Metacognition in Engineering Practice

Denny Davis, Michael Trevisan, Paul Leiffer, Jay McCormack,
Steven Beyerlein, M. Javed Khan, and Patricia Brackin

Engineering education continues to hear calls for significant change. National leaders and policy makers argue that students graduating from engineering programs must be able to contribute in the ever-changing work environment of a highly competitive global market (National Academy of Engineering, 2004, 2005; Sheppard, Macatangay, Colby, & Sullivan, 2008; Vest, 2006). Nontechnical skills, often referred to as professional skills—such as communication, ability to work in teams, professional responsibility, and lifelong learning—are the kinds of competencies needed to address major engineering challenges of the future. The National Academy of Engineering (2008) has identified challenges in the broad realms of sustainability, health, vulnerability, and joy of living that require engineers to apply the rules of reason, the findings of science, the aesthetics of art, and the spark of creative imagination to forge useful solutions for the future. Reflection and metacognition are essential for drawing upon and integrating these cognitive abilities for productive engineering problem solving.

This chapter will first describe the roles of reflection and metacognition in professional skills development in engineering education. We then discuss how reflection and metacognition are fostered through use of instructional strategies that integrate learning and assessment for each of three skill areas vital to engineering program accreditation: teamwork, professional development, and professional responsibility. These skill areas are incorporated into the Integrated Design Engineering Assessment and Learning System (IDEALS) that we developed as part of a National Science Foundation–funded project. IDEALS comprises a set of modules that house instructional strategies for each skill area, which will be presented in detail throughout this chapter. Further, we present examples of effective practices in diverse classroom settings to develop these professional skills. We also discuss assessment results validating that professional skills development is achieved through repeated practice of reflection and metacognition situated in an engineering project. We conclude by discussing how using this approach in engineering curricula can help students become practitioners of reflection and metacognition.

Metacognition (thinking about thinking) applied to learning involves active control over the cognitive processes engaged in learning: cognitive self-appraisal and cognitive self-management (Lawanto, 2009). Metacognitive learners are able to assess their learning processes and progress and to make decisions and take action that enhance their learning. Reflection is about making sense of situations and deepening learning through experimenting with tentative understandings. *Reflection-in-action*, triggered by an element of surprise during a performance, reshapes the action as it occurs. *Reflection-on-action*, after the action is completed, is analysis of processes to see what caused the surprise (Schön, 1987).

Engineering may be defined as the creation of responsible technological solutions that meet the needs of varied stakeholders while satisfying technical, financial, legal, social, and other constraints. Engineers create solutions to vaguely defined problems using ill-structured processes and deploying resources they select and access as needs occur. Therefore, engineers must be able to identify key stakeholders of a proposed technology and define the requirements to be met through a viable and attractive solution. Engineers must know the current state of related technologies and trends (technological developments, business climate, political environment, etc.) that affect the value of potential new technologies. They must be able to identify possible solution options—recognizing existing technologies that have potential value, adapting existing technologies to create better solutions, and creating completely new solution concepts. When evaluating different solution concepts, engineers must be able to model (sketch, construct, or describe mathematically or conceptually) and predict performances of solution concepts to assess their competitive positions relative to other alternatives. They also must be able to determine when solution development is "on target" and when it is not, perhaps requiring themselves and others to repeat previous steps to improve the solution being developed. All of these processes require engineers to reflect on previous activities and achievements, make decisions, initiate action, extract meaning, and test alternatives. Clearly these metacognitive and reflective abilities are vital to the success of current and future engineers.

Unfortunately, reflective and metacognitive skills have historically not been dealt with directly in the engineering curriculum as they are not explicitly required for program accreditation. However, by teaching these skills in the context of required professional skills development, engineering educators can prepare graduates more effectively for the complex challenges of engineering practice. Reflection and metacognition are imbedded in the IDEALS model.

PEDAGOGY FOR PROFESSIONAL SKILLS

The key to developing professional skills in engineering students is positioning this development in relevant parts of the engineering curriculum. The capstone design course, a culminating part of nearly every undergraduate engineering program, has been identified by many educators as the most reasonable place in the engineering curriculum for professional skills to be productively developed and assessed (Howe & Wilbarger, 2006; McKenzie, Trevisan, Davis, Beyerlein, & Huang, 2004). In capstone design courses, students work in teams to address a technically based need and are expected to use an identifiable design process to produce a defensible, tangible design solution, often for a real client (Howe, 2008). This semiauthentic professional work environment is the context for learning skills associated with the engineering profession (Lave & Wenger, 1991; Svinicki, 2004).

Because students tend to focus solely on project completion, instructors must find ways to encourage reflective practice and professional skills development. Typical of professional environments, these competing demands make students' design experiences an authentic professional environment for developing skills transferable to professional practice and for assessing real professional skills.

In summary, the pedagogy for developing and assessing professional skills must:

1. Trigger learning by presenting important challenges in the context of an authentic community of practice to enhance students' motivation and performance.
2. Interlace learning and assessment to provide students with frequent feedback, upon which to build higher performances.
3. Conduct assessment in authentic professional settings so that the results are indicative of performance in professional practice.
4. Use consistent outcome targets in a sequence of multiple assessments within a skill area to reinforce for learners the characteristics of high performance in the targeted outcomes and to enable them to reach high levels of performance.
5. Prompt students to practice reflection and metacognition to make them higher-performing practitioners.

The IDEALS model of integrated learning and assessment activities builds reflection and metacognition into professional skills development to achieve and document high levels of professional skills learning. The IDEALS model is constructed from a synthesis of learning and motivation theories applied to a team-based design project context (Davis, Trevisan, Davis, Beyerlein, Howe, et al., 2011). It incorporates formative (primarily for improvement) and summative (primarily for judging achievement) assessment with students' learning experiences to form an integrated, stepped learning and assessment cycle, as presented in Figure 4.1.

The six steps of the IDEALS learning and assessment model are explained in Table 4.1. These steps alternate between instructional practices and assessments. The first two assessments are formative (providing feedback to enhance learning), while the last one is summative (measuring final achievement). All of these steps are conducted in the context of the students' project, making them relevant and often complex.

The Initiate and Define steps take students to their first proposed action in response to the challenge, guided by tentative understanding of the challenge and its resolution. The Execute and Assess steps put responsibility on the students to implement or test their proposed actions to see where they fail to meet expectations. In the process, they can adjust their understanding of the challenge and its envisioned resolution. The Learn and Show steps offer students the opportunity to perform as professionals, applying refined knowledge to real problems and observing additional needs for revising their understanding. This knowing-in-action solidifies their understanding and gives

Figure 4.1 IDEALS learning and assessment model for professional skills development

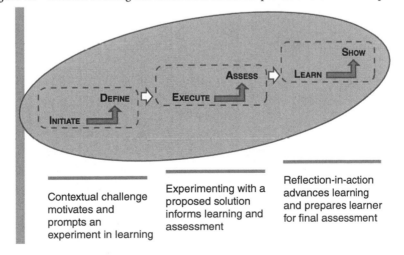

Contextual challenge motivates and prompts an experiment in learning

Experimenting with a proposed solution informs learning and assessment

Reflection-in-action advances learning and prepares learner for final assessment

Table 4.1　Steps in the IDEALS learning and assessment model

Step	Explanation of Step
INITIATE	A professional (e.g., teamwork, self-directed learning, or professional/ethical) challenge arises in the context of a team-based design project; this delays progress or limits performance and calls for assessment.
DEFINE	Through analysis of the problem and planning, students assess the situation, define important needs, set goals, and create a plan for achieving strong performance.
EXECUTE	Students take action, in concert with team and project goals, to implement their plan for achievement of strong processes and high-quality work products.
ASSESS	Students self-assess, peer-assess, or jointly assess progress toward goals and then revise plans as needed to enhance achievements.
LEARN	As students implement their plans and think reflectively and metacognitively, they practice knowing-in-action and achieve results more characteristic of professionals.
SHOW	Students document (show, explain, extend) their achievements in work products, skills development, and learning.

it contextual richness, which makes it more transferable to new situations (Schön, 1991, 1995). Thus, the model elevates knowledge to levels suitable for entry into professional practice.

MODULES FOR PROFESSIONAL SKILLS DEVELOPMENT

Because engineering faculty are generally unfamiliar with instruction that incorporates metacognition and reflection, we created modules (instructional materials and assessments) appropriate for specific professional skill areas. The modules are:

- Relevant to capstone or similarly complex design project work
- Short enough for completion in one class period (less than 1 hour)
- Suitable for use inside or outside of class
- Facilitation tools for useful feedback to students and instructors
- Engaging to engineering students
- Implementable in diverse classroom environments
- Structured to connect instruction to assessments in a logical and instructionally sound manner

IDEALS modules follow the "backward design" approach to curriculum design: learning outcomes guide assessment, which aligns with instructional materials and methods (Pellegrino, 2006; Wiggins & McTighe, 1998). Learning outcomes for a professional skill area are based on the profile of successful engineers (Boeing Company, 2008; Davis, Beyerlein, & Davis, 2006). IDEALS assessment questions are focused on barriers that prevent achievement of outcomes to help students reflect on those barriers and propose ways to improve their performance. Instructional materials and classroom activities guide learning and prepare students for effective assessment exercises (Davis, Trevisan, Davis, Beyerlein, McCormack, et al., 2011). An instructor's guide for each module provides background information and offers suggestions for effective use and follow-up for the module.

Each series of modules is designed to prompt students' reflection and metacognition surrounding their performance in a given skill area. The first module focuses on student understanding of outcomes for the professional skill: What does high performance look like, and how does my (our) performance align with that expected? A second (and possibly third) module in a skill area focuses on specific issues that are common challenges faced in reaching high performance in this area: How good is my (our) performance, and what can be done to improve performance? The final module in a skill area examines the student's performance, understanding of the performance, and ability to transfer this knowledge to professional practice.

The following sections describe how IDEALS modules have been used to develop and assess professional skills for each of the three skill areas. Each section first discusses the skills to be achieved and then gives examples of how modules were implemented to achieve desired outcomes. Examples are drawn from diverse classroom settings that depict different institutional cultures and instructor preferences.

Reflection and Metacognition in Teamwork

Content for teamwork

Because all large engineering projects in industry are carried out in teams, it is essential that engineering students learn the skills needed for working in teams. Each team member is assigned an individual role and contributes his or her individual skills, meshing with those of all other members to provide one part of a complex project. Team performance is important and can hit the pocketbook, as illustrated by this statement in a professional magazine article:

> Each individual's interpersonal skills become increasingly important as they increasingly work in teams. . . . Major employers of engineers such as Texas Instruments . . . don't give bonuses to individual employees, they give them to teams. The team decides how to divide the money among its members. (Borchardt, 1996, p. 22)

Effective teamwork requires members to contribute to the work of the team and depends on operating procedures that support the success of both individuals and the team (Imbrie, Maller, & Immekus, 2005; McGourty & De Meuse, 2001; Smith, 2007; Tonso, 1996). IDEALS teamwork modules propose a set of important team member contributions and team processes grouped under team climate and relationships, joint work achievements, individual contributions, and team information management. Readings, in-class discussions, and assessments structured around these types of contributions and processes help students organize their thinking about teamwork, and they prompt discussions that help students overcome discomfort or ineptness at initiating productive negotiations and enforcing good practices.

Four modules are used in the teamwork skill area, progressing from Team Contract to Team Member Citizenship, Teamwork in Progress, and Teamwork Achieved. These modules facilitate reflection and metacognition as team members grow their teamwork understanding and performance.

1. *Team Contract.* Members negotiate operating procedures and roles that will support effective teamwork and high productivity. The team submits a consensus "team contract" and receives feedback from the instructor identifying issues that may require additional consideration. Members reflect on their past team experiences, personal and team goals, member attributes, and the need for regulating team processes.

2. *Team Member Citizenship.* Members self-assess and peer-assess member contributions and their impact on teamwork. They submit individual assessments for one another that identify strengths and ways to improve contributions for the benefit of the team. Members reflect on team dynamics and the quality of feedback, and they plan specific actions that can strengthen team member performances.

3. *Teamwork in Progress.* Members review effectiveness of team processes in the light of their team contract. They prepare a consensus assessment of their contract and team performance, and they submit a revised team contract. They reflect on processes, contract language, and contract compliance, and they take action to improve their processes and contract.

4. *Teamwork Achieved.* Members evaluate their individual and collective teamwork, describe learning about teamwork, and discuss ways to transfer this learning to a professional work environment. They reflect on what was effective, what contributions were most important, and how they can regulate their future actions to support effective teamwork as professionals.

Example implementations for teamwork

Teamwork does not come naturally for many students, because most of their class work up to the senior year has been completed and evaluated individually, and some students prefer to work individually on projects. When teams are formed, individual personalities come into play, and disagreements over project approaches often surface. Instructors may brief the teams on communication strategies and conflict resolution, but these skills are really learned through practice. IDEALS teamwork modules facilitate this development, as illustrated by the following two classroom examples.

At Washington State University, all students in a two-semester entrepreneurial engineering capstone design course are assigned multiple IDEALS teamwork assignments to build and improve teams comprising several engineering and business disciplines. In this course, teams must produce a proposal for project funding from an outside agency, a business concept proposal video for a university-wide competition, a design solution prototype with test data, and a business plan for a university-wide competition. To help students develop effective teamwork, they complete a Team Contract (early first term) exercise, complete two Team Member Citizenship assessments (once each term), and submit a Teamwork Achieved summative assessment at the end of each semester.

At LeTourneau University, all senior engineering students carry out a two-semester team design project that begins with given needs, requires defining specifications, and culminates in a working physical system. Recent electrical engineering (EE) projects have included design of a high-frequency antenna coupler, a receiver for Digital Radio Mondiale broadcasting protocol, swarming robots, and simulation of an aircraft and carrier landing system using a global positioning system. Over the past few years, all of the EE project teams have used IDEALS Team Contract materials. Depending on the number of enrolled students, three or four EE teams each year also make use of the IDEALS Team Member Citizenship exercise as a formative assessment at the end of the fall semester or early in the spring semester. In this assessment, students reflect on the importance of several factors in teamwork and the contributions of each team member. They indicate the strengths of each team member, including themselves, and provide coaching suggestions for each member. Each student later receives a compilation of the ratings and comments, including encouragement, from the faculty. At the end of the spring semester, every engineering student in the program completes the Teamwork Achieved assessment as part of a continuous improvement process and outcomes assessment for ABET (formerly Accreditation Board for Engineering and Technology) accreditation.

At both institutions, student reflection and metacognition are evident in their written responses to teamwork assessments. For example, a student at LeTourneau University wrote the following in response to the Team Citizenship work:

> I think the thing that was the most help was the members' assessments of other members because for our project I was the team lead and so people would fill out assessments of other people and would go on to what they were assessing, and it was good to know what everyone thought about me (team leads are more susceptible to member dissatisfaction), and it was really interesting because some people's responses did not line up with others, and I thought I was treating everyone the same and it seems like they didn't all perceive things in the same way. It helped me recognize that different people come from different backgrounds and understand similar behavior differently.

A student at Washington State University specifically mentioned assessments and discussion as a beneficial component for the teamwork modules:

> Overall, I felt that the assessments and discussion by far provided the most benefits. The assessments that had us reflect on our team contributions were very valuable. In team situations, you want to critique your teammates and offer input, but it can be uncomfortable; being able to give feedback was good, and to understand your performance and personal assessments was good, too.

These responses illustrate student reflection on what worked and how it affected results. Metacognition is visible in descriptions of how learning occurred and how knowledge can be transferred to situations in which one will work in a team setting in the future. Instructors note that they have seen stronger and more productive teams when students have engaged in activities that facilitate their reflection on teamwork. This is discussed further in the section Validation of Professional Skills Achievement.

Reflection and Metacognition in Professional Development

Content for professional development

IDEALS professional development modules prompt student reflection and metacognition to grow knowledge, skills, or attitudes needed for successful project completion. As required for ABET accreditation of engineering programs, graduates of a program must demonstrate "a recognition of the need for, and an ability to engage in life-long learning" (ABET, 2011, Criterion 3i).

The IDEALS learning outcome for professional development makes more explicit a need for reflection and metacognition:

> While engaged in a challenging project, an individual identifies needs for professional development (in technical, interpersonal, or individual attributes), sets relevant personal development goals, self-assesses, and documents progress and appreciation for professional development. (Davis, Trevisan, Davis, et al., 2011, p. 5)

Engineering graduates must be capable of engaging productively in professional development to stay current and to contribute to technological innovation. To help students reflect on the breadth of professional development opportunities relevant to engineering practice, IDEALS modules present a list of attributes important to the engineering professional, defined as the profile of the high-quality engineer (Davis, Beyerlein, & Davis, 2005, 2006). These attributes include technical competencies, interpersonal skills, and individual attributes that support productivity and success in the professional workplace. Students are asked to assess their own performance and abilities needed for the success of their project, then set goals and create a plan to develop one or more of these attributes for the benefit of the project and team.

Three IDEALS professional development modules facilitate the assessment and advancement of students' professional development thinking and performances.

1. *Professional Development Plan.* Students self-assess (using personal inventories, etc.) and reflect on their personal attributes, compare these to abilities lacking in their team, and develop a plan to grow one or more abilities (knowledge, skill, or attitude) for the benefit of the team and project. Each student submits a professional development plan for instructor feedback.

2. *Professional Development in Progress.* Students self-assess progress toward their professional development goals. They have the opportunity to update personal professional development goals and revise their plans for achieving this growth. Each student submits an analysis and revised plan for instructor feedback.

3. *Professional Development Achieved.* Students evaluate their professional development achievements and reflect on the professional development process used. The students describe evidence of growth achieved, learning about professional development and their understanding of its transferability to the professional world. This evidence is used by faculty to assign grades and to document student achievements in professional development.

Example implementations for professional development

As part of their annual performance reviews, engineering professionals are expected to self-assess their performances and to establish professional goals for the next year. Most engineering students are unaware of these expectations and tend to be novices at establishing goals and monitoring progress for professional development. However, the complexity and duration of many capstone design courses offer the context and opportunity for expecting, practicing, and assessing professional development. Examples of reflection and metacognition to support professional development are discussed next.

Two-quarter capstone design projects in Mechanical Engineering at Rose-Hulman Institute of Technology are used to develop and assess students' achievements in professional development as evidence for satisfying ABET's student outcome for lifelong learning. Early in one term, students complete the IDEALS Professional Development Plan, self-assessing and developing a plan for personal professional development. In the next term, they complete the Professional Development Achieved assessment, providing evidence of professional growth and its impact on the team and explaining how their experience in professional development prepares them for future professional expectations of this type. Faculty use scores on the quality of the students' plans and descriptions of achievements as evidence that graduates have achieved the ABET student outcome for lifelong learning. The following student statements show reflection and metacognition associated with professional development facilitated by these modules:

Professional Development Plan. As a naturally competitive person, I have always been involved in activities that have a defined winner and loser . . . but that mindset is not conducive for industry. . . . [T]he need to have the best idea must be substituted for the need to reach a common goal. I must relate better to other points of view and ideas. . . . [H]earing a different opinion might spark something that would have been totally overlooked. To better my group dynamic skills I will keep meeting minutes of every brainstorming and design decision meeting . . . details of everyone's ideas and their reasoning. This act will accomplish two things: it will be a physical reminder that I should listen and consider the conversation as well as contribute to it, and it will also draw my focus on exactly what brought about these ideas, what usefulness they will have and why they are my teammates' choice.

Professional Development Achieved. After two quarters I have grown significantly. . . . In meetings with my team, I always tried to remain upbeat and keep everyone positive. I found that even if I was having a hard time personally or didn't quite understand why a decision was being made, it was much easier to discuss it if the tone of the conversation was light. In my team evaluations from the first and second quarter, all members mentioned my good-natured personality as being a positive contribution to the team. . . . The team meetings ran smoother and were more constructive. I can also measure my success by the increase of my rankings on the second team evaluation . . . from a variety of 3s and 4s on the first evaluation to almost all 4s. This professional development has affected my overall team interaction, both in and out of [the project]. In other academic teams and assignments, I have improved my ability to brainstorm and constructively design a solution.

Seattle University faculty in Civil and Environmental Engineering use IDEALS professional development assessments to document student achievement of specific outcomes required for ABET accreditation of programs in this discipline. Prior to completing the IDEALS professional development assessments, students are asked to complete a professional skills inventory. By knowing her or his level of professional skills development, a student can identify skill areas that need the most improvement. The following quotes illustrate student reflection and metacognition about leadership skills that have been developed:

The most significant professional development I achieved was within the field of leading others. I came to understand that meeting notes were useful in keeping track of decisions and past activities, getting other people the information or environment they needed effectively moves the team toward its goal, consistency allows everyone to rely on each other, and speaking up about problems is important. . . . Consistency, like regularly emailing finished documents as soon as finished, helped to make the project proceed. Unfortunately, I also learned about what happens when I was inconsistent—such as with meeting agendas—we got less done because of it. When people are not on the same page it needs to be mentioned. Unless project vision issues and personnel issues are named and resolved, the project cannot go forward. Each person must be heard.

Professional development is an ongoing process. Professional engineers have mentioned that they are working on the projects they are because they were curious, they asked about more than the project they were currently working on, and continued to learn. . . . [P]eople are your best resources. Books only help you understand a piece. The lived experience of the people wrestling with these problems tells a fellow engineer the most information, the quickest.

One faculty member at another institution has seen remarkable student growth from reflective and metacognitive activities: "When I read the written comments from the student, I react emotionally because I can see how the student has grown. The IDEALS approach enables a student to improve significantly and to recognize that they have improved." The following student comment is an example of those about which the faculty member was writing:

> When I look back at my [class] experience, I know that I will consider my professional development to be the most important thing I did. I would likely have done all of the design work anyways, because it had to be done for the [project]. The chance to practice serving professionally has allowed me to develop into a more motivated, organized, and mature person. A few days ago, for perhaps the first time in my life, someone called me grounded and mature. I also was told that I impressed those working on the [professional program] during my participation in their workshops. All of this positive feedback has taught me the power of focusing on professional development. I realize now that this development will not happen on its own. I have seen [IDEALS modules] can be used as an aid in the process. I may not use this tool in the future, but I will make sure to find a way to identify areas of improvement, form a plan, and follow my progress.

These examples illustrate student reflection on past experiences, relating causes and effects, making decisions on actions to achieve goals, taking necessary actions, showing new understandings emerging from experiences, and taking control of thoughts in order to be more constructive. The modules provided opportunities and prompts that produced this thinking and caused students to document their thinking. Improved submittals by students as their projects progressed demonstrated that when students practice reflection and metacognition, they become more skilled at reflection and metacognition while also achieving their professional development goals.

Reflection and Metacognition in Professional Responsibility

Content for professional responsibility

IDEALS professional responsibility modules challenge and grow students' professional responsibility in the context of a major design project. The corresponding student outcome required for engineering program accreditation is "an understanding of professional and ethical responsibility" (ABET, 2011, Criterion 3f). The IDEALS learning outcome for professional responsibility exhibits more of a need for metacognition:

> In a project with diverse stakeholders, an individual accepts professional and ethical challenges, considers impacts of possible actions, and acts responsibly in concert with professional codes and ethical norms. (Davis, Trevisan, Davis, et al., 2011, p. 5)

In design projects, reflections on professional responsibility are structured in the context of two sets of expectations: (a) professional codes and (b) generalized responsibilities. Students are directed to the National Society of Professional Engineers code of ethics (2007) as well as professional codes for their own engineering discipline so they know expectations of their professional community. Students are also asked to identify situations in their project that correspond to seven general responsibilities: honest communication; financial responsibility; health, safety, well-being; property ownership; social responsibility; sustainability; and work competence. When they are asked to relate their project to these different responsibilities (and professional codes), students consider different terminology, different stakeholders, and their own values and performances. Two modules are available:

1. *Professional Responsibility Formation.* Each student identifies a professional responsibility that was well demonstrated in his or her project and then reflects on the strong performance. The student also identifies a responsibility not being adequately addressed in this project and prepares a plan to improve this performance.
2. *Professional Responsibility Achieved.* Each student describes professional responsibilities that were relevant to his or her project, judging his or her performance relative to professional expectations. The student then envisions future professional practice challenges and reflects on how professional responsibility learning applies to future situations.

Example implementations for professional responsibility

At the University of Idaho, senior engineering students engage in a two-semester, industry-sponsored design project. Teams consist of students from multiple engineering disciplines (biological and agricultural engineering, computer science, computer engineering, electrical engineering, and mechanical engineering), which provides them a semiauthentic design experience modeled after engineering practice. This experience provides the venue for reflecting on professional responsibility in the context of their project work, which enriches the learning environment. The student projects are presented to the public at the Engineering Design Exposition each spring. During the exposition, alumni and representatives from regional industry serve as judges who query students about stakeholder needs, design requirements, engineering constraints, and solution impacts. High-quality responses include deep insights about project work throughout the year and a well-informed perspective about professional responsibility. Prior to the exposition, students engage in the Professional Responsibility Formation module and complete the assessment. In addition to preparing them to visit with exposition judges, this assessment is the basis for demonstrating the ABET student outcome for understanding professional and ethical responsibility.

The following example is a student response to the Professional Responsibility Formation assessment in which the student was asked to identify an area of demonstrated responsibility and to illustrate with an example what this responsibility means to him or her in this project. The student identified an issue, work competence, to describe.

> To me, work competence means that you understand the problem to the most reasonable level possible. In addition, you should also feel comfortable working toward a particular design option. If you are not comfortable, you should become so. For instance, we are going to be using an Arduino [microcontroller] in order to move the radial and angular portion of the cutter. As no one in the group has experience with these, it is our responsibility to become familiar with this system before we implement it. To solve our Arduino understanding dilemma, it is my responsibility to research and understand the device. I am in the process of working to understand how it works. I have sought out relative experts that have told me that this is an appropriate controller to use. I have also been reading the appropriate manuals on this product to figure out how it works. As budget is not a major concern, I have also ordered an Arduino to further my understanding. By doing this, we will not only know how to use the Arduino controller, we will also know how to use it effectively and efficiently.

In a second example, a student describes how honest communication was relevant to his or her project.

> In order to remain on time and efficient in our project planning and actual work, honest communication is very important. This ensures things get done on time and without overlap (more than one person doing the same thing). Mechanical design and electrical/control system design are taking place concurrently so by communicating honestly (and often) we are able to accommodate each other to keep each part going. If something was not able to be accomplished on time, then we make it known as soon as possible so that the other part of the project can find something else to do in the meantime to stay productive. Several times I have volunteered for individual tasks and have been asked when I will be finished/ ready for the next step related to that task. I gave an honest opinion/best estimate, despite possibly being longer than what some members may have desired. This is needed so that I have time to do a quality job on my task. Other team members are then able to find tasks that they can do in a similar time frame, and vice versa, so we move forward as a unit.

In these examples, students identified professional performances within their project work related to professional codes of conduct. They contextualized understanding of these performances and gave evidence of professional responsibility through their ability to supply project-specific details and to cite broad impacts of their actions.

Capstone course instructors view the pre-class and in-class resources for the professional responsibility module as essential preparation for elevating the richness of student responses in the professional responsibility assessment. This preparation consisted of forming groups of students from different design projects under way across the class, developing shared definitions for each of the seven areas of professional responsibility, and helping students visualize these responsibilities within projects where these were most compelling. Student performance in reflection and metacognition has been cited by faculty judges at the exposition in areas of design for customer requirements, awareness of realistic engineering standards and constraints, and broad impact of engineering solutions. Many judges rated student discussion of these topics as exemplary, observing that many students gave "thorough discussion of design features addressing all customer requirements along with some other considerations," while some students "prioritized engineering standards and constraints based on detailed analysis," and nearly all students were "able to identify and evaluate design alternatives that would minimize negative impacts related to the project."

MODULE UTILIZATION

For ABET accreditation of engineering programs, student outcomes must include teamwork, professional and ethical responsibility, and lifelong learning, which were addressed previously. When professional skills are developed in the context of a major design project experience, they must be learned in concert with the development of a design project solution. Therefore, the instructor must carefully select the skills to address in a required design course, hopefully for synergistic learning of both professional and design skills. Pursuing an overarching goal of developing students' abilities in reflection and metacognition is consistent with and can even enhance development of professional skills concurrent with development of a high-quality design solution.

Module Selection

From a practical perspective, faculty must select professional skills to fit the flow and goals of the course or projects that establish the context for professional skills development. The targeted skills may be developed and assessed over one or more academic terms. An intense approach is to develop teamwork,

Figure 4.2   Timeline for professional skills module utilization in a two-semester project

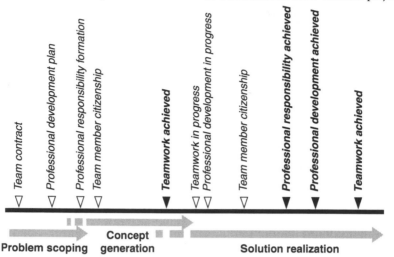

professional development, and professional responsibility skills in the context of one project that spans an academic year. A less-intense approach is to develop a subset of the professional skills in one major project course and develop others in other contexts.

Figure 4.2 shows a two-semester project timeline in which all of the teamwork, professional development, and professional responsibility modules are used in the recommended order. This schedule positions formative activities for each skill area prior to a summative assessment near the end of the project. In the teamwork area, students are asked to create a team contract, and later in the same term provide peer feedback, before completing a summative assessment at the end of the term. The second term begins with a review of the team contract, which is followed by more peer feedback, and ends with another summative assessment for teamwork. This sequence lays a foundation and gives students experience in reflection and metacognition before the final summative assessment; therefore, the final summative assessment typically shows significantly developed reflective and metacognitive skills in regard to teamwork. The use of formative and summative modules for professional development and professional responsibility similarly lays a foundation and provides feedback before the instructor completes summative assessments. Using modules in more than one skill area (as shown in Figure 4.2) reinforces and gives ample practice in reflection and metacognition so that final performances in the targeted skill areas are strong.

In summary, selection of professional skills for development and selection of module resources for each skill area require careful consideration of several issues:

- Modules that align with the skill areas of importance to the class will reinforce the importance of the skills and aid in developing and assessing those skills.
- Modules take student time away from what they see as their priority—completing their project—so modules should be used sparingly.
- Modules take instructor time to set up and to give useful feedback to students.
- Starting a skill area with a formative module and ending it with the corresponding summative module will produce and document improved student learning.

Module Facilitation

The impact of professional skills development activities will depend on their alignment with how students learn and are motivated (National Research Council, 1999; Pellegrino, 2006; Svinicki, 2004). To motivate students, skills development activities must be introduced and explained in terms of their value for preparing students to succeed in their projects and in their careers. In addition, activities for skills development must not distract unnecessarily from student achievement of personal and team goals, such as completing design projects well. Ideally, these activities should be viewed by students as contributing positively to team and project performances, which yield higher grades and greater acclaim from project sponsors and judges. Faculty are motivated when modules simplify grading and aid in preparations for ABET accreditation.

To enhance efficiency in module and assessment implementation, IDEALS modules are supported by a web-based interface[1] that makes module resources available and manages assessment assignments and data. The website gives instructors and students appropriate role-based access, as shown in Figure 4.3. The process begins when the instructor makes an assessment assignment online. Students then complete the assessment online, and data are moved to the database. The instructor next reviews the students' responses and provides feedback online, which goes to the database. The students then review the feedback on the system. The instructor is able to view summary data for a student or class by accessing the data for which he or she has access privileges. Instructors also can download resources, including an instructor's guide for each module. Students may access their work and feedback after the course is completed to support personal and career needs.

The value gained from conducting assessments is affected by the quality of assessment instruments and the ways in which students and instructors approach assessment (McCormack et al., 2009; National Research Council, 2001; Stiggins, 1997). Instructors and students gain the most when both see

Figure 4.3   Faculty and student access and data flows for online assessments

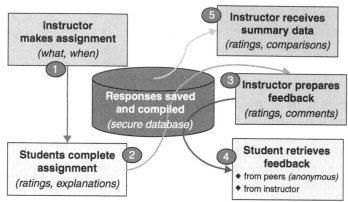

Figure 4.4   Assessment cycle used to facilitate learning from assessment

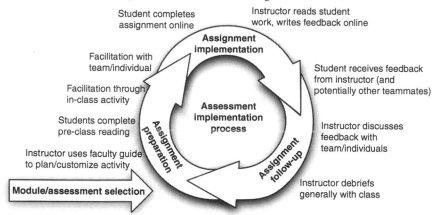

value in completing the assessment well and in interpreting results accurately. Experience with IDEALS assessments used in very diverse institutions and classroom settings has demonstrated that the instructor should follow the assessment implementation process shown in Figure 4.4 to see maximum gains.

After the assignment is created by the instructor, three major steps enhance learning and performance in the assessment. First, the students are *prepared* by learning (a) how the assignment enables success in class and in professional life, and (b) how to be successful in the assignment. Guided student discussions (using module resources) shed light on personal benefits and on what constitutes a high performance on the assessment. Second, the students *complete* the assignment—responding to questions online and viewing rubrics used for scoring responses. The instructor scores and provides written feedback online for the students. Finally, the students read and *cognitively processes feedback*—reading instructor scores and comments and discussing feedback with peers. Students see how their responses align with those of others and can revise their understanding to be more accurate.

As shown by educational scholars, learning is enhanced when students know the learning goals, see an organizational structure for new knowledge, can connect new learning to previous knowledge, receive regular and personalized feedback, and are motivated by learning in contexts authentic for the profession (National Research Council, 1999, 2000; Pellegrino, 2006; Svinicki, 2004). In addition, active engagement with others in the learning environment deepens understanding and helps to correct misconceptions (Prince, 2004; Smith, Sheppard, Johnson, & Johnson, 2005). By design, IDEALS module handouts and worksheets used in advance of assessments provide structure, context, and active engagement that enhance learning.

The instructor can most effectively facilitate learning through the module resource materials and assessments by:

- Reading the instructor's guide before a module is used, to understand its purposes and how instructional materials align with assessments
- Selecting instructional resources that align well with course goals and student interests
- Explaining to students the purpose of readings and discussions as they are assigned
- Familiarizing oneself with professional skill areas targeted by the selected assessments
- Highlighting for students the structure or organizing principles of the information being learned and around which assessments will be organized
- Identifying and reinforcing the metacognitive and reflective nature of assignments and the learning that is expected

VALIDATION OF PROFESSIONAL SKILLS ACHIEVEMENT

What evidence supports our claims that professional skills can be developed in capstone courses using modules that prompt reflection and metacognition? To be sure, evaluation protocols for IDEALS modules were specifically designed to assess professional skills attainment, and thus, most available validity evidence supports professional skills attainment. Growing evidence from several studies shows that students learn and value these professional skills as they transition to professional practice. At institutions that use one or more IDEALS modules in capstone courses, faculty report having observed significant professional skills development in their students and acknowledge its alignment with skills needed in professional practice.

Supporting data for the modules were obtained from formative and summative implementation of teamwork, professional development, and professional responsibility modules between 2009 and 2011. There are two categories of validity data. The first is student performance and implementation data derived from self- and peer-ratings by students and from interviews with faculty during and after assessment implementation (Davis et al., 2010; Davis, Trevisan, Davis, Beyerlein, McCormack, et al., 2011). The second is assessment instrument validity data, which include inter-rater reliability data that show the extent to which assessments can be scored consistently, student performance data showing growth in performance as they learned, and faculty and student perception data showing the value of the assessments to student growth and the perceived value the assessments provide toward the development of professional skills (Davis et al., 2010; Gerlick, Davis, Brown, & Trevisan, 2011; McCormack, Beyerlein et al., 2011; McCormack et al., 2012).

The faculty and student interview data provide a window into student reflection and metacognition. When former students (five months after graduation) were asked about the principal value of the modules, they often talked about the thought processes generated by the modules. For example, one student said:

> Assessments were the greatest value because it really forced you to look at yourself and look at how you're working from day one through the end of the program, and also having professor feedback so you know what you think you're doing is actually how you're coming across.

Another said:

> It was really interesting because some people's responses did not line up with others' and I thought I was treating everyone the same and it seems like they didn't all perceive things in the same way. It helped me recognize that different people come from different backgrounds and understand similar behavior differently.

Several others mentioned the greatest value they received was from the reflection process itself.

The majority of alumni interviewed indicated that modules were moderately helpful in their learning to think and act like a professional. Examples of how the modules had helped them include completing industry performance evaluations, setting goals, conducting self-evaluation and assessment, using self-reflection to "review one's own approach," examining how a team functions at different levels, reflecting on how to be a better leader, having stronger professionalism, interacting professionally with a liaison or an advisor, not dwelling on "petty human idiosyncrasies," understanding the importance of clearly defined roles and responsibilities, and writing peer evaluations. When asked if the modules helped them create a better design solution, one student stated:

> I don't know if [the modules] increased the quality of the final design, but they made it easier to get to that end result; made it smoother for teammates. The team members grew more as professionals than we would have without the IDEALS modules, even though this specific design may not have greatly benefited from it.

Alumni frequently stated that selected modules were found to be most useful in life after they completed their senior design course. They cited long-term value to interviewing, internships, and job performance as they applied skills in identifying strengths and weaknesses, self-reflection, setting goals, communicating, negotiating, networking, writing professionally, establishing clearly defined responsibilities and prioritizing, and building group skills. One alumnus commented, "I was better prepared in my current job to set my own goals and have them be specific, measureable, attainable, and reasonable after going through this [module] process." Another student remarked, "It just has given us the tools to continue that sort of personal development and knowing it is something you have to set a goal for; it's not something that's just going to happen."

Faculty who used the modules saw benefits in student learning and in the depth of discussions they observed in students. Faculty reported having discussions with students outside of class that indicated deep learning of the professional and design skills. Students were seen having in-depth discussions with teammates regarding the functioning of their teams, understanding of project sponsor or customer needs, and conflicting demands of different project stakeholders. Students were required to think beyond themselves, to problem solve, and to pursue different courses of action to deal with various tasks and activities.

In sum, students and faculty report that results from assessments represent the true state of performances and acknowledge benefits from using the modules and assessments, particularly for the Team Member Citizenship assessment for which the most comprehensive set of data exists (Davis, Trevisan, Davis, Beyerlein, McCormack, et al., 2011). In addition, former students report that the learning they gained is useful in professional practice, which further supports the validity of modules. The modules prompt students to write about their understandings, performances, plans, and judgments, exercising and revealing students' skills in reflection and metacognition. What can be said about the data is that they provide emerging validity evidence for the use of professional skills modules and assessments, and by implication, these assessments capture the development of reflective and metacognitive skills of engineering students. More work is needed to obtain comprehensive and defensible validity evidence for all modules and professional skill areas, particularly in regard to reflection and metacognition. This work would be enhanced by increasing the number of students involved, expanding the number and types of institutions that implement the modules and assessments, and developing data collection protocols that specifically address reflection and metacognition.

CONCLUSIONS AND APPLICATIONS TO ENGINEERING PRACTICE

This chapter has described ways in which reflection and metacognition are integral parts of student experiences in major engineering education design projects. We have explained the rationale for integrating instructional and assessment activities, using modules to support this integration, and adopting pedagogical practices that facilitate reflective thinking surrounding the development and assessment of professional skills important to engineering practice. Reflection and metacognition are introduced, guided, and practiced in this context. Finally, we have given examples of reflective thinking and metacognition that are facilitated and demonstrated by students who engage seriously in professional skills modules.

These design projects possess many of the activity types, expectations, and complexities of professional engineering environments. Consequently, design projects offer an environment for developing skills that are authentic to the profession, and assessment in this environment can yield results transferable to the engineering profession (Newstetter, Behravesh, Nersessian, & Fasse, 2010; Svinicki, 2004).

NOTE

1. See http://ideals.tidee.org.

REFERENCES

ABET. (2011). *Criteria for accrediting engineering programs*. Baltimore, MD: Author.
Boeing Company. (2008). *Desired attributes of an engineer*. Retrieved from www
  .boeing.com/educationrelations/attributes.html.

Borchardt, J. K. (1996). Navigating the new workplace. *Graduating Engineer, 17*(3), 22–26.

Davis, D., Beyerlein, S., & Davis, I. (2005, June). *Development and use of an engineer profile*. Paper presented at the American Society for Engineering Education Annual Conference, Portland, OR.

Davis, D., Beyerlein, S., & Davis, I. (2006). Deriving design course learning outcomes from a professional profile. *International Journal of Engineering Education, 22*(3), 439–446.

Davis, D. C., Trevisan, M. S., Davis, H. P., Beyerlein, S. W., Howe, S., Thompson, P. L., et al. (2011). *IDEALS: A model for integrating engineering design professional skills assessment and learning*. Paper presented at the American Society for Engineering Education Annual Conference, Vancouver, BC, Canada.

Davis, D., Trevisan, M., Davis, H., Beyerlein, S., McCormack, J., Thompson, P., & Howe, S. (2011). *Integrated Design Engineering Assessment and Learning System (IDEALS): Piloting teamwork and professional development instructional materials*. Pullman, WA: Washington State University.

Davis, D., Trevisan, M., Gerlick, R., Davis, H., McCormack, J., Beyerlein, S., et al. (2010). Assessing team member citizenship in capstone engineering design courses. *International Journal of Engineering Education, 26*(4), 1–13.

Gerlick, R., Davis, D., Brown, S., & Trevisan, M. (2011, June). *Establishing inter-rater agreement for TIDEE's teamwork and professional development assessments*. Paper presented at the American Society for Engineering Education Annual Conference, Vancouver, BC, Canada.

Howe, S. (2008, June). *Focused follow-up to 2005 National Capstone Survey*. Paper presented at the American Society for Engineering Education Annual Conference, Pittsburgh, PA.

Howe, S., & Wilbarger, J. (2006, June). *2005 National survey of engineering capstone design courses*. Paper presented at the American Society for Engineering Education Annual Conference, Chicago, IL.

Imbrie, P. K., Maller, S. J., & Immekus, J. C. (2005, June). *Assessing team effectiveness*. Paper presented at the American Society for Engineering Education Annual Conference, Portland, OR.

Lave, J., & Wenger, E. (1991). *Situated learning: Legitimate peripheral participation*. Cambridge: Cambridge University Press.

Lawanto, O. (2009, October). *Metacognition changes during an engineering design project*. Paper presented at the Frontiers in Education Conference, San Antonio, TX.

McCormack, J., Beyerlein, S., Brackin, M. P., Davis, D., Trevisan, M., Davis, H., et al. (2011). Assessing professional skill development in capstone design courses. *International Journal of Engineering Education, 27*(6), 1308–1323.

McCormack, J., Beyerlein, S., Davis, D., Trevisan, M., Lebeau, J., Davis, H., et al. (2012). Contextualizing engineering ethics in capstone projects using the IDEALS Professional Responsibility Assessment. *International Journal of Engineering Education, 28*(2), 416–424.

McCormack, J., Beyerlein, S., Feldon, D. F., Davis, D., Davis, H., Wemlinger, Z., et al. (2009, August–September). *Methodology for selection, sequencing, and deployment of activities in a capstone design course using the TIDEE web-based assessment system.* Paper presented at the ASME International Design Engineering Technical Conferences and Computers and Information in Engineering Conference, San Diego, CA.

McCormack, J., Davis, D. C., Beyerlein, S. W., Davis, H. P., Trevisan, M. S., Howe, S., et al. (2011, June). *Classroom learning activities to support capstone project assessment instruments.* Paper presented at the American Society for Engineering Education Annual Conference, Vancouver, BC, Canada.

McGourty, J., & De Meuse, K. P. (2001). *The team developer: An assessment and skill building program.* New York: Wiley.

McKenzie, L., Trevisan, M., Davis, D., Beyerlein, S., & Huang, Y. (2004, June). *Capstone design courses and assessment: A national study.* Paper presented at the American Society for Engineering Education Annual Conference, Salt Lake City, UT.

National Academy of Engineering. (2004). *The Engineer of 2020: Visions of engineering in the new century.* Washington, DC: National Academies Press.

National Academy of Engineering. (2005). *Educating the engineer of 2020: Adapting engineering education to the new century.* Washington, DC: National Academies Press.

National Academy of Engineering. (2008). *Grand challenges for engineering.* Retrieved from www.engineeringchallenges.org/.

National Research Council. (1999). *How people learn: Bridging research and practice.* Washington, DC: National Academies Press.

National Research Council. (2000). *How people learn: Brain, mind, experience, and school* (expanded ed.). Washington, DC: National Academies Press.

National Research Council. (2001). *Knowing what students know: The science and design of educational assessment.* Washington, DC: National Academies Press.

National Society of Professional Engineers. (2007). *NSPE code of ethics for engineers.* Retrieved from www.nspe.org.

Newstetter, W. C., Behravesh, E., Nersessian, N. J., & Fasse, B. B. (2010). Design principles for problem-driven learning laboratories in biomedical engineering education. *Annals of Biomedical Engineering, 38*(10), 3257–3267.

Pellegrino, J. W. (2006). *Rethinking and redesigning curriculum, instruction and assessment: What contemporary research and theory suggests.* Retrieved from www.activelearner.ca/activelearning_media/Pellegrino-Redesigning.pdf.

Prince, M. (2004). Does active learning work? A review of the research. *Journal of Engineering Education, 93*(3), 223–231.

Schön, D. A. (1987). *Educating the reflective practitioner: Toward a new design for teaching and learning in the professions.* San Francisco: Jossey-Bass.

Schön, D. A. (1991). *The reflective practitioner: How professionals think in action.* Aldershot, Hants, England: Ashgate.

Schön, D. A. (1995, November–December). Knowing-in-action: The new scholarship requires a new epistemology. *Change,* 27–34.

Sheppard, S. D., Macatangay, K., Colby, A., & Sullivan, W. M. (2008). *Educating engineers: Designing for the future of the field*. San Francisco: Jossey-Bass.

Smith, K. A. (2007). *Teamwork and project management* (3rd ed.). New York: McGraw-Hill.

Smith, K. A., Sheppard, S. D., Johnson, D. W., & Johnson, R. T. (2005). Pedagogies of engagement: Classroom-based practices. *Journal of Engineering Education, 94*(1), 87–101.

Stiggins, R. (1997). *Student-centered classroom assessment* (2nd ed.). Upper Saddle River, NJ: Prentice Hall.

Svinicki, M. D. (2004). *Learning and motivation in the postsecondary classroom*. San Francisco: Anker.

Tonso, K. L. (1996). Teams that work: Campus culture, engineer identity, and social interactions. *Journal of Engineering Education, 95*(1), 25–37.

Vest, C. (2006). Educating engineers for 2020 and beyond. *The BRIDGE, 36*(2), 7.

Wiggins, G., & McTighe, J. (1998). *Understanding by design*. Alexandria, VA: Association for Supervision and Curriculum Development.

5

"The Steps of the Ladder Keep Going Up"

A Case Study of *Hevruta* as Reflective Pedagogy in Two Universities

Mary C. Wright, Jeffrey L. Bernstein, and Ralph Williams

Reflective pedagogies, such as journaling or structured contemplation, have been found to have positive effects on postsecondary educational outcomes, enhancing leadership development and intellectual self-esteem (Astin, Astin, & Lindholm, 2011). However, few students report experiences in which such reflection was deliberately promoted in class (Astin, Astin, & Lindholm, 2011). Key challenges to reflective pedagogies include faculty's own lack of reflective time, the need for students and faculty to negotiate new instructional or learning roles, and difficulties that administrators face in facilitating or evaluating such teaching (Hansen & Stephens, 2000; Robertson, 2005; Savin-Baden & Major, 2007; Weimer, 2002; Winter & Yackel, 2000; Wright, Bergom, & Brooks, 2011).

Understandings of reflective learning are extensive and diffuse, embodying the terms *critical thinking, reasoning, problem solving,* and *inquiry* (Moon, 1999). Reflection is perhaps best conceptualized in the arena of experiential learning, such as cooperative education or service learning. For example, Dewey (1938) describes the importance of reflection, arguing that experience is a "moving force" (p. 31) that must be judged and directed, while Kolb's (1984) experiential learning cycle includes "reflective observation" as a key stage between concrete experience and abstract conceptualization. The importance of reflection is rooted in experiential learning theory, but there are questions about the transferability of these learning models to other pedagogies, such as text- and discussion-based study (Moon, 1999).

To develop a more widely applicable understanding, Moon (1999) constructed a more expansive definition of *reflection*, denoting the activity as a "mental process with purpose and/or outcome in which manipulation of meaning is applied to relatively complicated or unstructured ideas in learning or to problems for which there is no obvious solution" (p. 161). She describes five stages of reflection, with the first three associated with a surface approach to learning, where students' key motivation is to "cope with course requirements" (p. 122). In "noticing" (stage 1), "making sense" (stage 2), and "making meaning" (stage 3), a student moves from an emphasis on memorizing isolated facts to developing coherence and connections between ideas. In the final two stages, "working with meaning" (stage 4), and "transformative learning" (stage 5), students become self-motivated but benefit from dialogue to test and refine ideas. As an example of the final stage, transformative learning, Moon describes a "deeply satisfying discourse" that enables learners to "take a critical overview of knowledge and their own knowledge and functioning in relation to it" (p. 146). In its epistemological emphasis, Moon's work aligns with other empirical models, such as reflective judgment (King & Kitchener, 1994), but it also helpfully integrates motivational research on approaches to learning.

Here, we describe the use of one reflective pedagogy, *hevruta*, and discuss how this approach has been successfully adapted to promote reflection in two very different postsecondary settings: a large upper-level English literature course and a smaller introductory political science class. In both of these institutional contexts, faculty leverage *hevruta* to address the specific reflective challenges faced by their student bodies and embedded in their disciplinary learning goals. In each of these classrooms, students demonstrate reflective development in alignment with Moon's model.

HEVRUTA AND ITS IMPLEMENTATION

At its heart, *hevruta* is a pair-based "conversational give and take" (Halbertal & Halbertal, 1998, p. 460) that is central to the learning environment of yeshivas, Jewish schools that focus on traditional religious education. *Hevruta* learning in the yeshiva is characterized by sustained partnerships, or paired learners, who may work together over months or years. Although conversation is certainly not restricted to the *hevruta* partner, the sustained dyad is a key location for students to grapple with questions of interpretation and meaning over a close examination of religious texts. Lee Shulman (2008) has described this dialogical approach as a signature pedagogy in the yeshiva, which spotlights "the creative battles of interpretation and analysis engaged by the participants" (p. 12).

Another key feature of the approach in the yeshiva is that *hevruta* is both the key process and outcome of learning. There are no exams or papers, so the "evaluation of students and the ranking of their achievements occurs through the students' participation in the ongoing exchange" (Halbertal & Halbertal, 1998, p. 459). Although a teacher will often lead the full-group in a post-*hevruta* discussion, students will typically spend much more time in the paired conversation and come to the full-group discussion ready to debate and critically dialogue. In these religious contexts, there is some research documenting the benefits of the dialogical method for promoting student learning (Holzer, 2006; Kent, 2006; Segal, 2003).

Here we describe the adaption of *hevruta* in two classrooms at large public universities and the further adaptations made within each of these contexts to respond to student learning needs. To document the pedagogical approach, the first author conducted 60-minute interviews with both instructors, who are the second and third authors. Additionally, data about students' reflective learning were collected for both courses, and the process and key findings of these classroom research projects are described. In both cases, authors received approval from their institutions' human subjects review boards to conduct the research and student permissions to make their work public.

In these two classrooms, instructors implemented *hevruta* differently to enhance reflection among their students. In the first context, the method was used in a large English classroom at a research university to better foster student discussion and close reading of texts. In the second setting, *hevruta* was employed in a political science classroom, with undergraduates from more heterogeneous academic backgrounds, to foster students' political skills. However, in both classrooms, *hevruta* served as a highly adaptable method of enhancing student learning and reflection in the discipline.

Context 1: A Large Upper-Level English Course at a Selective University

Ralph Williams (coauthor of this chapter) incorporated *hevruta* in an upper-level English literature class at the University of Michigan (U-M) in the winter semester of 2009. English 313, "Of Human Bonding: Family, Race, Nation, Religion, University," enrolled 134 students. Topics addressed in the course were drawn from historical and contemporary literature and addressed wide-ranging issues such as race in America, the historical development of the family, religiosity, and diversity at the university. In this class, *hevruta* was employed by graduate student instructors (GSIs) in six discussion sections. Williams continues to teach with *hevruta* in other smaller courses at U-M, but here, we focus on his largest course taught with the method and the evaluation conducted in 2009.

In an October 2011 interview, Williams described his original rationale for using *hevruta* in his class. The goal was to meet student learning needs at a university that "recruits high-achieving students of high expectations, frequently of families of high expectations." (According to Cooperative Institutional

Research Program data [2011] about U-M students, 94% of incoming freshmen self-rate as above average in academic ability.) Williams notes that these high expectations often place limits on classroom discussions:

> Many high-achieving students come to the course very tense about "making a mistake" because it might lower their grade or lower them in their classmates' esteem. And there are characteristically, in a discussion group of 25, two or three others who are hypercontributors, who leap into any silence and, whether by intent or simply by fact of the pressure of time, dominate the discussion. Then there will be a number of students reticent by habit, who remain silent and defer to others. Often, genuine discussion doesn't occur at all. The teacher becomes the focus of all questions, and the session turns into a catechetical question-and-answer session, relatively absent of the sort of mode of learning that one wants.

In discussions with Michael Brooks, then the executive director of University of Michigan Hillel, Williams found promise in *hevruta*'s ability to promote a sense of "deep responsibility" for students' own learning and to emphasize that authentic listening is as important as impassioned speaking. These goals resemble the final stages of Moon's (1999) reflective learning model in their emphasis on self-motivation, transformation, and dialogue for experimenting with ideas.

In addition to these process goals, Williams reported that *hevruta* would best foster disciplinary learning objectives. Through paired discussions over assigned readings, students would develop close reading skills, a key disciplinary focus of many English literature classrooms. Additionally, because the class addressed several controversial issues (such as affirmative action), sustained partnerships could help develop the trusting relationship needed to grapple more deeply with complexities encountered in a text and with the partner's lived experience.

In the context of a large lecture class, Williams worked with his three GSIs to construct 50-minute discussion sections that were primarily *hevruta*-based. To prepare the GSIs, Williams met with them before and throughout the term to speak about "the mode of intellectual inquiry, about the socialization of the intellectual life which this represents, and about their being in the discussion and available without giving a sense of 'surveillance'." Additionally, he occasionally visited their sections throughout the term and previewed the final exam format with them. (For more on GSIs' preparation and experience teaching in a *hevruta*-based classroom, see Wright et al., 2011.)

On the first day of the term, Williams gave an introductory lecture to describe the *hevruta* approach and distributed the handout shown in Figure 5.1. Then, in each GSI's discussion section, students chose a partner

Figure 5.1   Handout on *hevruta* distributed during first day of class

HEVRUTA
ENGLISH 313 OF HUMAN BONDING

Winter Term 2009

Studying on the *hevruta* plan gives the chance for a priceless intellectual relationship—that, at the least asks, as with any special relationship, special responsibilities.

The basic requirements are three: intellectual engagement, intellectual honesty, and responsibility to your *hevruta* partner.

You will pair the first day of the section with a classmate whose discussion partner you will be for the remainder of the term. During the course of the term, there may be other temporary arrangements—discussions in three or four—but this relationship will be sustained and basic.

Each of you will be responsible to the other for making the best use of your and your partner's mind during the term. You will engage in reading and in the lectures to extraordinary detail and depth; you and your partner will support and challenge one another to unforeseen excellence. Like any worthwhile relationship, this one will take work, sensitivity to the other's perspective(s), developing the ways by which you can excite and fulfill the mind of the other, and, sometimes, patience. Its rewards in terms of added knowledge, intellectual engagement, and wider horizons are incomparable. Homer has a phrase for friendship—"two walking together." Essentially that is what *hevruta* is, and one of its best discoveries is that the two walking together may be closely bound not only by their arguments but also by their flexible and tolerant understanding of the grounds and mood of sustained disagreement.

The mode will be this: there is for each lecture a focal reading or set of readings, which each of us is asked especially to study, and a set of prompts for discussion. Each is asked to consider the material and prompts, to listen to the lecture, and then to write a communiqué of about one page in length to the *hevruta* partner presenting what he or she takes to be interesting and problematic issues which might emerge in the discussion in the next *hevruta* session. The communiqué should deal not so much with decisions and positions, but with questions—issues which one might discuss and debate. The communiqué should be sent by e-mail, with a copy to Professor Williams, to Mr. Brooks, and to Chris

Figure 5.1 (Continued)

Stauffer, by the Sunday evening previous to the *hevruta* discussion section. Then, after the *hevruta* session, by next evening at 10 p.m., there should be a follow-up one-paragraph review of the discussion, noting the lead ideas most interestingly treated.

At midterm, students will be asked to present for review a portfolio of their writings to that date.

At the end of the term, students will present a portfolio including all their communiqués and reviews, along with three other brief (1–2 pp. each) pieces: an evaluation of the *hevruta* experience jointly written with the *hevruta* partner; an individual response to *hevruta* by each student; and, based in a reading of one's own communiqués and reviews, an analysis of one's personal intellectual development over the course of the term.

At three times during the term, there will be opportunity for special evening sessions with the chance for more extended discussion, or for combining of *hevruta* groups.

The final examination of the course will be related to the *hevruta* method and will be described later.

For the first *hevruta* session, then, do read the article of the *hevruta* available to you on the course at the course tools site, and made available at the first lecture, and bring a copy of the article to your first discussion section.

(often by proximity), and this partner served as their *hevruta* discussant for the full term. As described by Williams, "The fact that it's sustained over a whole term means that issues of distaste for another person's way of thinking or way of life have to be negotiated." Williams met with students to negotiate conflict, but he notes that the "overwhelming response of the students in each class thus far has been one of finding the partnerships very fruitful." Student and GSI feedback did suggest that some partnerships were less helpful than others, but that students were able to negotiate this difficulty by re-sorting themselves when essential.

For each section meeting, students were assigned two ungraded papers: an initial communiqué, to preview each discussion; and a response, to reflect on the conversation and suggest new issues needing to be addressed. To help students prepare the communiqué, Williams distributed guiding ideas or questions in the lecture preceding the section discussion. (See Figure 5.2 for

Figure 5.2   Sample *hevruta* discussion prompt

READINGS FOR THE *HEVRUTA* SESSION
OF THE WEEK OF JANUARY 19

The following three pieces of material are among the most influential discussions of the issue of human bonding, and especially friendship, in Western culture. Each of them was a part of the backdrop of Professor Williams's lecture of January 12.

They are:

a) a portion of Plato's Symposium. The part presented here is Aristophanes's presentation in honor of love ("Eros"), with its myth of origins.
b) Books Eight and Nine of Aristotle's *Nicomachean Ethics,* arguably the single greatest and most influential work on ethics yet written. In it, Aristotle discusses the nature of "friendship."
c) Michel de Montaigne's brief essay, "Of Friendship." It is one of the most celebrated of such essays in the modern world.

Prompts:

1. For Plato's Symposium: What status has this account? It is, after all, a myth written by Plato and voiced through the work of a comic playwright. What might account for its continuing interest?
2. Which among Aristotle's distinctions about friendship seem to you most bound to his particular cultural moment? Which the least? What, in regard to this form of human bonding, seems to you most to have been lost over the centuries? Which characteristics seem still active in American culture?
3. Montaigne suggests that the sort of friendship he had with Etienne de la Boetie is of a depth which might occur only once in three hundred years. Why should we consider that friendship and its characteristics of interest to most of us?

a sample set of questions.) Students' communiqués responded to the guiding questions, and students also were prompted to note other issues they would like to discuss with their partners. In turn, the key purposes of the responses were for students to be "retrospective and analytical," as well as for them to reflect on "how we might go about this better in the future." These assignments assist with student goal setting and self-evaluation, which are important for prompting change in learners' assessments of themselves (Zimmerman, 1998).

Feedback from GSIs indicated that while they primarily utilized a *hevruta*-based classroom, for some classes they would alter the format, creating quads or having brief full-class discussions before and after the paired conversations. GSIs indicated that these changes were made in response to formative feedback from students.

Students also submitted reflective portfolios of their written work at mid-semester for formative feedback from the professor and GSIs. At the end of the term, students submitted another graded portfolio, with additional reflective papers that asked students to reread all of their own submissions for the course and to write an analysis of their own intellectual development over the term. Finally, GSIs led a final graded two-hour oral assessment of lessons learned from the readings, lectures, and *hevruta* discussions. Although grades were assigned by faculty members and GSIs, instructors attempted to deemphasize grades in order to encourage students to take responsibility for giving feedback to one another through memos and discussions.

Evaluation of students' reflective learning

To evaluate student experience in the course, an electronic survey was distributed to all students in the course near the end of the term (74% response rate), and a 90-minute focus group was held with 10 students in the course. The survey was adapted from one developed by Piontek (2004) to evaluate a much smaller *hevruta*-based English literature course taught by Williams in 2004. Both the survey and focus group addressed students' perceptions of the course's impact on their attitudes and behaviors, dimensions of the course that students thought most enhanced their learning, comparisons of this English course to other courses taken at the university, and students' suggestions for improvement. A separate 90-minute focus group was held with all three GSIs about their experience with the method. Here, we report briefly on the evaluation methodology and key findings, specifically on students' reflective development, but more detail on other learning outcomes, such as close reading and GSIs' reported growth from teaching with the method, has been published elsewhere (Bergom, Wright, Kendall Brown, & Brooks, 2011; Wright et al., 2011). Work from two students, a *hevruta* pair, is also provided to complement the student survey findings and illustrate learning dynamics in detail. These students enrolled in English 492/493, "Topics in Great Works of Literature: Primo Levi," which also was a *hevruta*-based course taught by Ralph Williams, but offered in the winter of 2012.

The student feedback suggests that *hevruta* was effective at prompting reflection along both of its dimensions: epistemological and motivational (Moon, 1999). First, on the survey, students described how the method prompted them to think more deeply about how knowledge is constructed. For example, one student noted that she learned "to question texts instead of accepting them as concrete, resolute documents," and another indicated that he will take away from the course the idea that "knowledge can be constituted in vastly different ways." Students also reported that they were better able to employ evidence to justify their point of view and to listen to other perspectives. This outcome was reflected widely among students on the survey as well, with the vast majority indicating they had developed an appreciation for different viewpoints (84%) and gained skills in debating and discussing (93%).

Second, the course fostered students' self-directed learning, a significant outcome given that in reflective learning, "knowing is a process that requires action on the part of the knower" (King & Kitchener, 1994, p. 66). Most survey respondents noted that they relied more on themselves (86%) or peers (80%) to help them learn, relative to other postsecondary experiences. As stated by one student, "Responsibility was the most important thing I took from this course, in a different sense than I knew it before." Another student reported in the focus group that the course was different because she learned that it was up to her to "create learning." Students noted that this greater sense of responsibility was attributable to the fact that they were encouraged to value the discussion for itself and to direct their attention toward responsibility to their partner rather than toward an extrinsic goal, such as a grade. To illustrate, a student frankly admitted that "left to my own devices, I probably would have skipped a lot of the readings and missed out on some material, but since I was responsible to my *hevruta* partner, I had to keep up enough to be able to have a good discussion."

Both of these reflective outcomes can be seen in student sample work, collected from a *hevruta* pair. In his final response for the course, a University of Michigan senior writes:

> At the beginning of a new semester, when presented with a syllabus for a new course in molecular biology or physical chemistry, and the like, I know exactly what I will do to succeed. . . . Facts, equations, protocols and theorems, while far from simple, are definite, substantial, and usable. . . . I find the humanities far more challenging. . . . You cannot simply search for answers in the written words, you must simultaneously probe for your own questions, and even more difficult, find the answers.

Here, the student appears to be grappling with epistemological questions raised by immersion in different disciplines. The student goes on to note that his partner, Taylor Wizner,[1] a first-year student, is helpful in this reflective process because she has a stronger background in the humanities, particularly poetry:

> I have always had a phobia when dealing with poetry. . . . When presented with a poem in high school, or my freshmen English class, it always escaped me how much analysis and reflection could be derived from a few short sentence fragments. . . . Luckily, Taylor was very interested in poetry and had a very strong background with this form of art. Out of respect for our growing relationship, I put extra effort into my reflections on the poetry selections for our discussion.

Indeed, this student's response papers throughout the term are replete with phrases acknowledging his partner's contribution, such as, "Taylor further refined this point," or "I really liked Taylor's words on the matter." These benefits were reciprocal. For example, in one response, Taylor notes how her partner's science background was helpful for reading *The Periodic Table*, written by Primo Levi. "As a science major, [my partner] expressed how fascinated he was with the book because of its link to the periodic table." She also notes that sometimes she addressed readings from a "feminist approach," while her partner helped to provide historical context.

In both students' reflections, themes of self-directed learning are also clear. Taylor writes, "We weren't simply working for a grade, but to continue an intellectual pursuit that we have been developing together." Similarly, her partner notes in his reflection:

> As a pre-professional student, ever conscientious of the importance of grades for progression, courses such as this one scare me. . . . [However,] it turned into a course that has been a great educational experience without cheapening the importance of personal growth and reflection that are part of pure learning. . . . While I have submitted many papers and taken many "blue book" exams, there are few courses that left me with a sense of accomplishment that comes with a deep sense of personal betterment.

This student reflection certainly seems to align with Moon's (1999) definition of transformative reflective learning with its emphasis on intrinsic motivation, personal growth, and critical perspective of disciplinary knowledge.

Context 2: An Introductory-Level Political Science Course at a Master's University

In the former case, *hevruta* was successfully used to negotiate the particular challenges of fostering discussion-based learning in a large research university English course. Now, we turn to a second adaptation of the method, to a very different student body. Eastern Michigan University (EMU), the affiliation of the second chapter author, Jeffrey L. Bernstein, is a large regional master's university, with a more heterogeneous student body. EMU draws a significant number of first-generation college students, and nearly half (40%) of seniors report working off campus more than 20 hours per week, according to the National Survey of Student Engagement (2011).

Since fall of 2009, Bernstein has employed *hevruta* in two lower-level political science classes. The first, Political Science 113, is an honors American government course, which typically enrolls about 20 first-year students and sophomores. The second course, Political Science 112, is a nonhonors section of American government, which typically enrolls 35 to 50 students, of whom at least 90% are nonmajors.

For these students, especially the nonmajors, Bernstein notes that "there's a real engagement challenge" with the traditional lecture model. Similar to the U-M classroom, Bernstein sought to give students more self-direction over their own learning: "What if I stepped back, put myself on the side and let *them* do it, let them run it?" Epistemological development was an additional goal with his use of the dialogical method, to give students "a chance to have me toss them into a controversy, into an ill-structured problem and just say to them, 'You figure it out, and you don't have to do it alone because you've got someone sitting there next to you who's also puzzling and figuring it out.'"

To adapt the *hevruta* sessions to learners with more heterogeneous backgrounds and abilities in an introductory course, Bernstein made several key changes. First, rather than comprehensive use of *hevruta*, Bernstein adopted a more punctuated approach, with strategic use of the method at select points in the term where he is addressing particularly difficult texts or issues. At other points, he employed interactive lectures, or active learning activities, like simulations, jigsaw groups, and small-group discussions.

Additionally, when utilizing *hevruta*, the EMU students are given more structure. Political Science 112/113 students first write a brief paper analyzing an article, on which formative feedback is given. Figure 5.3 presents a sample initial writing prompt for *Snyder v. Phelps*, a case about free speech, prompted by the picketing of a U.S. Marine's funeral by members of Fred Phelps's Westboro Baptist Church.

In addition to getting students "thinking a little bit about the issue," the initial paper serves as a classroom assessment device (Angelo & Cross, 1993), to flag "misconceptions . . . [and] also get a sense of where the class is coming down on a particular issue," enabling Bernstein to understand what perspectives most need to be surfaced in class.

Figure 5.3 Sample writing prompt

Jeffrey L. Bernstein
Political Science 113
Fall 2011

Controversial Issue Exercise 3: Preassignment

So, here is the assignment for the next issue exercise. On the reverse of this page is a summary of the *Snyder v. Phelps* case, involving the Westboro Baptist Church and their free speech issues connected with protests at the military funerals.

Now, whenever a case gets brought to the Supreme Court, the Court chooses whether or not to hear the case. It requires four out of the nine justices to agree to hear a case. This is called *granting cert* (more formally, *granting a writ of certiorari*). Generally, the justices will grant cert if they believe the case raises important issues, or new issues, or speaks to an area of law that is unsettled and unclear. If it is not a potentially important case, they often choose not to hear it.

For this assignment, I would like you to write a one-page memo (addressed to the other justices of the Supreme Court) for why the Court should grant cert and agree to hear the case. Convince your fellow justices that this case raises important issues that the Court should address.

This assignment is due on Tuesday, November 1, 2011, by noon, to the Dropbox. We will discuss the case in class that day, and this memo will hopefully get you prepared for the discussion.

Have fun!

Another point of divergence with the U-M classroom is that Bernstein structures the pair conversation more by assigning new texts and by ending the session with a full-group discussion. Sustained partners are not used, for reasons that differ for the two classes. The honors students are already a cohort with high levels of interpersonal comfort, while the academic heterogeneity of the nonhonors section, and higher rates of absenteeism, often resulting from family obligations or work requirements, make it necessary to allow students to switch partners. In class, students discuss a series of new texts, which often include primary sources about the issue, such as a newspaper article, YouTube clips, or reasonably dense legal texts. Because some of these texts, particularly the ones focusing on constitutional interpretation, can be "pretty difficult" for students, the paired discussion can "force them to go line-by-line with a partner and say, 'Okay, what's going on here?'" (See Figure 5.4 for examples of discussion questions used to help the students get started.) Afterward, he leads a full-group discussion, to help "keep students focused a little more" and assist them in navigating the more difficult readings.

Bernstein also uses the full-group discussion to prompt further development of students' reflection and metacognition. By dialoguing with students and often asking them to play "devil's advocate," he uses this forum to encourage students to think not just about their conclusions, but also how they reached these decisions and what evidence they could mobilize for their positions. Often, he concludes a discussion by modeling his own reasoning process, noting, "I will often, at this point, share with the students how I think through these issues and how I reason through the contradictions in the articles—in modeling my behavior, I hope to model my own metacognitive processes."

He finds the sequential nature of the discussion (pairs, followed by large group) to be especially helpful in moving forward student learning: "I think one of the things I very much associate with *hevruta* is this idea that the pairs first come together to go over text, which then, later on, the full class will come together to explore." For Bernstein, the paired dialogue, followed by the large-group discussion, culminating in a written analysis, cumulatively helps

Figure 5.4   Sample discussion prompts

Discussion Item for Text 1 (Amendment I to the U.S. Constitution)

1. According to the Constitution, can Congress make a law abridging the freedom of speech?

Discussion Items for Text 2 (Explanation of time, place, and manner restrictions on free speech from http://legal-dictionary.thefreediction ary.com/Time,+Place,+and+Manner+Restrictions)

1. According to Text 2, what are the circumstances under which Congress can make laws abridging the freedom of speech? What is the difference between restrictions based on time, place, and manner, and those based on content?
2. How do you interpret this decision in the context of free speech rights of teachers? Do you believe that teachers have free speech rights in their classrooms? And, if so, do you believe this speech can be limited?

develop analytical thinking, and the "steps of the ladder keep going up." He observes this culminating group discussion to be very participatory and of high quality, because students have had time to process their ideas and "get really confident in what they're going to say."

After the class, a graded short paper is assigned. Figure 5.5 presents the final short paper assignment associated with the *Snyder v. Phelps* case. For example, students might be asked how the U.S. Supreme Court should rule based on what was discussed about public school teachers' right to free expression. By this time, students have acquired the tools for argumentative writing, or "different ways to argue one side or the other and then it's a matter of asking them, 'Choose which side you're going to argue, make those arguments, address the criticisms in your argument.'" To give additional structure to students' learning in the term and to focus on material not covered in any

Figure 5.5　Second sample writing prompt

Jeffrey L. Bernstein
Political Science 113
Fall 2011

Controversial Issue Exercise 3: Postassignment

Okay, hope today's exercise was fun.

Now, having gone through this exercise, I'd like to invite you to write your own opinion on *Snyder v. Phelps*. The opinion should be approximately 1,000 words (3–4 pages). Assume that Justice Roberts has written the majority opinion and Justice Alito has written the dissenting opinion. Your assignment is to write an opinion that agrees with either Roberts or Alito. The opinion should express why you agree with one of the opinions, highlighting the arguments that are most critical to you. *It should also directly address the arguments made in opposition to yours and show convincingly why those arguments are incorrect.* I think this second piece is the most important part of the assignment.

This assignment is due on Tuesday, November 8, 2011, by noon, to the Dropbox. I hope you'll have a good time writing it—I'm happy to answer any questions you have as you are working on this.

Have fun!

of the four *hevruta* discussions during the term, Bernstein's American government students also complete in-class midterm and final examinations.

Evaluation of students' reflective learning

To evaluate student learning in the course, Bernstein designed a rigorous multipronged assessment, consisting of (a) pre- and postsurveys about disciplinary thinking, skills, and attitudes (adapted from Colby, Erlich, Beaumont, & Stephens, 2003), distributed to American government honors students, as well as students in six other political science classes at EMU; and (b) the survey distributed in the U-M class (described previously), distributed to the honors students in the fall of 2009. As in the prior example, short samples of student work are provided to illustrate the quantitative findings. For all of the surveys, there was a 92% response rate in the *hevruta* sections and an 87% response rate in the control group courses. Here, we focus particularly on the student outcomes related to student reflection, but more detail on other outcomes can be found in Bernstein (2010). As with the Williams course, Bernstein's students demonstrated outcomes consistent with the epistemological and motivational development seen in reflective learners (Moon, 1999).

Pre- and postsurvey data clearly indicate that students found *hevruta* useful for prompting disciplinary analytical skills and use of evidence. For example, there was a statistically significant increase in students' assessment of their skill levels over the term in how well they could "explain their political views to others," "persuade others on political issues," and "weigh the pros and cons on political issues." Gains made in these areas in the *hevruta* course were also greater than those in other EMU political science classes, at a statistically significant level ($p < .05$).

Although based on disciplinary thinking skills, these outcomes are tightly connected to reflective thinking, because, using one example from Bernstein, "a reflective student is able to read the newspaper and identify the contradictions and identify the holes in an argument." In their writing assignments, students also connected the *hevruta* exercises to development of more reflective and analytical thinking. In particular, students indicated that both the peer discussion and the variety of texts were helpful in promoting these gains. To illustrate, one student noted that the discussions helped "clarify my views," and another appreciated the in-class reading packets, reporting:

> I think it is important to hear from a variety of sources and different occupations. In some classes, we have one book that does not have any contrast and that we read for the whole time, which I feel does not teach me as much as I would know if I were seeing different perspectives.

EMU students also reported very high levels of agreement that Political Science 112/113 fostered self-directed learning. A large majority of survey respondents agreed or strongly agreed that they relied more on themselves (70%) or peers (70%) to help them learn, compared with other college classes they experienced. For example, one student wrote that the collaborative component of the course was critical for her learning: "Without being able to ask my peers questions about the subject, I don't think I would have had such a comprehensive understanding of the information."

CONCLUSION

In both cases presented here, faculty adapted *hevruta* to best meet students' evolving learning needs in their disciplinary and institutional contexts. Both instructors prompted student reflection through a dialogical process, as well as structured assignments designed to prompt deeper engagement with texts and the *hevruta* partner. However, there are also two key differences, which reflect the instructors' adaptations to their institutional contexts: (a) whether *hevruta* partnerships are sustained throughout the term and (b) the degree to which class discussions are structured by the instructor. Despite these variations, classroom research suggests that the U-M English and EMU political science students demonstrated reflective learning. In particular, both groups of students reported developing epistemologically, as well as increasing their skills for self-directed learning, key components of Moon's (1999) reflective learning model.

Innovative pedagogies are often portrayed in the literature as "one size fits all," working on any type of campus. Our experience in implementing *hevruta* in two distinct classrooms illustrates that innovative classroom interventions address different problems and issues in their own settings, and that their results are best understood within the context of different student needs. Although *hevruta* was implemented to deepen student reflection and reduce student concern with grades at one selective university, it was also successfully used to engage students in class and encourage more attention to classroom work in a comprehensive setting. Kent (2006) described *hevruta* learning as a "negotiation [between partners] about how they will go about their learning" (p. 217). Similarly, while faculty implementing *hevruta* share a commitment to dialogue and discussion, they are also attentive to specific institutional contexts and constraints when negotiating their implementation of the pedagogy.

NOTE

1. Students' preferences for attribution of their written work—anonymous or named—are utilized here.

REFERENCES

Angelo, T., & Cross, P. (1993). *Classroom assessment techniques: A handbook for faculty* (2nd ed.). San Francisco: Jossey-Bass.

Astin, A. W., Astin, H. S., & Lindholm, J. A. (2011). *Cultivating the spirit: How college can enhance students' inner lives.* San Francisco: Jossey-Bass.

Bergom, I., Wright, M. C., Kendall Brown, M., & Brooks, M. (2011). Promoting college student development through collaborative learning: A case study of *hevruta. About Campus, 15*(6), 19–25.

Bernstein, J. L. (2010, January). *The boundaries of our knowledge: The hevruta method in introductory political science courses.* Paper presented at the Annual Meeting of the Southern Political Science Association, Atlanta, GA.

Colby, A., Erlich, T., Beaumont, E., & Stephens, J. (2003). *Educating citizens: Preparing undergraduates for lives of moral and civic responsibility.* San Francisco: Jossey-Bass.

Cooperative Institutional Research Program. (2011). *The American freshman.* Los Angeles: Higher Education Research Institute. Retrieved from www.heri.ucla.edu/tfsPublications.php.

Dewey, J. (1938). *Experience and education.* New York: Macmillan.

Halbertal, M., & Halbertal, T. H. (1998). The yeshiva. In A. O. Rorty (Ed.), *Philosophers on education: New historical perspectives* (pp. 458–469). London: Routledge.

Hansen, E. J., & Stephens, J. A. (2000). The ethics of learner-centered education: Dynamics that impede the process. *Change, 32*(5), 41–47.

Holzer, E. (2006). What connects "good" teaching, text study and *hevruta* learning? A conceptual argument. *Journal of Jewish Education, 72*(3), 183–204.

Kent, O. (2006). Interactive text study: A case study of *hevruta* learning. *Journal of Jewish Education, 72*(3), 205–232.

King, P. M., & Kitchener, K. S. (1994). *Developing reflective judgment.* San Francisco: Jossey-Bass.

Kolb, D. A. (1984). *Experiential learning: Experience as the source of learning and development.* Englewood Cliffs, NJ: Prentice Hall.

Moon, J. A. (1999). *Reflection in learning and professional development: Theory and practice.* Sterling, VA: Stylus.

National Survey of Student Engagement (for Eastern Michigan University). (2011). *Mean and Frequency Report* [Data file]. Retrieved from http://irim.emich.edu/ia_surveys.php.

Piontek, M. (2004). *Summary of survey of students in English 407.* Unpublished manuscript. Center for Research on Learning and Teaching, University of Michigan, Ann Arbor.

Robertson, D. R. (2005). Generative paradox in learner-centered college teaching. *Innovative Higher Education, 29*(3), 181–194.

Savin-Baden, M., & Major, C. H. (2007). Using interpretive meta-ethnography to explore the relationship between innovative approaches to learning and their influence on faculty understanding of teaching. *Higher Education, 54*(6), 833–852.

Segal, A. (2003). *Havruta study: History, benefits, and enhancements. Notes from ATID.* Jerusalem: Academy for Torah Initiatives and Directives.

Shulman, L. S. (2008). Pedagogies of interpretation, argumentation, and formation: From understanding to identity in Jewish education. *Journal of Jewish Education, 74*, 5–15.

Weimer, M. G. (2002). *Learner-centered teaching: Five key changes to practice.* San Francisco: Jossey-Bass.

Winter, D., & Yackel, C. A. (2000). Novice instructors and student-centered instruction: Understanding perceptions and responses to challenges of classroom authority. *Primus, 10*(4), 289–318.

Wright, M. C., Bergom, I., & Brooks, M. (2011). The role of teaching assistants in student-centered learning: Benefits, costs, and negotiations. *Innovative Higher Education, 36*(5), 1–12.

Zimmerman, B. J. (1998). Developing self-fulfilling cycles of academic regulation: An analysis of exemplary instructional models. In D. H. Schunk & B. J. Zimmerman (Eds.), *Self-regulated learning: From teaching to self-reflective practice* (pp. 1–19). New York: Guilford Press.

6

Implementing Metacognitive Interventions in Disciplinary Writing Classes

Mika LaVaque-Manty and E. Margaret Evans

This chapter will describe metacognitive interventions in two advanced undergraduate writing courses, one in psychology and one in political science. These interventions significantly improved student engagement with the material in our courses and, because the interventions are discipline independent, we believe they offer similar promise in a wide array of course settings. We introduced these strategies when our courses became sites of a Teagle and Spencer foundation–supported research project on meta-cognition.[1] Our goals, even before the implementation of the interventions, had been metacognitive in one sense: we wanted to foster greater student awareness of disciplinary conventions and of differences between disciplines. We each had taught our respective courses before and, by the standard indicators, reasonably successfully. But each of us felt things could be improved. Furthermore, there was another type of metacognition we hadn't been thinking about as much: the students' reflection on their own writing *processes*.

Partnering with the researchers on the project—the editors of this volume—we implemented metacognitive strategies using a three-stage model of metacognition drawn from work done by Schraw (2001), who notes that three essential skills—planning one's learning, monitoring it, and evaluating it—are required for successful self-regulation of cognition. Specifically:

- In the planning stage, students had to reflect on what they already knew and what they still needed to learn in order to complete the particular assignment.
- During the actual writing, students monitored their own writing choices by commenting on their own texts.
- In the evaluation activities, students reflected on what had worked, what hadn't, and what they learned for future assignments.

This approach also drew on work by Lovett (2008), whose work on "exam wrappers" modeled the value of adding metacognitive components to existing assignments. (See also chapter 2.) The strategies were easy to implement, and they can be offered independently of one another, using diverse techniques and technologies. Students' experiences of them varied, but we argue that the strategies have significant virtues. By giving students a way to reflect on their concrete writing processes, the strategies foster broader reflection on what gives an academic discipline its particular characteristics. And perhaps most surprisingly, they significantly improved our other pedagogical techniques. One of these was student peer review: the metacognitive interventions gave the students a new mode of communicating with one another as authors and commentators. Additionally, the interventions fostered a sense of "meta-" communication, as instructors and students reflected together on the writing process itself and its disciplinary norms and on ways to communicate that new understanding.

Given our own satisfaction with the strategies, we have continued to use them in our courses even after the end of the research project. LaVaque-Manty has begun using one of the techniques in *all* of his courses, from large freshman introductory classes to graduate seminars.

We describe herein the techniques and our own experiences of them in detail. We begin with the settings of our courses. This is *not* because the techniques are only useful in courses like ours. Quite the contrary: the differences between our courses alone show that the techniques travel well.

THE SETTING: THE UPPER-LEVEL WRITING REQUIREMENT AND "THINKING LIKE A PSYCHOLOGIST/POLITICAL THEORIST"

In the College of Literature, Sciences, and the Arts at the University of Michigan (U-M), students' writing requirements come in two stages. First is the familiar "freshman comp," the first-year writing requirement. Second, students must take one course that satisfies an upper-level writing requirement (ULWR). These are usually disciplinary courses with a substantive focus, but also with a substantial amount of writing. For a course to count as a ULWR course, at least half of the writing done in it must be revised, and writing instruction has to focus on writing as a process. One goal for the ULWR courses is that they allow students to learn disciplinary norms and conventions or, as we framed it in our courses, "What it means to think like a psychologist (or a political theorist)."

Psychology: Research Methods in Developmental Psychology

Course overview: Goals

Psychology (Psych) 351, Research Methods in Developmental Psychology,[2] is an upper-level methods and writing course that is one of several offered by the psychology department. The course is capped at 60 undergraduates, with each of three graduate student instructors (GSIs) running a lab comprising 20 students. As part of the course requirements for an undergraduate degree in psychology, students are required to take two research methods courses, with one of them being a formal course, such as this one, and the other often following more of an apprenticeship model, such as working as an assistant in a research lab. Statistics is a prerequisite for the formal courses. In the methods courses, students are provided with training in the skills necessary for designing, conducting, evaluating, and communicating research in psychology. At the conclusion of the course, they should have integrated the theoretical demands of the discipline with the more practical concerns of conceptualizing and running a research study. Thus, students should be able to write and think "like a psychologist." As these research methods courses are required for graduation, students are often less than enthusiastic about signing up for them. In the case of the developmental methods course, the curricular demands are heavy, with students reporting that it requires more work than 75% of the other courses offered at U-M. Despite these constraints, they are often pleasantly surprised by the material, with one student reporting that the course was "surprisingly digestible."

Course organization: Assignments and writing feedback

Over the semester students complete four major writing assignments, each of which carefully builds on the skills acquired in the previous assignments. The first is a dissection of a research article (article evaluation). The next two assignments consist of two research papers, one an observational study and the other an experimental study; for both of these assignments, students collect data. The culminating activity of the class is a research grant proposal on any topic in developmental science, to be chosen by the student, for which they do not actually collect data, but do provide a data analysis plan (see Table 6.1 for details). Each research paper follows the conventions set by the American Psychological Association (APA), with one of the required books being the *Publication Manual of the American Psychological Association*. Students have to learn to craft a careful evidence-based argument in the introduction, ending that section with specific hypotheses regarding the research question that

Table 6.1   Writing assignments in Psych 351

Assignment	Length (in words)	Peer Review
Article evaluation	2,100–2,400	None
Observation paper	2,100–3,600	First draft
Experimental paper	2,100–3,600	First draft
Research grant proposal	2,100–3,600	First draft

is central to their argument; this is followed by methods and results sections, which detail the measures, data collection, and analyses used to investigate the hypotheses. In the final discussion section, the students restate the core research question in nonnumerical terms, interpret the data, and describe limitations and future directions. In addition, there is a short abstract in which the entire paper is summarized. In essence, students have to sustain a complex argument, based on evidence from peer-reviewed sources and current data, throughout each research paper. Students get comments and other writing feedback on all of their writing, both from the instructors and from their peers.

One unique aspect of this course is that the students gather data in real time—in a nearby preschool for the observational study, and in a nearby elementary school for the experimental study. Overall, students are very enthusiastic about these hands-on components, often finding them to be the most valuable aspect of the course.

The GSIs comment on and grade the papers. During Evans's lengthy weekly GSI meetings, student papers are discussed in detail. For each assignment, Evans asks all GSIs to grade and provide feedback on the same sample paper in order to establish that they are using the same criteria. In addition, Evans provides extensive grading rubrics for each paper. From an instructional point of view, one of the challenges is to help the GSIs, who are mostly second- and third-year graduate students, learn how to give appropriate feedback, and shared commenting and grading protocols are a key element of this component. The undergraduates, as well, are instructed on optimal commenting procedures during their peer-review sessions. These shared experiences give rise to what is best described as a metacommunicative process, as discussions of the kinds of reasoning that go into disciplinary writing foster communication among all class members.

Political Science: Twentieth-Century Political Thought

Political Science (Polisci) 409, Twentieth-Century Political Thought, is an advanced undergraduate lecture course with a prerequisite specifying that a student have exposure to a previous political theory course.[3] When it is taught as a ULWR course, its enrollment is capped at 50; there is one GSI whose responsibility is to grade a substantial amount of student work, engage in one-on-one tutoring, and talk about writing-related issues in class. The course's primary pedagogical purpose is to introduce students to some of the key political themes in twentieth-century politics through the study of a variety of texts, some explicitly scholarly, some not. These are the course's learning objectives as they are spelled out in the syllabus:

> The two primary purposes of this course are to introduce you to the key ideas of twentieth-century political thought and help you learn to think like a contemporary political theorist. Political theory is a type of social inquiry that studies arguments made in texts. The purpose of this course is to introduce you to some of the most important arguments made in the twentieth century, and to teach you to *interpret* and *analyze* the texts and *evaluate* the arguments. Most of the steps require your own expressive skills, particularly in your own writing. This means that while the *knowledge* objectives of the course are limited to the theories we study, mastering the *skill* objectives will make you prepared more broadly.

In terms of writing pedagogy, the greatest challenge in Polisci 409 is what we call the "genre challenge": most of the readings are *not* examples of how professional political theorists in the early twenty-first century write. Although Max Weber's lecture *Politics as a Vocation* or Antonio Gramsci's *Prison Notebooks* are significant scholarly texts, they are not exemplars of how we would want today's students to write to succeed as academics. Students also read some samples of contemporary academic writing, and the course tries to turn the variety of genres into a pedagogical advantage by making the students aware of the differences. In general, in getting the students to write like contemporary academic political theorists, the goal isn't to turn them into political theorists, but to foster genre and audience awareness and to get the students to understand that different modes of inquiry come not only with different methodologies but also with different modes of expression.

The logic for the writing assignments in the course is to allow students to practice, in a focused way, the various "modules" that comprise academic writing in political theory before putting them together in a sustained, freestanding academic essay. The modules include relatively straightforward paraphrases, summaries, and elaborations as well as significantly more demanding elements, such as analyses, interpretations, counterarguments, and applications of concepts. Table 6.2 lists the writing assignments in the course.[4]

Table 6.2   Writing assignments in Polisci 409

Assignment	Length (in words)	Peer Review
Modular paper 1	500	No
Modular paper 2	500	First draft
Modular paper 3	500	First draft
Term paper	2,500–3,000	No

IMPLEMENTATION

Because our interventions were unfamiliar to the students, we spent considerable time introducing them. Our syllabi, which were sent to the students electronically before the semester began, contained the following:

> Metacognitive Writing Activities: Research suggests that self-monitoring of learning can improve student performance. For that reason, we are asking you to complete brief metacognitive writing activities as part of the major assignments: (i) a planning activity for each assignment, (ii) a monitoring activity, as part of each paper, and (iii) an evaluation activity for one assignment. Completion of each activity will count toward your grade on that assignment (and help you understand the concepts).

Furthermore, in the first lecture of the semester the students were introduced to the metacognitive activity in more detail with several slides shown devoted to the theory behind the activity (see Figures 6.1 and 6.2) and to our expectations. In the psychology course, it is usually in one of the first labs of the semester that the students are given a handout (see Appendix A) in which the major metacognitive activities are described in detail. This handout is also posted on a class website, and as the semester proceeds the weekly assignments are posted under a weekly announcement (with the relevant handouts attached electronically). In the political science course, the process is the same except that because the course doesn't have discussion sections the instructor and the GSI devote a substantial portion of one of the early class sessions to explaining the details.

The metacognitive activities come in two forms: (a) planning and evaluation activities, which are done before and after an assignment, respectively, as well as (b) a self-monitoring activity, which is embedded in the assignment. We discuss the planning and evaluation activities together because the evaluation activity for one assignment can be connected to—or simply be—the planning activity for the following assignment.

Figure 6.1   Basic metacognition model

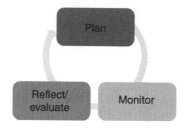

Simple model: Metacognition

Figure 6.2   Detailed model for metacognitive interventions: planning and evaluation activities

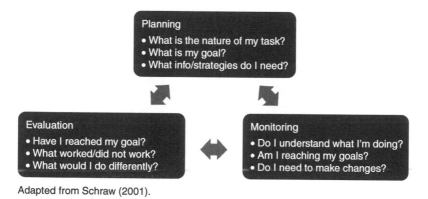

Detailed model: Metacognition

Planning
• What is the nature of my task?
• What is my goal?
• What info/strategies do I need?

Evaluation
• Have I reached my goal?
• What worked/did not work?
• What would I do differently?

Monitoring
• Do I understand what I'm doing?
• Am I reaching my goals?
• Do I need to make changes?

Adapted from Schraw (2001).

Planning and Evaluation

In Psych 351, one of the great challenges of introducing metacognitive activities is that the course is already full of activities with weekly due dates, and it is very easy to overwhelm the students, even if each activity does not take too much time. Evans has tried several methods over the years that she has been working with the metacognitive approach. As part of the Teagle–Spencer study, all student work was submitted electronically, so the metacognitive activity responses were also submitted on a special website (using a basic online survey tool). Each assignment was introduced along with handouts in the Thursday labs; then, on the following Sunday, students had to complete a metacognitive planning assignment and, where appropriate, a metacognitive evaluation of the previous assignment, answering planning and evaluation questions like the ones listed in Table 6.3. The process was, again, more or less the same for the political science course.

Table 6.3   Planning and evaluation questions in Psych 351 and Polisci 409

	Psychology	Political Science
PLANNING	1. In what ways will this assignment help you think and write like a psychologist? 2. Thinking of assignments you've done in the past, what did you learn that you can draw on in completing this assignment? 3. What do you need to have clarified to complete this assignment successfully?	1. Which skill will you be practicing in this assignment? 2. Why did you choose this particular skill? 3. In what ways will this assignment help you think and write like a political theorist? 4. Thinking of other assignments you've done in the past, what did you learn that you can draw on in completing this assignment? 5. What do you need to have clarified to complete this assignment successfully?

We responded to the students' planning and evaluation exercises in class. In particular, we tried to address general, pressing issues using class time and using other means (such as e-mail) for more idiosyncratic issues. Here are a few sample comments from the students in Psych 351, written between the initial article evaluation and the observation study paper:

- "I learned that it is more difficult than expected to dissect an empirical article. It takes a great deal of analysis to pick out the authors' intentions at times. This can be extended to the observation assignment."
- "That I need to look for underlying information not just surface."
- "It will help me write a better argument in my future assignments and taught me how to think scientifically."
- "I learned that I have a lot to work on as far as paying attention to detail and avoiding plagiarism. I also learned that I may need to put more time into editing my next paper so I won't make the same mistakes as before."
- "I learned that my hypotheses and variables need to be very clearly defined. It is best to state the variables in simple, scientific terms instead of trying to elaborate too much in the same sentence. It is also important to define the levels of the variables."

These comments seem to reflect a sense of discovery or surprise at the complexity of the task at hand. Students discovered that they have to look beneath the surface features of an argument to discern the intentions of the author, as shown in the first two comments. The latter comments reflect a growing realization that writing a scientific argument requires careful and detailed analyses at multiple levels.

Here are some examples of student planning responses from the political science course:

- "I chose to work on the summary because I believe my writing weakness is primarily in my inability to succinctly and accurately explain what I have read and this is a very important skill to master."
- "I have been struggling with this idea of summarizing: as I've stated before, I tend to write in hyperbolic, flowery prose. I know this is one of my worse [sic] habits, and thus I'm trying to practice writing succinctly and effectively for my unknown reader. I think this is a very important skill, and thus I'm hoping that practice will one day make perfect."
- "I enjoy thinking about the concepts in a text, and the issues it raises. I think George Orwell's observation is interesting, and would like to analyze the implications of it."
- "I chose this skill because I liked Orwell's Shooting the Elephant and felt that it would be the most interesting to write about. I also enjoy analyzing texts."

Comments like these tell us quite a bit about the students' own sense of their strengths and weaknesses (the first two) and interests (the last two). They also give us a sense of how deep or sophisticated these self-understandings are. For example, the first and the fourth are relatively general, while in the second and third examples the students are able to *describe* their weaknesses ("hyperbolic, flowery prose") or *specify* what interests them (the *implications* of Orwell's observation).

In subsequent semesters, we streamlined the logistics by incorporating the planning and evaluation aspects of the cycle into in-class activities. This reduced the number of online assignments, which eased the workflow for both the students and the instructors. As we will discuss, there are some drawbacks in using the planning and evaluation as a kind of homework, whereas doing the activities (at least occasionally) in class provides variety in assignments and gives both us and the students more immediate feedback. In a way, bringing the planning and evaluation into collective class time is a form of a "flipped" classroom (in which facts and concepts are studied outside class time and "worked with" during class), and, in our view, an efficient *and* effective use of face-to-face contact time. In Psych 351, Evans introduced the concept of an "action paper" given in a lecture. The action paper has two components: a series of questions related to the lecture as well as the

Figure 6.3 Streamlined planning and evaluation process, Psychology 351

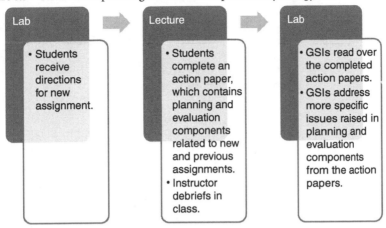

metacognitive activities. This served to break the lecture into subsections and gave the students the opportunity to commit their planning activities to paper and then discuss their thoughts with the faculty member. For all but the first assignment, Evans combined the evaluation and planning exercises so that students evaluated how the previous assignment contributed to the current assignment and stated what else they needed to know to complete the current assignment. Evans debriefed aspects of this assignment in lecture and then GSIs further addressed issues in the lab sections. Figure 6.3 details this process.

Once the undergraduates became used to this routine, the majority of them made good use of the opportunity to get their questions answered. Importantly, they began to realize that it is a good idea to review and reflect on each of the assignments long before it is due—one of the hoped-for outcomes of this approach. Additionally, this gave the GSIs the opportunity to anticipate problems students might have interpreting the assignment and deal with them early in the process. Thus, the GSIs and the instructors themselves became more metacognitive and reflective about the nature of their own students' learning. (We return to this point in the following discussion.)

Similarly, in Polisci 409, LaVaque-Manty has experimented with turning the planning exercises into in-class group activities. He has done this in several ways and varies them from assignment to assignment. The simplest is to let the students spend some time in small groups discussing the kinds of questions we listed previously, and then debrief the entire class. This method allows common concerns to arise, but it also allows students to get answers to questions they may not have thought about. A slightly more complicated approach is to give the students a paper survey with a few planning questions, ask them to fill it in, and either collect it for later feedback or, more fruitfully, put them directly into small groups and encourage them to agree on either common or most important concerns. Once again, these discussions can then be collectively debriefed or collected for later feedback.

Self-Monitoring

The metacognitive self-monitoring activity was done through comments students inserted into both drafts and final versions of their papers (see Appendices A and B for details). Students learned how to use the review function in Word for each of their writing assignments. In the comments box, they would highlight three or four issues that were metareflective in nature, and the grader of the paper would respond to these comments in his or her feedback.[5] Part of the GSI training time during the semester was spent reviewing optimal ways of responding to these comments. The responses should not be too didactic but should themselves be reflective, encouraging a dialogue with the student.

Students also inserted monitoring comments into drafts that were to be peer reviewed, and peer reviewers were asked to respond to those comments. In some cases, the student author–peer/editor dialogue became extremely substantive—and substantial. Consider the following exchange from Polisci 409, which is only the first of five such "conversations" in a student's 500-word paper on Michael Walzer's theory of dirty hands in politics. The author adds comments to his 90-word introduction to which the peer/editor replied at length. Figure 6.4 is a screen shot of the actual paper, showing how the dialogue appeared.

We return to the idea of a dialogue at several points in the following section. First, we report on student perspectives.

Figure 6.4 Screen shot of peer dialogue

Michael Walzer deals with the issue of 'Dirty Hands' though the lens of it being a dilemma that every politician faces sooner rather than later. Walzer puts forth his opinions on cases in politics that deserve to be termed cases of dirty hands along with responding to the broad overall question of whether politicians are justified in carrying out these 'dirty' actions. Walzer's argument is full of hypothetical real-world scenarios that he considers to be dirty hands and this paper is aimed at analyzing another real-world case through Walzer's eyes.

Comment [1]: Given the prompt of the assignment, I was unsure how to structure the paper, especially the way in which to start. Should I have started with my example first? Maybe a deeper analysis of Walzer's theory? Is this too broad?

Comment [2]: It might be interesting to start your paper with an example and really work with the way Walzer would react to this example. Then, maybe the introductory comments could be rendered unnecessary because your illustration would be clear enough to take care of this explanation. On the other hand, if you leave it this way you could cut down the explanation by giving a more explicit one line definition of dirty hands (i.e., Michal Walzer's concept of dirty hands is the idea that politicians can't succeed without having to face difficult moral dilemmas; thus, they are justified for partaking in an action that they would dub immoral in their personal lives.) Then you could go straight from that and begin explaining your illustration all in the first paragraph.

FINDINGS

Student Perspectives

The Teagle–Spencer project has collected significant amounts of data on the interventions we (and one other) instructor implemented. We include some summary data here, for the obvious reason that student perceptions matter when instructors consider whether to try new pedagogical strategies.[6] Table 6.4 provides student assessments of each intervention. Students were also asked to assess the value of feedback from their instructors and peers. Of the three interventions, students found the monitoring intervention to be most valuable, and at levels similar to the value they placed on peer and instructor feedback.

Students' qualitative comments explaining their assessment of the monitoring intervention revealed two primary themes about the benefits students perceived it to offer: (a) insight into their own writing process, and (b) dialogue with their readers. These comments were typical:

- "When I made comments on my own writing, I was able to reformulate my thoughts to make them more logical and clear." (Political theory student)
- "I really like metacognitive comments because they make me think more about what I'm writing and give the reviewer a better idea of what I'm thinking." (Psychology student)

Students' qualitative comments indicate less positive views of the planning and evaluation activities. However, some students reported finding the planning activities useful, particularly if they prompted specific instructor feedback that further clarified the assignment. In our discussion in the next section, we offer a conjecture on the lower level of enthusiasm for the planning

Table 6.4 Student assessment of metacognitive interventions

Statement: "X . . . was valuable"	Psychology	Political Science
Planning	2.11	2.42
Monitoring (Comments)	3.39	3.5
Evaluation	1.97	2.61
Feedback *to* Colleagues	3.05	3.44
Feedback *from* Colleagues	3.24	3.64
Feedback from Instructors	3.58	3.75

1 = Strongly Disagree; 4 = Strongly Agree.

Table 6.5   Impact on student disciplinary thinking

Statement: "I have a clear understanding of what it means to think like a . . ."	Pre	Post
Psychologist (2010)	2.74	3.29*
Political Theorist (2010)	2.76	3.14*

1 = Strongly Disagree; 4 = Strongly Agree.
*Difference of means (paired sample) is statistically significant at 0.05 level.

and evaluation activities and suggest a way of making them more appealing. Also, given our—and the ULWR program's—goal of encouraging disciplinary awareness, we include student perceptions of it in Table 6.5.

Qualitative responses to the question "What does it mean to think like a . . . ?" also show movement after the class activities in students' alignment with *our* perspectives. For example, in political theory, LaVaque-Manty defines "analyzing the construction of arguments" as a crucial element of the discipline. In their postresponses, many more students echoed this theme. That this seems evidence of a "priming effect" is, of course, a feature of the approach, not a bug: our very goal is to get students thinking of the disciplines in the way expert practitioners think of them, and using the same language is a sign of steps in the right direction.

Instructor Perspectives

Our sense of the interventions reflects the students' perspective to an extent: we find the metacognitive monitoring comments most valuable. But we also find the planning and evaluation strategies worthwhile; we will discuss those first.

We believe that the seeming student dissatisfaction with the planning and evaluation activities is less a response to the strategy in general than to the way we administered it during the Teagle–Spencer project. Because of data collection needs, we administered both the planning and the evaluation instrument for each paper, always digitally with a survey tool and always with the same set of questions. It seems to us that this relatively quickly became a rote activity to the students: students began to "go through the motions," instead of really thinking about what they already knew and what they would want to know.

As we pointed out, we have continued to use the planning and evaluation activities, but with a variety of approaches, and not for every assignment. The variety and selectivity seem to reduce students' "instrument fatigue" while encouraging reflection. And although the original version of the planning and evaluation activities could be somewhat tedious, they yielded one important and unexpected positive outcome: they greatly increased communication among faculty, students, and the GSIs. The students were delighted to have their questions answered, and the GSIs and the faculty instructors found a new way to communicate directly with the undergraduates, even the shy ones, given that office hours usually serve that purpose for only a few students.

It is for this reason, in fact, that the self-monitoring comments inserted in student papers were so successful. They further fostered communication between students and instructors. As the following comments (from Psych 351) indicate, students were appreciative of feedback on their marginal reflections from their peers as well as their instructors:

- "The metacognitive comments were very helpful. In the areas where I had questions, it was nice to have them directly answered."
- "The instructor feedback was helpful also, because I did not realize how much information I did not understand."

In assignments that involved peer review, students emulated the instructor commenting models and responded to the questions in ways that were clearly appreciated:

- "I learned that I need more thoughtful metacognitive comments. My peer pointed out that a few of my comments were capable of being answered if I spoke to my GSI."
- "My peer feedback was really helpful to me because my peer editor was able to answer my metacognitive questions."

Even this activity required instructional reinforcement. Just as with the planning and evaluation activities, some students seemed to insert marginal reflections simply because they were required to do so. (And some needed reminding that they had to.) In those cases, in particular, the students' questions and comments were not necessarily helpful, either for the students or for us. We had to encourage students to ask substantive as opposed to superficial questions, and we especially had to discourage questions with "yes/no" answers (e.g., "Is this what Weber thinks?"). Such questions signal that the author is thinking of the assignment in terms of "right" or "wrong" answers. To be sure, our assignments did have such elements: Evans's requirement that the papers conform to APA style or LaVaque-Manty's requirement that each short paper be of a particular kind ("a paraphrase," "an analysis") clearly indicate to the student that there are right and wrong ways of doing things. So some "right/wrong" questions were reasonable. At the same time, such questions might be better dealt with through different resources. (For example, Evans creates a handout summarizing APA style and makes it available to her students at the beginning of the semester.)

The greatest value of the metacognitive reflections emerged when students asked substantive questions or wrote substantive commentary on their own thinking process. The marginal reflections occasionally helped us see that the student had indeed understood the matter at hand. That may be because the commenting "genre" itself may seem less daunting to the students. When a student believes she has to write a particular type of academic prose and isn't yet fully confident in her abilities, she may have a harder time expressing herself than when she is simply explaining to her instructor or peer what she *tried* to do. Almost invariably, substantive questions allowed us to give the student authors specific and, we believe, constructive feedback.

DISCUSSION

Levels of Reflection

As we pointed out earlier, metacognition worked at two levels in our courses. On the one hand, each course was designed to encourage student reflection on and understanding of disciplinary specificities and thereby differences between disciplines. On the other hand, the specific interventions we have described—planning, self-monitoring, and evaluation—brought about metacognition on the writing *process*. These two are related. The latter is the mechanism through which the former comes about. The logic for this is straightforward: when students become attentive to a variety of details in the writing process, they see what gives that discipline its character and, ideally, also understand the reasons behind disciplinary differences and academic conventions in general.

This happens both for the relatively basic elements in disciplinary conventions (e.g., citation styles) and for the fundamental differences. In the political science course, the self-monitoring of marginal reflections clearly shows that at least some students are mindful of the differences between *theoretical* and *empirical* arguments, even when—or perhaps especially when—they are not entirely sure how that distinction works. Comments on this may come in the form of questions, such as "Is it okay to bring in this outside evidence?" to more sophisticated ones, such as the following, where the student realizes different types of claims require different types of evidence, depending on the audience:

I'm not sure about bringing in outside information like this. I figure it augments my argument, and when speaking to a group of political scientists, it shouldn't require citation, but I was hoping to get your thoughts on the appropriateness of just stating this part.

These two levels of reflection, where the more procedural level is the mechanism that facilitates the broader disciplinary level, are what make these specific metacognitive interventions useful *and* transportable. As we have shown, our courses are quite different, but the very same interventions worked well in both. We see no reason to think that the interventions could not be successfully used in any type of course that involves writing. In fact, LaVaque-Manty has introduced some aspects of the interventions into all of his courses, including graduate seminars and very large (300-student) introductory courses.

We want to go further and suggest they can work across the disciplinary spectrum and maybe even beyond academia. In fact, they are already in practice here and there, even if they are not called "metacognition." Every time a computer programmer comments on her code, as all good programmers do, she is doing what we call self-monitoring. Also, when we remember that some of the research on self-regulated learning, of which metacognition is an element, comes from the study of athletes (Cleary & Zimmerman, 2005; Zimmerman, 2008), we might suggest that these interventions can be adapted to activities and skills that have nothing to do with academia. To be sure, working on your jump shot is not the same as writing a paper, and the specific tools for self-monitoring are going to be different from what we have described. But the general ideas are the same in all the practices:

1. Plan for the task by thinking about what one already knows or can do and what else one needs to complete the task.
2. Pay attention to one's execution of the task and somehow communicate what one takes oneself to be doing.
3. Evaluate how one did, particularly in light of external feedback on the execution, and what one learned from the execution and the feedback.

Communication and Peer Review

Someone might object to our example of the computer programmer. A programmer, the objection goes, comments on her code not to reflect on what she is doing but to *communicate to others* who will also have to work on the code.

Our response is that she does both. That these metacognitive activities are a form of communication is one of their greatest virtues.

One of the reasons students seem to find academic writing frustrating is that assignments require them not only to communicate ideas but to *demonstrate* their knowledge to instructors who already know more about the material than the students. In other words, despite their different form and supposedly different purpose from examinations, students' writing assignments are just a type of exam. We think this is reasonable and sometimes necessary, but it is nevertheless helpful for instructors to remember it and also make the purpose of each writing assignment explicit to their students. It is for this reason that the metacognitive interventions and their communicative function can be particularly fruitful.

For example, in the political science course, LaVaque-Manty frames the writing assignments and the metacognitive interventions, particularly the self-monitoring comments, as follows:

> You are not writing these papers to me or the GSI, but to an imaginary audience [specified for each prompt]. I and the GSI are your senior collaborators, people a bit more familiar with the discipline, audience, and the material. In your drafts, you communicate to us what you are trying to do, ask questions where you want help and, in general, involve us in your writing and thinking process.[7]

This kind of framing not only gives the students a sense of how to use the metacognitive activities, but importantly shapes the classroom relationships. It does not pretend that there aren't hierarchies—such a pretense is, in our view, pernicious—but it makes it explicit that writing and learning are collaborative activities, even in hierarchical settings. As the courses' purpose is to get the students to "think like psychologists" or "think like political theorists," we think it appropriate that the course setting emulate the collaborative relationships junior scholars such as graduate students or junior faculty might have with more senior colleagues.

This collaborative model influences student peer review as well, as we discovered somewhat to our surprise. As our previous example of peer communication shows, the communication between a student author and his peer can become very substantial and substantive. It is of course different from the students' communication with the instructors in the sense that the students are less certain of their command of their material. We see this particularly in peer comments: "I'm not sure I understand Foucault either, but I thought . . ." or "I thought the dirty hands problem refers to . . ." We nevertheless see this as a virtue. First, it makes the value of peer learning evident. Students work together to understand the materials. And thereby, second, it reminds the students that often understanding the material is not as much about "getting it right" as about learning to offer reasons for one's understanding. And, third, successful instructor comments on student reflections often aren't just factual corrections—"No, you have misunderstood Foucault"—but attempts at fostering an ongoing dialogue.

Sometimes students ask what they should say or whether their readings of texts, for example, are correct. We find that it is often more helpful to tell them something along these lines: "Well, it depends on what you want to argue; I see the following two options. . . ." That kind of dialogue helps the student understand that there is no single right answer she must demonstrate to us, but that she has agency as a writer.

Interestingly, in addition to these external dialogues, metacognitive techniques explicitly foster internal dialogues as well. The student who takes a third-person perspective on his or her own work has added a level of conscious objectivity that might not have been evident beforehand:

> It provided the opportunity to step back and read my paper objectively while analyzing and critiquing my arguments, structure, and logic. I will utilize this strategy in future papers I write. (psychology student)

CONCLUSION

We conclude by summarizing some considerations for successful implementation.

These strategies require training students. Students need to have the purpose of the tools explained to them, and they need specific examples of how to use them successfully. For example, as we pointed out, it may take a while for the students to understand why substantive, as opposed to "yes/no," questions are better.

Students need to be rewarded for the use of the tools. From a student perspective, some type of grading incentive generally works best, at least in the first instance. But as our discussion of "instrument fatigue" suggests, whether or not they get points for the use of a tool, they will cease to engage it meaningfully if it is seen as rote busywork.

The strategies do not have to be used all the time, for every assignment, or in a similar way. The primary consideration for when and how to use a tool should be a pedagogical one: the planning, evaluation, and self-monitoring activities should be used when the instructor thinks it makes sense. But instructor, student, and infrastructural resources must of course also be considered. For example, the planning activity might only be used once a term, on the first assignment, for example, or for a major assignment such as a term paper. This might optimize pedagogical benefit while simultaneously preventing instrument fatigue and instructor overwork. Similarly, a planning activity might take place in the classroom as group work. Here, the value of peer learning goes together with the idea of a "flipped" classroom, that is, that instructor-moderated student interaction can be a more valuable way of using instructor–student contact time than the conventional "talking at" students.

These alternative strategies come with costs, too. Evans's action paper strategy for eliciting student responses has resulted in her role as a communicator becoming minimized. With the new approach, she is not necessarily responding to student questions and comments in real time, but instead often brings in questions provided by students from previous semesters. Trying to get students to communicate their concerns during a lecture does help, but this does not get around the problem of the many students who do not want their perceived ignorance of the assignment revealed to their peers. One solution has been the use of vastly improved website tools that have recently become available. The psychology course website now has forum and chat tools that allow more of an ongoing discourse. Thus, in addition to the action papers, Evans can add a chat tool to the website and encourage students to post at least one of their metacognitive responses per semester to the site and answer the question both online and during lecture. Still, every semester Evans has included a question about usefulness of the action papers in the midterm feedback, and about 99% of the students have enthusiastically endorsed the low-tech approach.

So these tools come with challenges, trade-offs, and contextual considerations. But from our perspectives, the metacognitive interventions have been a great success. We are convinced that they are a valuable tool for increasing student metacognition. As we have argued, they increase it at two levels: By making students pay attention to and reflect on writing as a process, we can get them to understand what it means to engage in writing and inquiry in this particular discipline, whatever the "this" is. As we have also argued, these interventions have shaped the way we teach our courses and, we believe, the way both students and instructors experience our courses.

We would like to be able to demonstrate significant differences in students' learning outcomes and in their critical thinking. Comparison of assignments in our courses before and after the interventions would be the most obvious natural experiment, especially for assignments and prompts that have remained constant, as some have. That evaluation would require a double-blind comparison, which in this case would mean the assessment of anonymized student work by a competent evaluator who has not been an instructor in our courses. We have not had the financial resources to undertake that evaluation, although we hope to do so in the future. However, even if we could show that the interventions improve the quality of students' critical thinking, it would not automatically entail greater student learning. Perhaps the higher quality of student work elicited by the interventions might be a simple function of the increased time the interventions cause students to spend on their papers. If this were the case, however, it would be a positive outcome.

And perhaps that is all we should hope for. Working more does not mean working better, of course, but our own sense is that when implemented well, these interventions do make students work better and improve their critical-thinking abilities. This is because they direct them to the elements of the writing process that are important for successful writing. Put another way, when students learn to use tools that allow them to reflect on their own learning, they have learned something important both for their discipline and for their future.

NOTES

1. The Impact of Meta-Cognitive Strategies Within Writing in the Disciplines was funded by the Teagle Foundation and Spencer Foundation's grant: Systematic Improvement of Undergraduate Education in Research Universities.

2. Developmental psychology focuses on psychological changes over time across the life span, from cradle to grave.

3. Political theory is one of the four subfields of political science. The others are American politics, comparative politics, and world politics.

4. Compared to Psych 351—or many other courses—the writing load seems light. But in political theory, conceptual and analytic precision as well as textual evidence and argumentative logic are the key methodological criteria for quality. This means that allowing, indeed forcing, students to think about every word they write is important. Related to this, the course tries to get students to understand the value of succinct expression, and here the 500-word papers serve an important function. In fact, excessive length is penalized in grading the short papers, and some students struggle to keep their papers focused and prose tight.

5. In Psych 351, a sectioned course, the paper grading was done by the GSIs. In Polisci 409, LaVaque-Manty graded about a third of the papers, the GSI the rest.

6. We are grateful to the editors of this volume for making this material available to us.

7. This message is given in in-class discussions of the writing assignments. It is not a verbatim quotation, but because LaVaque-Manty has given this message at least half a dozen times, it is pretty close to verbatim.

REFERENCES

Cleary, T. J., & Zimmerman, B. J. (2005). Self-regulation differences during athletic practice by experts, non-experts, and novices. *Journal of Applied Sport Psychology, 13*, 185–206.

Lovett, M. (2008). Teaching metacognition: Presentation to the Educause Learning Initiative annual meeting. Retrieved from http://net.educause.edu/upload/presentations/ELI081/FS03/Metacognition-ELI.pdf.

Schraw, G. (2001). Promoting general metacognitive awareness. In H. J. Hartman (Ed.), *Metacognition in learning and instruction* (pp. 3–16). Dordrecht The Netherlands: Kluwer Academic.

Zimmerman, B. J. (2008). Investigating self-regulation and motivation: Historical background, methodological developments, and future prospects. *American Educational Research Journal, 45,* 166–183.

Appendix A
Psych 351: An Overview of the Metacognitive Writing Activities

I. Metacognitive Planning Activity

A planning activity consists of two to three questions to be answered by you in lecture (as part of the action paper), just after each assignment is given out (e.g., Article Evaluation, Observation Study, Experimental Study, Grant Proposal). Your GSIs will go over the issues you raise in lab.

II. Metacognitive Monitoring Activity: Examples of Prompts

Once you've written your paper, you will take a step back and think about any questions or comments you have about what you've achieved in your writing (for the Observation Study and the Experimental Study).

Use the "comment" function in Word to insert at least three questions or comments in the margins of the paper *that you submit online*. This is your opportunity to communicate with us and your peer evaluators "backstage" about the choices you've made, to make your thinking more explicit. You might note places where:

- you've made your primary argument—why that argument and why there?
- you've drawn on key concepts from the course—why that concept, what does this concept help you do/understand/achieve in this paper?
- you feel uncertain about whether you've gotten your point across, and why.
- you are struggling with or confused about a particular concept, and why.

The following sample marginal comments have been taken from papers that were submitted in this course last year. In each sample, the writer explains what he or she is struggling with or justifies a choice he or she has made. We encourage you to experiment with a range of comments and question types represented in the previous list to determine which ones offer you the most useful feedback.

1. "We, however, predicted that non-sharing behaviors would occur in inverse proportion to sharing behaviors, so the population that exhibited the most sharing behaviors would exhibit the least non-sharing behaviors."

2. "If this were the case we would probably see a smaller variance between age groups in scores on the semantically related list, and a larger variance between age groups in scores on the random ordered list (assuming that in this list the older elementary children's increased metamemory skills played a larger role). This interaction was not actually found at a significant level, however."

3. "For each of the two groups, the scores are divided by 30 to calculate the mean number of aggressive behaviors per group of students."

III. Metacognitive Evaluation Activity

At the conclusion of one of the assignments you will complete an evaluation activity that consists of one question to be answered by you in lecture (as part of the action paper).

NOTE: Each of the activities contributes one or more points to your overall grade on each assignment.

Appendix B
Samples of Short-Paper Prompts in Polisci 409

The writing pedagogy in Polisci 409 uses short, 500-word papers to have students practice the different types of "modules" that make up a freestanding, full-length academic article in political theory.

The following are examples of prompts students could choose from. There were altogether 15 possible prompts, given in weekly sets of three, and students had to write two papers.

- **Interpretation.** On p. 140, Frantz Fanon writes:

  The Negro is a toy in the white man's hands; so, in order to shatter the hellish cycle, he explodes. I cannot go to a film without seeing myself. I wait for me. In the interval, just before the film starts, I wait for me. The people in the theater are watching me, examining me, waiting for me. A Negro groom is going to appear. My heart makes my head swim.

Offer an interpretation of this passage. Unlike an argument paraphrase, in which you basically restate the argument in simpler terms and do not draw from other parts of the text, here you need to tell your reader what you think Fanon *means*. For that, you may well have to draw from other parts of the book.

- **Comparison.** Identify one aspect or a dimension on which the anti-colonial positions of Orwell and Fanon are different, and offer a hypothesis (with reasons) on what explains that difference.
- **Counterargument.** Fanon thinks that White racism causes a "collective neurosis" in non-White subordinated people. Write a paper in which you argue that "pathologizing" political phenomena—that is, thinking

of them as a kind of health issue—is a bad idea. (This assignment is very difficult!)

- **Explanation of a concept.** The subtitle of *Eichmann in Jerusalem* is *A Report on the Banality of Evil.* Explain what Arendt's concept "banality of evil" means.

- **Defense.** When *Eichmann in Jerusalem* first came out, many readers said, "She is basically exonerating Eichmann." Write a paper in which you defend Arendt against the charge. (You may, of course, think the charge is correct; you can still do this exercise.) Note that you don't have much space, so try to focus your defense on some key aspect. You will also need to explain—very briefly—why someone might think Arendt is exonerating Eichmann in the first place.

- **Comparative counterargument.** Adopting Weber's position from *Politics as a Vocation*, write a paper in which you offer one critique of either Walzer's or Hollis's argument. Note that you have to write *very* economically, as you will need to make clear to your reader what Weber's *and* either Walzer's or Hollis's argument is.

- **Illustration and analysis.** Describe an example of your own that illustrates the so-called "dirty hands" problem in politics, and apply an analysis from either Walzer or Hollis to the case. Be sure to identify all the relevant features of the case and what makes it a case of dirty hands.

7

Designs for Writing

A Metacognitive Strategy for Iterative Drafting and Revising

E. Ashley Hall, Jane Danielewicz, and Jennifer Ware

Design plans were first introduced by Wysocki and Lynch in their composition textbook *Compose, Design, Advocate* (2006). By making rhetorical principles—such as audience, purpose, genre, materials, and arrangement—explicit, a design plan encourages writers to use metacognition while inventing, planning, and producing a composition. We have adapted the design plan and use it as a pedagogical intervention to help students achieve prolonged metacognition, or systematic thinking, about composing decisions. The key components of design plans are described in Table 7.1.[1] This chapter will first expand on the metacognitive features of design plans. We then describe the varied course contexts in which we have used design plans. Finally, we describe our practice for implementing design plans, sharing examples to illustrate how this approach unfolds.

DESIGN PLANS AS METACOGNITIVE STRATEGY

Metacognition has been defined in a variety of ways, but one of the most common definitions is "cognition about cognition" or "thinking about thinking" (Flavell, Miller, & Miller, 2002, p. 175; Shamir, Mevarech, & Gida, 2009, p. 47; Veeman, Van Hout-Wolters, & Afflerbach, 2006, p. 5). Based on this somewhat simplistic definition, we can already distinguish the metacognitive quality of Wysocki and Lynch's design plan from other invention and planning techniques such as freewriting, outlining, brainstorming, and cluster mapping, which are all focused on the lower-order cognitive process[2] of generating content. Wysocki and Lynch describe the process of creating a design plan as "rhetorical" because it calls attention to the relations among rhetor, audience, and text and because it offers a way for composers to "systematize

Table 7.1 Design plan template

Statement of Purpose	An active statement that succinctly explains: • the author's purpose (*I want to inform, persuade, convince, prove, debunk, explain . . .*) • the author's audience (*to whom*) • the author's strategy (*by doing x, y, and z*)
Audience Declaration	A brief description of the readers (or viewers/listeners/etc.) you imagine reading or experiencing your text along with some notes about the attitudes, beliefs, assumptions, and/or cultural or professional practices members of this group share.
Context	The immediate context for your work is the specific place of publication or how your work will be shared with your audience. This may be as straightforward as "turning in my essay to my instructor." Or if you will be sharing your work with an outside audience, your context may include a community service partner's website or an academic journal such as *Young Scholars in Writing* or *College English*. The broader context includes the academic, scholarly, public, or popular conversation to which you are contributing and joining by producing your work.
Genre	A brief description of the genre that has been assigned or that members of your target audience would expect given your purpose and context for composing. In your description, make note of the features multiple documents in the same genre have in common along with a brief summary of the communicative purpose that documents in this genre typically address.
Media/Materials	A brief description of the materials you will use to complete the project and how you will use them (not necessarily how you will arrange your materials but more so the role each item will play or the purpose it will serve to help you accomplish the goals defined in your statement of purpose).
Arrangement Strategy	A description of how the content will be organized, including: • the specific sections of your document • the key claims that will be made in, or be the focus of, each section • the types of evidence or materials you will use to support or illustrate those claims An explanation of why you believe this strategy will be effective and help you accomplish the goals defined in your statement of purpose.

their thinking" about designing and producing a text (p. 29). John Flavell, the developmental psychologist who coined the term, defines *metacognition* as "any knowledge or cognitive activity that takes as its object, or regulates, any aspect of any cognitive enterprise" (Flavell et al., 2002, p. 175). Applying Flavell's definition to Wysocki and Lynch's description is the basis for our claim that design plans have a metacognitive quality. In the context of this chapter, we use metacognition to mean a composer thinking about the decisions, choices, and use of intellectual strategies that happen before, during, and after writing. Our application of the term *metacognition* to writing has five components:

1. Awareness of one's own thinking
2. Articulation of the thinking process
3. Reflection
4. Questioning and challenging previous choices
5. Using components 1 to 4 to evaluate, guide, and regulate present and future composing decisions

A defining characteristic of our implementation is that we use design plans in all phases of the composing process, not only during invention and planning but also while drafting and revising and even when reflecting on completed work at the end of a semester. When a design plan is used in a sustained, iterative manner throughout the composing process, it fosters the "reciprocal flow between monitoring and control" described by developmental psychologists Shamir et al. (2009, p. 48). Metacognition, they argue, "regulates cognitive activity by enabling students to be aware of how they think and by guiding them in the strategies they are to employ in order to solve a problem during learning" (p. 48). Using a design plan to gain awareness of and guide thinking while they are composing helps students create more complex and sophisticated texts.

EXAMPLES FROM OUR TEACHING

We have used design plans in a variety of courses at the University of North Carolina, Chapel Hill, three of which are presented here. In the examples provided, we demonstrate that the design plan is a flexible tool, applicable to all types of composing projects—written, oral, multimodal, and digital—whether the project spans an entire semester or lasts only a few weeks. Design plans are easily adaptable to many disciplines, and instructors can use them without any special training. However, design plans are most effective when instructors devote significant time in class to model the metacognitive process and, most importantly, for students to complete, share, and discuss sections of the design plan regularly. When students work on design plans in class, the instructor should create a thoughtful sequence of activities that scaffold metacognitive knowledge and skills progressively. We recommend more overt instruction—introduction of a model, discussion, application or experimentation, and reflection or revision—at the beginning so that students learn through practice how design plans support the reciprocal flow between monitoring and control that helps them regulate their composing decisions with greater intention and more effectiveness.

First-Year Composition

A small number of sections of first-year composition courses in our writing program are designated as research exposure sections. In these classes students work on an extended 16-week written project with the aim of producing original undergraduate research. Instructors use design plans to help students navigate the new discourse communities they are joining and to guide them through composing in new genres such as conference proposals, conference presentations, and academic journal articles. Students begin creating their design plan in the first week of class and iteratively revise it over the entire semester. They alternate between working on the design plan and writing in the target genre.

This example illustrates an extensive use of the design plan. Approximately 15% of class time throughout the semester is typically spent workshopping the individual sections of the design plan in these classes. During these workshops, time is devoted to small-group discussion and reflection, and students are given time to make updates to their plans in class. Devoting class time to iteratively revising the design plans places emphasis on the metacognitive habits of the mind we aim to instill by using design plans as a pedagogical intervention.

Additionally, the design plans are useful during one-on-one conferences when students and instructors discuss midstage composing choices and brainstorm new ideas. Students often need time to think before they can articulate their goals and thoughts about a project. Since students who are using a design plan have already spent time thinking about these points and have written their thoughts on paper, the limited time spent together during a conference can be focused on helping students evaluate their thinking and helping them understand how such evaluation, when it is systematic and iterative, can be used to monitor, regulate, and *improve* their composing choices.

At the end of the semester, students submit a portfolio of their work, including the most recent design plan and a process letter[3] that explains how the design plan guided their choices while composing each of the three unit projects. The process letter is an opportunity for students to reflect on and concretely document what they have learned about learning how to write in new genres. The design plan provides them with a record of their thinking process, while the process letter provides an opportunity to articulate in their own words how their thinking processes changed over time while they completed the project. As a writing-to-learn activity, writing a process letter about using a design plan helps students understand how they were able to monitor and regulate their composing decisions with progressively greater expertise and confidence. Like all writing, using a design plan to focus on metacognition while composing is a skill that requires practice. We have found that by the end of the semester, when students assemble their portfolios, they have consistently gained an awareness of and articulated the ways in which the design plan supported better writing and thinking throughout the composing process. Our hope is that by undertaking a final reflection by means of the process letter, students will make a deliberate choice on future occasions to use a design plan, or some other technique, to systematize their thinking about composing decisions while they write.

First-Year English Honors Seminar

We've also used design plans for projects that are smaller in scope, in this case a 5-week new media composition (see Appendix A for a sample design plan worksheet). In this class, students were composing new media personal essays that took the form of either a video or a website. During week 1, these students only made slight revisions to their design plans, using the document primarily for invention and planning. After choosing their medium in week 2, students used the materials and arrangement sections—critical to a visual rhetoric project—to keep track of what raw materials they needed to gather, to generate ideas for modifying and incorporating visual materials, and to manage logistical details while they drafted. For new media projects, where visual elements are often more important than textual ones, a design plan helps students realize that choices such as color, layout, and shot selection are rhetorical choices that affect the overall message of the project (Blair, 1996; Wysocki, 2003). The design plan was essential in guiding students through the composing process in a medium that was less familiar to them and therefore more challenging than producing a written text. This less-intensive but equally strategic use of the design plan was also effective.

A Writing-in-the-Disciplines Course

We consulted with a communication studies professor who taught an upper-level service-learning course (see Appendix B for a sample design plan overview with examples). The community partner for this project was Carolina Community Gardens, which requested that students create a wide range of projects, including instructional materials designed for volunteers as well as educational videos and a professional website for the organization funding the garden project. In this class, design plans for each of these projects were used for 8 weeks after initial contact between students and the community partner had been made and after preliminary research had been conducted. The professor reported that design plans especially helped coordinate groups of students who were working on projects that had vastly different genre conventions and goals. Given the logistical challenges these diverse projects represented, the professor reported that without the design plans, she would have had to mandate that all students work on the same genre. But such a restriction would have disappointed the community partner and limited students' composing experiences, greatly diminishing their contribution to the community partner.

INTRODUCING STUDENTS TO A DESIGN PLAN

We begin by introducing students to the concept of a design plan. Many student writers are already familiar with informal genres created primarily for the dual purposes of invention and planning, such as mind maps, cluster charts, and outlines. When students are initially presented with a handout listing the sections of the design plan (see Table 7.1), we call their attention to the purposes a design plan serves and we highlight key differences. We explain that whereas an outline documents and organizes *content*, a design plan is a tool that documents and organizes a writer's *thoughts*; in other words, a design plan often captures thoughts *about* content but not the content itself.

Another important distinction between an outline and a design plan is that the design plan offers a conceptual and rhetorical overview of a writing project that evolves over time. Although an outline is created before a draft, creating a design plan is an extended endeavor coupled with the drafting process. For example, the life span of an outline is limited to the planning of a draft. After an outline is generated, student writers rarely return to and update it, even though the argument may change shape or take a new direction. By contrast, the life cycle of the design plan is extended through the duration of the project. We help students use the thoughts recorded iteratively in the design plan to evaluate their composing choices and guide (or metacognitively regulate) future decisions throughout the writing process.

HELPING STUDENTS CREATE A DESIGN PLAN

Students begin the design plan by drafting a statement of purpose. In many cases, when a composition is first assigned, the main goal students have is to complete the work and obtain a desired grade. Other possible self-defined goals beyond simply completing the assignment remain implicit. But asking students to consider and define a specific goal for their work outside of "getting a good grade" launches them into metacognition. We use the design plan in this early stage to help students gain awareness of their thinking about their own goals for the project (the first component in our applied definition of *metacognition* on page 149). When students write these goals down to complete the first section of the design plan, they are articulating (component 2) those thoughts on paper. Next, we ask students to discuss what they have written in small groups, giving them time to reflect (component 3) on their thoughts. Over time, they will return to the initial goals they have set and question or challenge them (component 4) in light of new ideas that are generated while conducting research and drafting the project. When students use all four components, they use metacognition to guide or regulate their composing decisions.

Some students, we have found, have never thought about their independent goals for a writing project and therefore have never stopped to consider how their own goals may align with or differ from those defined by the instructor. For these students, a first attempt at drafting a statement of purpose often results in a paraphrase of the assignment prompt; even this minimal response is valuable because it helps students consider the possibility that they may indeed have (or at some point in the future will come to have) a different set of self-directed goals. Even when "completing the assignment" is the only purpose students can generate in the early stages of a project, asking them to record this simple goal in the design plan will help them track and document changes in their thinking over time. When students iteratively revise their goals together in class, the design plan makes explicit the more theoretical notion that self-directed goals for writing change and evolve over time. If we can help students become more aware of their goals (metacognitive monitoring), we can subsequently help them develop intentional strategies designed to accomplish their goals (metacognitive control).

We often ask students enrolled in the research exposure sections of first-year composition to write a literature review about a scientific topic if they are trying to do research in the natural or applied sciences. We have often seen students working on these projects replace their initial goal of completing the assignment with a more focused goal of learning about a particular scientific topic, such as climate change (see Appendix B's "A basic statement of purpose" for an example). These kinds of early-stage revisions are practical and show progress in the students' thinking. As students continue to work on their project, they conduct research, identify sources, take notes, and evaluate which sources they will use in their projects. Throughout this process, students are prompted to update and revise their goals. For example, a student whose early-stage goal was to learn about climate change might now state that he or she wants to "present the latest findings about the impacts of carbon emissions on the average oceanic temperatures and sea levels over the past two decades as reported in leading scientific journals by a series of independent research teams from three separate universities" (see Appendix B's "A better statement of purpose" for a fuller example). Learning to set more advanced goals is, in itself, evidence of intellectual growth on the part of the student writer.

Encouraging students to set personal goals for their writing at the outset of the project serves two complementary pedagogical aims. First, students are invested with greater autonomy as composers because they are not just responding to externally imposed requirements but instead are active agents co-constructing the desired outcome of their work. Second, the intervention is designed to shift students from low-order cognitive processes to a higher-order metacognitive level earlier rather than later in the composing process. Unlike writing a post hoc process letter, using a design plan to achieve metacognition in the midst of composing allows students to have more time to benefit from the intervention.

Once students have sketched[4] a statement of purpose, we prompt them to move on to the next section of the design plan by drafting an audience declaration. Teachers often direct students to "pay attention to audience" as they write, but we have found that students sometimes find it difficult to imagine their teacher as "an audience." We have also found that some students have trouble defining someone other than the instructor as a potential reader. These students find it challenging to transform overt directive instruction such as "pay attention to audience" into practical or applied knowledge. To address this, we use the following audience analysis heuristics to guide students through the metacognitive sequence:

1. Name one specific person (not the instructor) who would read or view this document.
2. What professional groups does this person belong to? For instance, is this person a biologist? A historian?
3. Within this larger group, is there a more specialized group who would be interested in reading this project? For instance, neurobiologists? Feminist historians?

4. Now that you have identified a particular group of readers, what sources can you consult to learn more about them? What professional websites, e-mails, interviews, and so forth will help you discover what these people share in terms of values and professional practices?

As students gain audience awareness (component 1), they articulate (component 2) their thoughts in the audience declaration section of the design plan. Having these thoughts concretely documented helps students when they engage in small-group discussions about audience in class. When students make their existing knowledge about audience explicit, they can more easily recognize what they already know and, more importantly, discern and reflect on (component 3) what they still need to learn. With this understanding in place, students can systematically monitor and regulate their thinking about audience, using it as a guide while they compose. Prompting students to record the steps they follow while analyzing the audience helps them document and understand their learning process. This metacognitive awareness (not just who the audience is but how they came to know and understand that audience) is a form of concrete and transferable knowledge that students can draw from in future composing situations, such as when they progress to subsequent sections of the design plan or when they work on a new project with a different audience.

As students turn their focus to the genre section, they are challenged to apply the five components of the metacognitive routine by studying the documents they collected while conducting audience analysis. To study genre is to analyze the "typified rhetorical actions based in recurrent situations" (Miller, 1984, p. 159). Rather than simply responding to a series of teacher-generated heuristic questions about the documents, students are called on to relate knowledge gained through audience analysis and to begin to define the conventions of genre they believe will be most effective given their target audience and evolving self-directed goals for the project. This involves a slight reduction in overt instruction at this stage so that students have an opportunity to practice metacognition more independently. To accomplish this, we ask students to reflect (component 3) on the thinking and learning process they used while conducting audience analysis and relate it (component 4) to thinking about genre. This helps students and instructors assess how well students are able to transfer and apply metacognitive skills when they are presented with a new thinking challenge. We support the students as they progress to more independent metacognition by delaying the use of heuristics. When we intervene later in the thinking process, our goal is no longer to help students get started but rather to extend and expand on their initial thoughts, in this case about genre. To do so, we use a series of questions we have adapted from the genre analysis heuristics developed by Bawarshi (2003). We ask students:

- *How do members of the target audience group use particular documents?*
- *What are the documents?* Prompt students to compare the kind of documents they have discovered while conducting genre analysis on the kind of document they are planning to create. Ask students to compare the similarities and differences. Ask students to consider several different kinds of documents created by members of their target audience. Ask students to identify and describe any themes or patterns they find in these documents.
- *When are the documents created?* Ask students to look for a particular event or context that prompts the creation of a particular kind of document. Ask students to find an occasion that would call for the kind of document they are trying to create.
- *For what purposes are the documents created?* Prompt students to compare the purposes they discover with their own purpose and to use the comparison as a trigger point for revision and adjustments to their current statement of purpose.
- *By whom are these documents created?* Prompt students to reflect on their position as composers addressing the same target audience.
- *For whom are these documents created?* Prompt students to return to the audience declaration and capture new thoughts about how this particular discourse community functions.

When students are asked to compose new and unfamiliar kinds of texts, thinking metacognitively about genre can help them compose more effectively. Rather than following a specified set of instructions about how their documents should be formatted, students have a heightened sense of why a particular document functions in certain ways. Ideally, students are able to articulate a rationale for some of their own composing decisions based on what they learn through genre analysis, and ideally they apply these insights to regulate future choices such as what materials they will need to be successful and how they will use those materials most effectively.

We saw the design plan supporting this kind of thinking in the first-year English honors seminar when students created a design plan in tandem with composing a new media personal essay. Prior to beginning this project, students practiced composing in a variety of life-writing genres, including autobiography/memoir, autoethnography, and biography. Although they tended to be familiar with these genres as readers, writing in these genres was new and unfamiliar for most students. Because they had already developed a routine of learning how to detect conventions of genre, students were well prepared for the additional challenge in the fourth unit when they were presented with both a new genre and a new medium. They used design plans to keep track of their notes and ideas while they studied the new genre to develop their projects.

As students in the class worked on the genre section of their design plans, they also considered some heuristic questions posed in the assignment prompt including:

- What is the essay?
- What are the conventions of the essay as a piece of writing? As a form of new media?
- How is the personal essay different from a journal or diary?
- What makes the essay personal?
- How do new media choices inform the personal?

One student began the project with the idea of a video about setting personal learning goals and accomplishing them. But over time, she revised her project and decided that the best way to meet the expectations of her audience and conform to the conventions of genre was to set a new learning goal for herself and record the experience of accomplishing it. She decided to make a video essay documenting her experience learning how to ride a bicycle, something that, even as a first-year college student, she had not yet learned to do but would master by the end of the semester.

Having determined her goal, she then began reflecting on the genre itself, comparing the features of this new genre (new media personal essay) to other familiar genres. Comparing the video essay to a biography, she commented that a biography is a story *about someone else*: the biography writer presents research and materials with a particular angle and shapes the story, but the focus is on someone else who is the subject of the biography and the object of study. On the other hand, this student said, a personal essay is written by and about the author. But, she pointed out, it's not just a journal or diary. A personal essay has a story arc, and there is something about the personal story that should resonate with readers (or in this case, viewers) and be more meaningful, more complex, than an account of the writer's mundane day-to-day life. One day might be the lens for the essay, she explained to her group, but not simply to say what happened on that day. In a personal essay, she noted, the point is to connect that one day to a bigger part of the life story.

These insights guided the student as she considered several possible ways to approach her video. For example, she discarded the idea of a video blog series, concluding that it was too similar to a journal or diary and was therefore not well suited to her composing goals. She also rejected the idea of a documentary video in which she would be interviewed by a friend about her learning process.

Finally, she decided on an approach that she felt was appropriate for the genre and purpose of the project and that aligned with her self-directed goals for the video essay. She decided that she needed video footage from two points of view: (a) an observational perspective with the camera placed on a tripod that would record her performance learning to ride a bicycle and (b) a personal perspective with the camera taped on the bicycle showing what she saw while she was learning to ride the bike. She also decided to record the voice-over using her own voice to maintain the personal quality necessitated by the genre conventions of the personal essay.

In this example, we can see a student writer composing with a great degree of agency and with an expanding sense of self-confidence when balancing the prescribed goals, defined by the assignment prompt, and her personal goals, defined and tracked in the design plan. We can see how the student applied metacognition by relating her prior knowledge about life-writing genres to help her think through the possibilities afforded by composing in a new medium. She used metacognition not only to gain awareness of her thinking process while composing but also to guide her composing choices. Each iteration of her thinking process described previously further illustrates the metacognitive reciprocal flow: alternating between awareness and control. She used the design plan to maintain awareness of her thoughts about audience expectations, personal goals, genre conventions, materials, and arrangement and used this awareness to regulate or guide her composing choices as she produced the final project. Working through each section of the design plan also helped systematize her thinking while she was in the reciprocal flow of metacognition.

We can see how the intellectual routine being prompted by the design plan supports a gradual progression in which students depend more heavily on the structure of the document and the heuristic prompts to help them think metacognitively at the beginning, until eventually the intellectual routine is established and students sustain metacognition in a more independent fashion. For example, after the student concluded the genre section of the design plan, she had already started thinking about the materials she would need to complete the project: a video camera, a tripod for the medium shots, duct tape for the personal shots, a bicycle, a flat landscape free from obstacles to practice riding and to film the process, a friend to help her, and a script for the voice-over.

When she moved from the genre section to the materials and arrangement sections of design plan, she had already put a good deal of thought into what tools and texts she needed to collect, so she could spend more time thinking about how she would use those materials most effectively to accomplish her goals, appeal to her audience, and match the genre conventions.

We prompt students to return to the materials section of the design plan frequently while they are conducting research. As students find new academic sources or media resources, they iteratively update the design plan by adding the new items to their list of materials. For traditional academic sources, this serves the same function as an annotated bibliography by recording the citation in conjunction with a brief summary of the source and a critical evaluation of how the source is useful. Other materials students have documented in design plans include a primary text and secondary sources such as scholarly articles for humanities research; observational data for social science research; laboratory results for scientific research; and images, clips, sounds, fonts, and so forth for multimedia compositions.

Using the materials and arrangement sections of the design plan to help students organize their thoughts about their projects was particularly important in the upper-division service-learning course, where important ethical considerations surfaced that required instructional guidance. One group of students had been asked by the community partner to make an informational video to help raise awareness among students, faculty, and staff about the Carolina Community Garden. When the group tasked with making the informational video started listing their materials and explaining how they planned to use them, they mentioned that they had learned that "more than three hundred active volunteers have provided labor for the garden and have grown more than eight thousand pounds of produce that have been distributed to over ninety [UNC] housekeepers at weekly distributions."[5] The group felt that one of the most important goals for their video was to help raise awareness about the members of the campus community "who don't earn enough money to necessarily be able to afford these wonderful vegetables" if it weren't for the garden. When they presented their design plans to the class, the group explained their plan was to attend and observe one of the distributions so they could film and possibly interview the housekeepers as they received their free vegetables. Interviews, they explained, would be the best way to convey to viewers how important the gardens are to the housekeeping staff. The teacher used this as an opportunity to discuss research ethics and human subject research with the students. After learning more about the ethical stakes of their video, the students worked with the Carolina Community Garden leaders and the housekeepers to determine the best way to handle this.

They agreed to only film a small portion of the distribution; they announced their presence and explained their purpose for creating the video to the housekeepers present at that day's distribution. They asked for and received permission from all of the recipients who appear in that portion of the video. And they were careful to limit the filming of the distribution to make sure that anyone who preferred not to be filmed still had ample opportunity to receive fresh vegetables. By using the design plan to monitor the students' thinking as it progressed, the teacher was able to intervene early in the composing process and provide students with an opportunity to think through the ethical issues that arose. The teacher's mentoring, facilitated by the design plan, helped ensure the positive outcome of the project.

Once students have listed their materials, we prompt them to engage in metacognition by asking them to write a rationale for why those materials will be helpful and what led them to this belief. The rationale comprises a strategy statement for each item or group of items listed in the materials section. Asking students to sketch brief strategy statements for items listed in the materials section of the design plan provides a foundational scaffold for the more complex analytical thinking that will be necessary as they move on to the next section of the design plan in which they develop an arrangement strategy for their project.

In the arrangement section of the design plan, students progress from thinking about how they will use items listed in the materials section as individual sources to developing a comprehensive strategy for using resources in concert with one another to accomplish the goals specified in the statement of purpose. In some ways, asking students to complete the arrangement section may seemingly resemble asking them to write a traditional outline. What's different is the focus on strategy that is fostered by metacognition. When students create an arrangement strategy, they are not just arranging content but gaining awareness of their thinking process as they consider different arrangement options (component 1), articulate their thinking process in writing by updating the design plan (component 2), reflect through small-group discussion and face-to-face conferences (component 3), question the merits of different approaches (component 4), and use this sequence to regulate composing decisions (component 5). We don't want students to outline the content point by point in the arrangement section of the design plan. Instead, we shift their attention to maintaining awareness of the decisions they are making about what information to provide and how that information should be grouped and presented to the reader (viewer, listener, etc.) to achieve their defined goal(s) with the maximum success.

We recommend another slight reduction in overt instruction at this stage. This provides another occasion for assessment of how well students are able to use metacognition to improve their writing. For example, we use more limited heuristics to launch students into the metacognitive reciprocal flow of monitoring and control. We begin by selecting a sample text to use as a model for analysis in class. Students are guided through the process of identifying the different sections of the text and describing their rhetorical function. For example, if we have selected a scientific journal article for analysis, we might mention the IMRAD (introduction, methods, results, and discussion) structure commonly used to organize articles in the sciences. We prompt students to work in small groups to discuss the logic for why such articles would be arranged in this manner. Next they analyze the purpose each section serves independently and how the individual parts work together in the context of the larger article. We discuss their thoughts as a class and complete a cursory outline of the article to demonstrate the method of reverse outlining. For homework, we ask students to find a text they would like to use as a model for their own project. They create a reverse outline in which they visually map out the different sections and explain how the sections work together to form an arrangement strategy. We use the following heuristics:

- Identify and list the different sections of the text.
- What are the moves being made in each section?
- What are the goals of the project?
- How do the moves in each section make progress toward those goals?

When they return to class, students present their work to their group mates and brainstorm ideas for how they could apply this arrangement strategy to their own project using their own materials. Next, we ask students to question and challenge how well this arrangement strategy aligns with their goals, how well it would meet the expectations of their audience, and how well suited it is to the conventions of genre for their project. We also ask them to reflect on how well suited the arrangement strategy is to the materials they plan to use. Are crucial materials missing? Would a different arrangement strategy work better for the materials they do have? Finally, with an awareness that there are a wide range of options to choose from, students articulate their thinking process for deciding on a particular option by describing their arrangement strategy in the design plan and explaining why they believe it will be effective.

DESIGNING AS A REFLEXIVE PROCESS

When students produce a project in tandem with creating a design plan, updating one section, such as the arrangement strategy, triggers students to reflect on and possibly revise other previously completed sections. Some of these connections are readily apparent but others are more implicit. We prompt students to think about the more subtle connections with the following heuristics:

- Based on your most recent discoveries about your audience, are there any revisions you can make to your purpose or goals that will help you meet the expectations of your readers?
- Is there anything new that can be added about audience or genre at this point given the materials you've collected?
- Based on what you've learned so far about the audience and genre, is there anything critical missing from your list of materials?
- As you find new materials, can you refine your goals for the project?
- At what point would readers from your target audience group be satisfied with the depth of research necessary to accomplish the goal you have defined? How does your research compare to this standard?
- Based on the arrangement strategy that you are planning to use, are the materials you have collected sufficient or do you need to find additional materials?

Making connections between different sections of the design plan reinforces the dynamic and interdependent relations inherent to the design plan. Our ultimate goal is for this reflective habit of the mind to become second nature. As soon as students acquire new information, their first impulse should be to return to the design plan in order to rethink their strategies and goals and to use these new ideas to regulate their composing decisions. This routine exemplifies the reciprocal flow between awareness and monitoring that we believe is necessary for composers who wish to use metacognition to improve their writing.

REVISING DESIGN PLANS ITERATIVELY

We want to be able to compare the first draft of each section of the design plan with subsequent attempts so that we can measure the students' progress at the conclusion of the project. Each time we ask students to update their design plan, we ask them to append new information rather than overwrite their

Figure 7.1 Design plan with multiple, date-stamped iterations of the audience declaration

---

Audience declaration: week 1

First attempt at audience declataion would be recorded here. For example, "writing for my teacher."

Audience declaration: week 3

Updated audience declaration would be recorded here. For example, "writing for my clasmates, especially those who are interested in climate change."

Audience declaration: week 6

Another updated audience declaration would be recorded here. For example, "students majoring in environmental sciences are who are interested in ocean temperatures as an indicator of climate change."

---

earlier work. We also ask them to add a date stamp for each revision. Figure 7.1 shows multiple iterations of a design plan's audience declaration.

Over time, the design plan becomes an archive of the students' discoveries and the dates illustrate the frequency of the iterations. These textual features of the design plan as a rhetorical artifact make the intellectual routine being developed explicit. Students can see how many times they have revised a particular section (awareness); they can trace the development of their thinking over time (articulation); and they can easily compare their initial thoughts to later, more sophisticated ideas that would not have emerged if they had been relying entirely on memory (reflection). The date annotations in the design plan record moments of pedagogical intervention or intellectual breakthroughs, allowing both students and instructors to see the concrete benefits of metacognition.

As a result of deliberately tracking developments in their thinking, students should be able to articulate not only why they believe their final draft is successful but also how they came to that conclusion. Likewise, students who use a design plan to craft their argument strategically should be able to explain why they decided to use the specific evidence they selected; why they believe that evidence should be persuasive to the target audience; and also how the presentation of that evidence aligns with the audience's expectations, the genre conventions, and the goals defined in the statement of purpose. We argue that students' abilities to articulate such a strategy demonstrate an elevated level of metacognitive development. Both students and instructors can measure the degree and quality of the students' intellectual development by comparing first attempts to later-stage goals and strategies, all of which are tracked in the iterative versions of the design plan.

CONCLUSION

In closing, we turn to Jenny Edbauer's (2009) notion of rhetorical ecologies. Rhetorical situations are complex, dynamic, and highly interdependent and can be described as rhetorical ecologies. The design plan is a similar sort of ecology. When new insights about one section, such as arrangement, are used to develop new ideas about another, such as materials, students are functioning automatically within the system or ecology of the design plan. For example, as students conduct research about their target audience and capture these details in the design plan, they may also discover project-specific outcomes—desired changes in cultural beliefs or practices, for instance—that can be used to revise the statement of purpose.

This interplay of the design plan ecology creates two strategic pedagogical opportunities. The first calls students' attention to the iterative and interactive nature of the design plan as a document that is intended to be unfinished and open to perpetual revisions and additions throughout the composing process (Faigley & Witte, 1981; Flower, Hayes, Carey, Schriver, & Stratman, 1986). The second highlights the ways in which one section of the design plan can (and should) be revised in response to additions or revisions made to another section. As an iterative pedagogical intervention, the design plan implements the dynamics of rhetorical ecologies through sustained metacognition. Throughout the process of conducting research and composing a text, the design plan operates as an interactive framework for helping students gain deliberately prolonged awareness about their thinking process. Teachers provide heuristics to help students practice using this awareness to guide their composing choices. When students begin making unprompted revisions to the design plan because they realize that an update to one section suggests new ideas and new possibilities in another section, they demonstrate intellectual growth made possible through applied metacognition. At the conclusion of a project, we ask students during conferences to compare early-stage to later-stage goals. We have found that, by discussing the differences between their initial goals and their final goals for the same project, students are frequently able to demonstrate the magnitude of their intellectual development over time.

We find the metaphor of a rhetorical ecology helpful for describing the way design plans function because of its generative connotations. An ecology is a living thing that grows, expands, and is inherently messy; no clearcut distinctions exist among the different parts. As soon as you zoom in on one thing, you find a connection to something else. Complexity is integral, relentless, unavoidable—but also necessary. Similarly, the design plan itself is a living and dynamic system that grows and expands over the duration of a writing project. Design plans are inherently messy and purposefully so. The distinctions among the different sections of the document are not clear-cut and, as we have shown, they are temporary; one change in any section initiates many other changes elsewhere. Thus, a design plan acts like an incubator for complex thinking. Since instituting them in our classes, we have been astonished by the overall quality of our students' work. With the aid of a design plan, students are able to achieve progressively higher levels of metacognitive intellectual development as they move through successive drafts to arrive at a polished final product that often exceeds the teacher's expectations.

NOTES

1. The sections we use have been adapted and are not identical to the original elements proposed by Wysocki and Lynch.

2. We want to acknowledge a parallel development regarding metacognition across the disciplines. In math education, for example, scholars refer to lower-order and higher-order levels of cognitive development (National Council of Teachers of Mathematics, 2000) and design pedagogies (Oregon Mathematics Leadership Institute, 2005; Smith & Stein, 2011) to move students from simply answering a question through a series of cognitive steps that refine the students' skills. This enables them not only to respond, but also to learn how to strategize to answer the question, challenge and defend their answer, and then make abstract connections to larger sets of similar problems. These higher levels of discourse are reached only when students make explicit connections between prior knowledge and newly acquired knowledge. This process parallels the design plan with its iterative drafting stages in which we ask students to revise sections of the document based on newly acquired knowledge within the various sections.

3. A process letter is a document that asks students to reflect on what they have learned while working on a particular project and to articulate what they would do in the future to improve their writing. It is a common practice for composition instructors to assign a process letter at the conclusion of a semester.

4. We explain that we realize the statement of purpose is unfinished and needs revising. Prompting students to stop midstream while composing and revisit individual sections of the design plan can help them discover new intellectual resources—thoughts and ideas that may have been unavailable to them at the start of a project.

5. For complete project see www.youtube.com/watch?v=CjsKSGUGW5E.

REFERENCES

Ball, C. (2004). Show not tell: The value of new media scholarship. *Computers and Composition, 21*(4), 403–425.

Bawarshi, A. S. (2003). *Genre and the invention of the writer: Reconsidering the place of invention in composition.* Logan, UT: Utah State University Press.

Blair, J. A. (1996). The possibility and actuality of visual arguments. *Argumentation and Advocacy, 33*(1), 23–29.

Edbauer, J. (2009). Unframing models of public distribution: From rhetorical situation to rhetorical ecologies. *Rhetoric Society Quarterly, 35*(4), 5–24.

Faigley, L., & Witte, S. (1981). Analyzing revision. *College Composition and Communication, 32*(4), 400–414.

Flavell, J. H., Miller, P., & Miller, S. (2002). *Cognitive development.* Englewood Cliffs, NJ: Prentice Hall.

Flower, L., Hayes, J. R., Carey, L., Schriver, K., & Stratman, J. (1986). Detection, diagnosis, and the strategies of revision. *College Composition and Communication, 37*(1), 16–55.

Miller, C. (1984). Genre as social action. *Quarterly Journal of Speech, 70*(2), 151–167.

National Council of Teachers of Mathematics. (2000). *Principles and standards for school mathematics.* Reston, VA: NCTM.

Oregon Mathematics Leadership Institute. (2005). *OMLI classroom observation protocol.* Portland, OR: RMC Research.

Shamir, A., Mevarech, Z. R., & Gida, C. (2009). The assessment of meta-cognition in different contexts: Individualized vs. peer assisted learning. *Metacognition Learning, 4*(1), 47–61.

Smith, M., & Stein, M. (2011). *5 practices for orchestrating productive mathematics discussions.* Reston, VA: National Council for Teachers of Mathematics.

Veeman, M., Van Hout-Wolters, B., & Afflerbach, P. (2006). Metacognition and learning: Conceptual and methodological considerations. *Metacognition Learning, 1*(1), 3–14.

Wysocki, A. (2003). With eyes that think, and compose, and think: On visual rhetoric. In P. Takayoshi & B. Huot (Eds.), *Teaching writing with computers: An introduction* (pp. 181–201). New York: Houghton Mifflin.

Wysocki, A., & Lynch, D. A. (2006). *Compose, design, advocate.* New York: Pearson/Longman.

Appendix A
Creating a Design Plan Step-by-Step

This worksheet is intended to function as a guide to help you formulate a design plan and begin planning your composition. The product of this worksheet will be a series of individual sections you could put together in a new document as your design plan. Remember that a design plan is not an outline; it is more of a roadmap that will guide your drafting choices as you write/compose/create.

Part 1: Thinking About Purpose

What is your purpose for this project? What are you trying to accomplish with this text? What do you want your audience to know/believe/feel/do after reading your article?

For example, sometimes when I write, I have carefully analyzed my audience and thought about what they already know, feel, and believe about teaching first-year writing. I want them to do something specific (consider alternative teaching strategies), so I want them to know how to do this, feel that it is important to do so, and then actually do it. This means my statement of purpose usually has at least these three elements.

Write a *Statement of Purpose* here:

Part 2: Thinking About Audience

Take a minute to think about the audience(s) you imagine reading/seeing/ hearing/encountering your project. Who is the literal audience? Who is your intended (imagined) audience? Out of all the students and professors on our campus who could potentially encounter your project, whom are you trying to speak to?

For example, when I write articles, I often imagine that I am writing to other instructors who teach first-year writing. Because I also teach first-year writing, I have a deep understanding about what their interests and concerns are. By speaking directly to this audience in my text, I can make my argument more clear and compelling to this target audience.

Write an *Audience Declaration* here:

Part 3: Thinking About Genre

Take a few minutes to reflect on the audience declaration section of your design plan. Based on what you know about the documents your target audience creates and consumes, start to think about their expectations for the document you are creating.

What kinds of documents do members of your target audience *read*?

When are these documents created?

Why are these documents created? What purpose do they serve?

What kinds of documents do members of your target audience *create*?

When are these documents created?

Why are these documents created? What purpose do they serve?

Who reads the documents created by members of your target audience?

Write a few sentences to explain what you think your target audience expects the document you are creating to look like, what kinds of materials or evidence your target audience expects to be in the document, and how they expect the document to work.

Write a few sentences explaining how you are trying to meet the expectations you have described.

Part 4: Thinking About Context

Take a few minutes to think about the conversation you are joining or to which you are responding.

The *Immediate Context* for your project is your intended place of publication. This might be our course website, an undergraduate research journal, a student magazine, the Undergraduate Research Symposium, YouTube, etc.

The *Broader Context* is the conversation you are joining. How does your project fit in with other texts in the same genre? Or with other genres dealing with the same issue? Write a description of the *Broader Context* for your writing here.

Part 5: Thinking About Media and Materials

What objects, files, formats will you use to convey your message with your project? Remember that a big part of some new media projects is to explore the ways you can communicate without relying primarily on alphabetic expression in traditional essay format.

Write a brief description of the media you will use and how you will use them (not necessarily how they will be arranged, but more so the role they will play in communicating your message). I will show the reader _____ with _____. I want the reader to feel _____ and I will use _____ sounds to create a sense of _____.

Part 6: Thinking About Arrangement

6.1 Look at the rhetorical analysis you drafted for today's class. What was the writer's arrangement strategy? Look at how each of the blocks on your reverse outline fit together. Describe the overall organization of the article and the rhetorical moves the writer makes in each section of the article.

Use your evaluation of whether these moves are effective (or not) to guide you in thinking about how to organize your own article.

6.2 Take a minute to think about the sources or examples of similar projects you have collected so far. How are those pieces structured? Will you arrange the structure of your piece in a similar way? If so, how? What will the most important similarities be and why? If there will be differences, what will they be? And how will they accomplish the goal you have set for this project? Once you have an idea in mind about how you will structure your project, map out the key sections of your text.

Now that you have listed the key sections, explain how you will organize these sections. Write out your *Arrangement Strategy* here:

Appendix B
Supplemental Instructional Resource for Teachers

What Are the Parts of a Design Plan?

There are no fixed definitions of what must be included in a design plan, but an effective plan will often contain some mixture of the following elements. Since this is a document that writers use to develop a strategy for composing, you can work on this in parts and arrange the parts in whatever way makes the most sense given your rhetorical situation and your composing goal.

Statement of Purpose: an active statement that succinctly explains:

- The author's purpose (*I want to inform/persuade/convince/prove/explain...*)
- The author's audience (*to whom*)
- The author's strategy (*by doing x, y, and z*)

Audience Declaration: a brief description of the audience you envision for your writing and their interests/backgrounds.

Immediate Context: the specific place of publication described briefly.

Broader Context: the conversation you are joining summarized briefly.

Materials/Media Plan: a brief description of the materials you will use and how you will use them (not necessarily how they will be arranged but more so the role they will play in communicating your message).

Arrangement Strategy: a description of how the content will be organized, including:

- the specific sections of the document;
- the main claims that will be made in or the main focus of each key section;
- the types of evidence that will be used to support each claim or communicate the main idea (pictures, text, narration, sound, etc.).

Add a brief summary articulating why you think this strategy will be effective given your purpose and audience.

For Instructors

Statement of purpose notes and ideas

A basic statement of purpose: *I will inform a group of scientists about new research findings related to global warming published in the recent scientific journals by giving facts about recent studies.*

A better statement of purpose: *I will present the latest findings about the impacts of carbon emissions on the average oceanic temperatures and levels over the past two decades as reported in leading scientific journals by a series of independent research teams from three separate universities. Each team specializes in oceanographic data collection and research and conducted independent long-range studies funded by grants. The results of the three studies will be synthesized and summarized with the key data from each study represented in a table that will allow the reader to quickly understand the similarities and differences between each team's results.*

Audience declaration notes and ideas

Audience awareness is a familiar concept in composition textbooks that take a rhetorical approach. Relating the idea of audience to the concept of joining a particular discourse community and negotiating entry into and membership within that discourse community will be a new and interesting addition to that more traditional approach.

Begin by having a class discussion, asking the students to define the discourse community they are writing for and giving some examples to help get them started. Then, have them write descriptively about the audience as a discourse community, exploring what they already know about it. Guide them to doing more research about their audience to deepen their knowledge about whom they are writing for. Use examples that include reading academic blogs, listening to podcasts on iTunes, going to professors' websites, going to academic journals, using Twitter hash tags, looking at YouTube or Vimeo channels, and so forth so that they have a whole range of traditional and new media approaches synthesized (Ball, 2004).

This is one way to bring in the new media that helps the students get a deeper understanding of the audience they are writing for (more rigorous than they are used to) but doing so in an interesting and engaging way that doesn't "feel" like research and that aligns to a very traditional rhetorical and pedagogical concept (audience awareness).

Another benefit relates to assessment. The teacher can assess what the students learn about the community being targeted as the audience as a separate component, without having to assess how well the students integrated the use of new media. In other words, the design plan opens the door to new or unfamiliar forms of composing such as new media but limits the risk. Introducing new media as another aspect to explore in the design plan reduces intimidation for instructors who are just getting their feet wet with this new form of composition. They don't have to be experts in the field or navigate (explicitly) the scholarly versus nonscholarly debate about how to assess new media compositions. Student questions such as "Can I cite Wikipedia in my project?" or "Can I use this blog post as part of my research?" can be addressed independently. Instructors should acknowledge the rich variety of content that is available on the web and give the students a way to explore it and use it but not in the most superficial way as a "source."

Materials/media plan notes and ideas

Ask students to start by making a list of all the artifacts they think they will need to complete their projects. Depending on what they are trying to accomplish, this may include a wide variety of materials ranging from specific research articles to online texts such as images or videos. Some students will need to list equipment they may need to borrow or check out from the library to produce their own audio, images, or video.

A media plan is often a running list of items that expands continually as students work on their projects, developing new ideas and refining their approaches. Gradually adding new items to their collections will help them keep track of all their materials (this is especially useful when the students are nearing a deadline to submit their work and need to cite their sources). It often helps writers make connections among their materials that they don't immediately notice when thinking about each item one at a time.

Provide students with a sample media plan listing materials and descriptions of how the materials will be used. It is also helpful to illustrate how to cite nontraditional resources such as images or sounds.

I will show the reader _____ with _____. I want the reader to feel _____ and I will use _____ sounds to create a sense of _____.

Arrangement strategy notes and ideas

The following can be used as a homework prompt to help students begin thinking about arrangement after conducting an in-class workshop to demonstrate how to reverse outline a journal article:

> By now you've read several articles that relate to your project. Pick one of those articles and reverse outline it. Highlight how the document is arranged and then write a short summary of why the arrangement works for that particular subject. Now, try arranging the structure of your project to parallel the reverse outline. Repeat the process with a second article: create your reverse outline; then arrange your project in the same order. Think about each arrangement strategy and decide which one would be more effective for your project. Write a few notes to explain why. You can repeat this process as many times as necessary until you find a strategy you believe will be the most effective.

8

Reflection, ePortfolios, and WEPO

A Reflective Account of New Practices in a New Curriculum

Kathleen Blake Yancey, Leigh Graziano, Rory Lee,
and Jennifer O'Malley

Expertise—and the notion of the expert—provide an anchor for reflection in rhetoric and composition and, as we will see, for the teaching of writing, especially in the course we profile in this chapter. In the 1970s, for example, researchers studying composing processes identified reflection as an important component of composing; and then, because teachers want students to behave as expert writers, they began asking students to reflect as a part of their composing, too. The form that pedagogy in reflection has taken has varied, however. Early on, Jeff Sommers (1988) asked his students to create "Writer's Memos" intended to "go behind the paper," that is, to document what the student was thinking as she or he composed. Sommers then used that account of writing—and the student's draft—as the centerpiece for a conference intended to help the student create a second draft. In a more common application, other faculty have asked students to write portfolio letters introducing readers to a portfolio of work. In this case, rather than supporting the development of individual texts, reflection is used as a culminating and synthesizing activity.

In her *Reflection in the Writing Classroom* (1998), Kathleen Blake Yancey brought together both kinds of reflective practice—the episodic practice linked to separate texts and the culminating reflective text—combining them into a comprehensive theory of reflective practice for college writers. Influenced by Donald Schön's (1984) work on reflection in various disciplines—including education, architecture, and medicine—Yancey defines *reflection* as both practice and product. In method, Yancey says:

Reflection is dialectical, putting multiple perspectives into play with each other in order to produce insight. Procedurally, reflection entails a *looking forward* to goals we might attain, as well as a *casting backward* to see where we have been. When we reflect, we thus *project* and *review*, often putting the projections and the reviews in *dialogue* with each other, working dialectically as we seek to *discover* what we know, what we have learned, and what we might understand. When we reflect, we call upon the cognitive, the affective, the intuitive, putting these into play with each other: to help us understand how something completed looks later, how it compares with what has come before, how it meets stated or implicit criteria, our own, those of others. (1998, p. 6, emphasis in the original)

In terms of classroom practice, Yancey documents three "moments" of reflection. First, there is "*reflection-in-action*, the process of reviewing and projecting and revising, which takes place within a composing event." Second, writers engage in "*constructive reflection*, the process of developing a cumulative, multi-selved, multi-voiced identity, which takes place between and among composing events." And third, in preparing portfolios, writers engage in "*reflection-in-presentation*, the process of articulating the relationships between and among the multiple variables of writing and the writer in a specific context for a specific audience" (1998, p. 200, emphasis in the original).

Yancey's model of reflection has also provided the point of departure for more recent research on reflection, which has focused on identifying ways curriculum can be designed to support students' transfer of knowledge and practice, that is, their ability to take what they have learned about writing in one setting and use it appropriately in another. As the National Research Council's volume *How People Learn* (Bransford, Pellegrino, & Donovan, 2000) suggests, teaching the development of mental models, as one of the distinguishing features of expertise, is central to such support:

The ability to monitor one's approach to problem solving—to be metacognitive— is an important aspect of the expert's competence. Experts step back from their first, oversimplistic interpretation of a problem or situation and question their own knowledge that is relevant. People's mental models of what it means to be an expert can affect the degree to which they learn throughout their lifetimes. A model that assumes that experts know all the answers is very different from a model of the accomplished novice, who is proud of his or her achievements and yet also realizes that there is much more to learn. (p. 50)

What's interesting here, relative to writing, is how an expert-based theory or mental model of writing that students develop—or don't develop—can affect how they approach writing tasks.

As Yancey, Robertson, and Taczak (forthcoming) point out, one way of thinking about this aspect of learning is to say that an expert's mental map is very much like a larger road map that allows one to see different locations and routes to those locations (and connections among those routes):

> With such a map, one has a fair amount of agency in deciding where to go and how, at least in terms of seeing possibilities and how they relate to each other—precisely because one can see relationships across locations. Instead of maps, of course, many people now use a GPS device, which can be enormously helpful in getting from A to B, and, depending on the model, can offer various routes from A to B (the quickest, the most scenic); traffic alerts; and alternative routes. Still, all a GPS offers is the route from A to B: one doesn't have much sense of how the route is situated or its relationship to other routes or places. The analogy, though imperfect, is probably self-evident: at some level, without a large road map of writing, students are too often traveling from one writing task to another, using a definition and map of writing that is the moral equivalent of a GPS device. It will help students move from one writing task to another, but it can't provide them with the sense of the whole, the relationships among the various genres and discourse communities that constitute writing in the university, and the accompanying agency that a fuller map contributes to—nor will the GPS support the development of expertise. (n.p.)

Given this new understanding of reflection and its potential to help students' writing development, we have included in our reflective activities a request that students behave as experts in this regard as well, in this case with the aim of helping them develop their own theories, or emergent mental maps, of writing.

A NEW WRITING ENVIRONMENT: WRITING IN PRINT AND ONLINE

In 2010, the English Department at Florida State University (FSU) introduced a new major: Editing, Writing, and Media (EWM). A highly structured major, EWM includes three junior-level gateway courses, including Writing and Editing in Print and Online (WEPO), a writing course that is unique in its explicit attention to three spaces of writing—(a) the traditional space of the page; (b) the newer space of the (nonnetworked) screen, including composing spaces and genres such as presentation software (e.g., PowerPoint, Prezi) and video essays; and (c) the newest space, the network arena of blogging, Wikipedia, texting, and Twitter—and to the relationships among these spaces.

Six course outcomes especially important in a multisectioned course taught by a variety of faculty are:

- Explore and learn theories of composing and designing and the rhetorical principles that guide the composing and designing of texts for different environments (in print and new media).
- Employ these theories and principles to create works appropriate to various media, including print, screen, and network, and understand how these texts can be repurposed for new environments.
- Develop a metacognitive awareness of rhetorical principles that enables you to understand how these works can be repurposed for new environments.
- Write with and against styles conventionalized within different genres— in public realms as well as in the academy.
- Examine and apply the art and techniques of editing.
- Develop a theory of composing.

Students are expected to repurpose at least one text for another medium, that is, to revise and/or rewrite the original text to take advantage of the affordances of a new medium (e.g., print to screen; network to print). Students then conclude the course by creating an electronic portfolio (ePortfolio).

Like its print antecedent, an ePortfolio is marked by two principal characteristics: first, the processes of collection, selection, and reflection contributing to its creation; and second, the inclusion of student commentary on learning, as indicated previously, in a "reflection" that could range from narration of processes or experience to self-assessment of texts or an account of the development of the self as writer. For the WEPO class, however, we are especially interested in the sixth course outcome: using reflection to support the development of a theory of writing, in the process relying primarily on two integrated formats for reflection: reflection-in-action and reflection-in-presentation. At the same time, this ePortfolio—given that it lives in a digitally networked environment—also taps multiple affordances keyed to the "electronic" in an ePortfolio and congruent with the new kinds of curricular projects students create. These affordances include (a) the ability to include many different kinds of projects in multiple media (from print and presentation software to audio podcasts and videos), (b) multiple options for arrangement, and (c) the potential to be hosted on the web and thus available for wide circulation (Yancey, 2004b).

Our WEPO course helps students learn to behave as experts through both signature pedagogies and social pedagogies: it lives at the intersection of both.

Signature pedagogies, as defined by Gurung, Chick, and Haynie, "invoke the core characteristics of a discipline to help students think like a biologist, a creative writer, or a sociologist, rather than simply expecting them to passively accept analysis or findings of an expert who already thinks like a biologist, a creative writer, or a sociologist" (2008, p. 4). (*Social pedagogies* will be defined later.) As suggested in this definition, our WEPO course, in addition to providing multiple opportunities for practice, includes theory that is meant to help students understand the logic and history of the practice. Put another way, WEPO incorporates theory, both about composing—which, given the various writing practices of the twenty-first century (e.g., texting, posting updates, writing with images in presentation software), is continually evolving (Yancey, 2004a, 2009)—*and* about ePortfolios, which as object and practice, are likewise in the process of definition. At the same time, the inclusion of theory in an undergraduate course is neither unique nor specific to our major: rather, it's part of a national trend in signature pedagogies intended to help students *think like*. Put simply, we in higher education understand now in ways we had not previously how important it is for students to understand the links between theory and practice, that is, to explore and take hold of the why of an action in order to perform the action well.

Here, we share our experiences teaching in three versions of the WEPO class, each keyed to the three spaces of writing and the six outcomes mentioned before, but each also emphasizing a somewhat different aspect of WEPO's key concepts. In the first version of the course, the emphasis is on students' theorizing of composing: the key question thematizing the course is "Based on our readings, your writing, and our discussions, what is your theory of composing?" Students thus *think like* the scholars they are studying; for the students, as for the scholars, a key question is how composing is changing given the new spaces we are composing in and for.

In the second version of the course, students' attention is drawn to the role of audience in the three different spaces, especially in the networked space, where an audience can be simultaneously intimate and anonymous; here, students *think like* scholars considering how classical Aristotelian notions of audience are changing given the capacity and complexity of networked audiences.

In the third version of the course, students are asked, "How can this new knowledge about composing help you create a professional identity?"—an important question in a world where Monster.com is a recruiting vehicle for many. Here, then, students *think like* faculty exploring how identity is shaped by representation, especially in multiple media.

As important, the portfolio and its accompanying reflective activities are *central* to the course: the model of ePortfolio highlighted here is a semester-long project that is woven throughout and integrated *into* WEPO, in this sense serving as a site for both learning-in-process and learning accomplished. Our use of the portfolio thus parallels development in reflection. As previously indicated, reflective pedagogy was initially conceived of as an episodic event, tied to individual assignments *or* to a culminating portfolio. But as with reflection, which is woven throughout the course, so too is the ePortfolio; all three sections of WEPO that we share here are what we call *portfolio courses*, whose intent via signature pedagogy is to foster the students' ability to construct and practice their own understanding of course material in personally inflected, academic, digital, and networked portfolio representations. We learned about this application of ePortfolios from a colleague in the United Kingdom who developed a portfolio course for her teacher education students (Hughes, 2009). Although the original purpose of Hughes's ePortfolio model was to support student teachers as they made the transition from school to the workplace, her purpose for the ePortfolio quickly became larger: to provide a continuing space for students to "document learning as it occurs" (p. 53). More typically in a U.S. setting, ePortfolios are compiled at the term's end, their purpose being to document learning that has *already* occurred, but we were taken with Hughes's more continuous model and its capacity for supporting thinking in process, so we adapted it for our WEPO classes.

We believe a portfolio course could be useful in other disciplines as well, and for three reasons: in part because Hughes's model was itself conceived of in another discipline, teacher education; in part because in the Canadian context there is a similar model being developed in accounting and financial management (Penny Light, Sproule, & Lithgow, 2009); and in part because of the capacity of such a model to support students as they shift from one content set to another inside a course or from one setting to another (e.g., a class to an internship), a shift that we see in several disciplines.

Our signature pedagogy is also very much like what Randy Bass and Heidi Elmendorf call *social pedagogies*. In their definition:

> *Social pedagogies* [are] design approaches for teaching and learning that engage students with what we might call an "authentic audience" (other than the teacher), where the *representation of knowledge* for an audience is absolutely central to the *construction of knowledge* in a course. Social pedagogies build in iterative cycles of engagement with the most difficult material, and through a focus on authentic audience and representation of knowledge for others, help students deepen their understanding of core concepts by engaging in the ways of thinking, practicing, and communicating in a field. (n.d., Précis, para. 2, emphasis in the original)

Social pedagogies are particularly sensitive to audience, as Bass and Elmendorf observe. Although not stipulated, a Vygotskian notion seems to underpin social pedagogies; it's through and in the *representation of knowledge for others* that students explain it to themselves. Those others—the audience—are a central feature of all composing courses and of WEPO as well, although again, somewhat differentially. In our first version of WEPO, students think like experts as they dialogue with their instructor about their emerging theory of composition; in our second iteration, students think like networked compositionists as they write and dialogue with peers, teacher, and the world; and in our third instantiation, students think like their future selves as they create a portfolio keyed both to their future selves and to future employers.

We turn now to these three versions of the courses, paying special attention to the role of reflection and portfolio in each.

THINKING LIKE AN EXPERT: LEARNING AND APPLYING THEORY

All three ePortfolio models were conceived as sites of articulation, specifically as sites where students create an archive of their own documents and synthesize what they think they are learning in terms of course content and writing practices, especially as they reflect on both over the course of the term and in the ePortfolio itself.

In our first model of ePortfolio, which is keyed to theorizing the course material, students crafted a site that positioned them in terms of the course material and that also asked them to behave as developing experts of the course material as they composed their own theory of composition. Moreover, because the portfolio assignment is designed to be a semester-long project, we planned activities and writing exercises that would prepare students both to construct the portfolio and to articulate the meaning they've made from the course material in their reflection. One strategy to accomplish this goal is having students post to the class blog frequently, in this case every Friday, in response to a specific blogging assignment. This repeated assignment creates both a rhythm for theorizing and a set of reiterative opportunities to resee and expand their theories on the basis of new work in a public reflection-in-action. Put another way, the blog prompts ask students to write a brief theory of composition informally; the posts engage students in a reiterative practice through which they revisit their initial theory several times throughout the semester—and they do so in the public setting of the blog in a kind of peer-review mode. They have a real audience for their writing and can build on each other's insights. In addition, because the timing of the blog posts often corresponds with conceptual landmarks in the course—landmarks such as the role of technology in composition, the impact of visual rhetoric, and the significance of remediation, all themes that students speak to in their portfolios, as we shall see—students take the opportunity to incorporate new concepts and perspectives into their evolving theories. Consequently, when it comes time for students to write the final, formal version of their theory of composition in their reflection-in-presentation, they have a variety of texts and "concept papers" to work with and include.

This scaffolding, of course, is intended to prepare students to craft their final theory of composition for their portfolio. It also serves as a heuristic, providing a context for students to *collect* certain documents during the semester as well as cues as to which documents to *select* for the portfolio. (See Figure 8.1 for the directions students received with respect to selection.) The second goal of the portfolio—providing a theoretical synthesis—occurs in the reflection, which takes the form of the theory of composition. Students are asked to write a theory of composition that isolates a theme—one that exemplifies how they've made meaning of the course material—and that traces that theme through the three composing spaces of the course: print, the screen, and the network. Finally, students situate their portfolio documents within their theory, demonstrating how the work they've done in the course enacts that theory.

Valentina's ePortfolio

In creating their ePortfolios, many of the students relied on templates made available by their chosen software to organize their work, but Valentina created

Figure 8.1   Directions for the ePortfolio

Choosing what goes into the portfolio is entirely up to you. You will, however, want no more than 10 documents. And, most importantly, you want to select a range of texts. Simply put, consider the different kinds of writing we've done during the semester: journals; group mapping and visual exercises; individual projects for the course and the major process memos that go with them. Thus, you want to choose texts that represent the thinking you've done inside and outside of class, individually and collaboratively. In addition, as you'll see in my goals, I'm interested in seeing your applications of the course material to other areas of your life, particularly nonacademic, so you are more than welcome to choose texts from outside the course. But, you want to find a balance between the texts you include.

her own portfolio navigational structure (see Figure 8.2 for a screenshot that shows her flyer, her reflection on her flyer, and the menu bar for her navigational system). Likewise, many of the students used one of the suggested themes for the portfolio. These themes, like "WEPO is a play in three acts," can help provide both a structure and a theme for the portfolio. Instead of adapting a given theme, Valentina created her own, one that helped organize her work while giving it meaning, a much more complex task than simply organizing work by chronology or outcome, which are acceptable but more rudimentary approaches. Borrowing from Marshall McLuhan's "The medium is in the message," Valentina employed "Meaning Through Medium" as her theme for *thinking like* an expert about the course material (see Figure 8.3 for a visual representation of her theme). In sum, we focus here on Valentina's portfolio because it is exemplary in these two ways.

In terms of artifacts, Valentina's portfolio is rich, offering six documents and two reflections (see Figure 8.4 for an excerpt from one of Valentina's reflections). The first reflection, a comprehensive review comprising more than 2,500 words, is a substantive synthesis of Valentina's composing experience as seen through the theoretical lens of "Meaning Through Medium." Interestingly, though, this is not the only piece of reflection in the portfolio. The second is connected to a flyer Valentina made for the print media project;

Figure 8.2   Valentina's introduction to her flyer

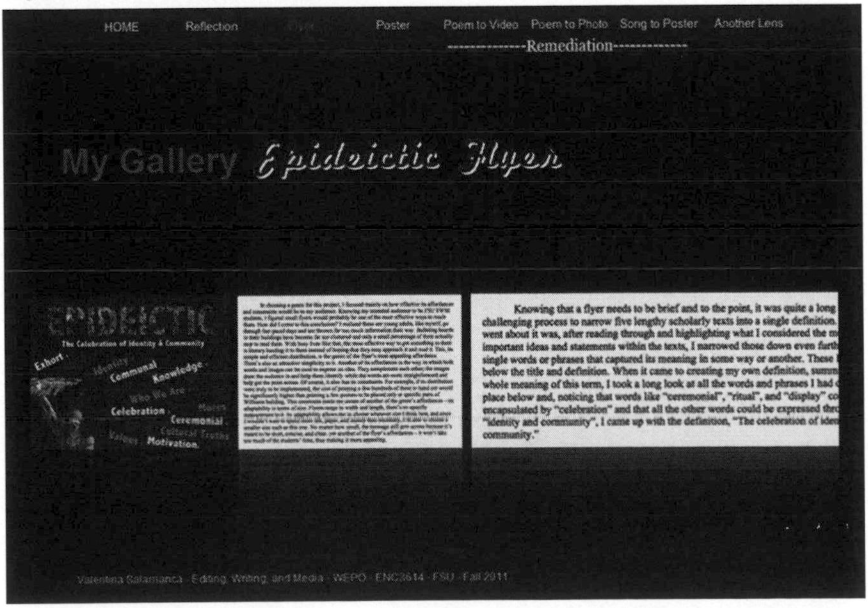

Figure 8.3   Valentina announcing her theme visually

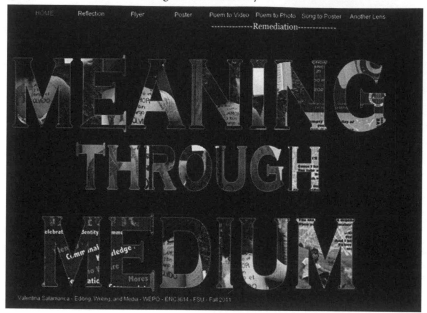

Figure 8.4   An excerpt from Valentina's reflection-in-presentation

> You sit, staring at the empty screen. An endless task, you think, and you've hardly written a word. It feels endless because that is what composition is, an ongoing process of communication. Does it reach its end in the form of a final draft, a polished version, or a published piece? It doesn't matter how hard we try to fix a message into a composition, its meaning will continually be shifted, adjusted, and redefined across audiences. The content itself may not change, but its meaning will also be altered, adapted, and revised through varying spaces.
>
> Valentina

the reflection-in-action process memo that went along with the assignment is likewise included so that her audience can better understand the rhetorical choices she has made. Valentina devotes the remainder of her portfolio to pages about remediation because she sees it as the exemplar of her theme: meaning through medium.

In terms of the *kinds* of exhibits it includes, Valentina's portfolio is also rich, pointing us to a diverse representation of documents: two texts from

Figure 8.5   Valentina's poem remediated from page to body to screen to network

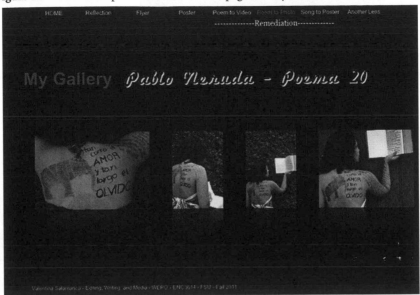

the course and then a range of academic and nonacademic documents (e.g., a poster Valentina made for the photography club she belongs to) that enact the content of the course as she defines it in her theory of composition. Her theory of composition integrates her documents within her discussion and definition of her theory, and Valentina uses course readings to substantiate and frame her argument. Each document in the portfolio speaks to this theory of composing. The first is her remediation project for the course, which Valentina completed by transforming a poem into a music video focusing on graffiti. To show the remediation, Valentina includes both the original text and her remediated text. Her next example is another remediated poem, but this time Valentina has used her own body as a medium: lines of poetry are written on her body as an animated slideshow demonstrates (see Figure 8.5). Her final example is a remediation from song to poster. Thus, to show the pervasiveness of composing, Valentina includes exemplar artifacts from the course, but she primarily directs the reader's attention to the different rhetorical situations in which medium and meaning are inextricably connected.

Valentina's reflection provides the larger context for the portfolio: in this model of ePortfolio, the audience—principally the teacher—can, as Edgerton, Hutchings, and Quinlan (1991) suggest, see through the *combination* of reflection and artifacts how successfully the portfolio and reflection work together.

(See Figure 8.6 for Valentina's reflections on audience.) Speaking of teaching portfolios, Edgerton et al. explain why both artifacts and reflection are needed:

> General reflection, divorced from evidence of actual performance, fails to capture the situated nature of teaching. Work samples [e.g., syllabi, assignments, and graded sample work] alone aren't intelligible. But work samples plus reflection make a powerful formula. The reflection is grounded by being connected to a particular instance of teaching; the work sample is made meaningful and placed in context through reflection. (p. 9)

In our case, reviewing the portfolios composed by Valentina and her colleagues, we look for the depth of the reflection, the way the documents are situated within the students' theoretical framework, and the way they support that framework. In addition, we read to see how students chose to accomplish various assignment goals by exploring, including, and citing compositions in a variety of settings.

Figure 8.6   Valentina's theorizing about audience in her reflection-in-presentation

Audience should be taken into consideration at every step of the way: when selecting a medium, through choice of language, aesthetics, details, and most importantly, throughout revision. If we compose to transfer meaning, the message should feel as fitting to the sender as it is to the receiver.

I use the term *receiver* in the loosest sense of the word. The audience doesn't only perform the task of receiving but also of interpreting, and it is here where its significance stands. Audience is necessary for meaning to, not only be transferred, but exist. The inner workings of the composition process at the level of reader and text is made more clear by the understanding that, "What you see is seldom what you get if all you're seeing (seeing even now) is just ink and paper. . . . In the end, what you get is what you give" (McCloud 136). This concept allows us to see just how dependent the medium is on its audience. In a sense, this is good because it means a deeper involvement, but if the audience holds back and decides not to participate in the medium, then the text isn't a text but simply lines and shapes on paper or screen, and neither the message or its meaning will get across.

                                                                      Valentina

Valentina's reflection is sophisticated, and two aspects of it are particularly impressive. First, she identified and enacted a provocative theory of composition: meaning through medium. In working with this theme, Valentina crafted a focus requiring a deep understanding of genre and the rhetorical situations from which texts emerge. Second, Valentina employed the theory of the course to write a text addressing the relationship among composition, meaning, and medium. Most students had one paragraph at the beginning of their reflections that attempted to develop such a theme, but Valentina sustained her analysis for her entire composition. Within her theoretical discussion, she referred and linked to her portfolio documents, illustrating how they enact principles of her theory, as well as to class or blogged discussions of how this theme could be identified or traced in each of the three composing spaces of print, screen, and network. In addition, as we see in Figure 8.7, Valentina did not simply rely on the theories of the course; rather, she extended and

Figure 8.7   Valentina's challenging of course concepts

New technologies lead to new genres and an expansion of spaces. Devitt explains, "Genres develop, then, because they respond appropriately to situations that writers encounter repeatedly. In principle, that is, writers first respond in fitting ways and hence similarly to recurring situations; then, the similarities among those appropriate responses become established as generic conventions" (576). For instance, we have discovered other types of prints composed through automated aid, such as the camera, which later evolved to fit the screen, and subsequently was implemented into the web. Many of these technologies, as it has been mentioned before, were and still are resisted. With the camera, for example, "Pictures were accused of offering an overly simplified view of the world, a view that lacked interpretation" (Faigley). If we stop and think about it, any and every type of rhetoric, whether visual, written, or oral, give us an "overly simplified view of the world." Anything we try to communicate will always be distorted by the lack of one thing or another because not everything can be encapsulated into words in the same way that not everything can be caught in a photograph. And even if we did have the ability to encapsulate everything we mean to get across into words or photos, the action of interpretation must be done by both the sender and the receiver of a message, meaning the message will always lack interpretation until it's been received.

Valentina

challenged them. Beginning with a summary of the position of a relevant scholar, Valentina made her own claim, challenging the conclusions of our course readings. Besides demonstrating a deeper understanding of how to use source material, this composing shows Valentina's rigorous critical thinking.

Through her ePortfolio, Valentina thus theorizes her understanding of composition keyed to three spaces by presenting that theory to her audience, chiefly her teacher, but she includes explanations for others as well. To illustrate her theory, Valentina uses a small selection of course documents and then ventures out into texts she has created in other contexts, academic and non-academic, to illustrate the pervasiveness of her theory throughout all forms of composition. And for each example, she includes the original text, lyrics, and audio or video, placing them alongside her own composition. Valentina's ePortfolio thus clearly demonstrates that she did more than simply complete a set of assignments; instead, we see her understanding of composition and the ways that very different compositions can be transformed through the practices of remediation and of "remix," the integration and synthesis of older texts with new texts, often in a new medium.

THINKING LIKE A NETWORK COMPOSITIONIST: THE ePORTFOLIO AS NETWORK NODE

Marilyn's ePortfolio

We highlight our second model of portfolio—this one keyed to the notion of audience, especially as it is embodied on the web—by looking at Marilyn's portfolio composition, in part because she took risks with her ePortfolio design and content and in part because she was willing to grapple with the material. She had never created a portfolio before and by her own account found it daunting. At the same time, she found that the structure of the class, which included creating a provisional ePortfolio midterm and participating with her peers in a peer-review process of that provisional portfolio, was very useful. According to Marilyn, "Having the time to reflect on my own portfolio, and discuss how other people see it, was very important during the creation and organization process." More generally, students also found this peer review useful because they had the opportunity to ask peers questions about technology issues such as, "How did you upload that image?" or "Can you show me how to do _____ ?"

Beginning with the opening page of her ePortfolio, Marilyn includes her navigational scheme at the top as she composes her portfolio by calling upon several composing abilities—including designing visuals, creating font style and size, and incorporating various kinds of texts into the supertext of the portfolio. The portfolio is thus differential in its contents but unified both visually and conceptually; each of the artifacts is introduced by its own reflection. Marilyn organizes her ePortfolio by creating categories based on the themes she abstracted from the course goals, and she creates an effective multimodal presentation by making use of the affordances of Wix, a website-building software. Her hypermediated ePortfolio is alluring. It includes considerable content, and the content is appealing because of the way Marilyn has shaped it with purposeful visual organization.

Marilyn's ePortfolio consists of eight separate pages. The home page functions as a welcome page, inviting her audience to explore her ePortfolio: "[Y]ou have the freedom to observe my growth as a writer, editor, and designer over the course of this semester." While reading the "About" page (and perhaps listening to the subtle instrumental song Marilyn has chosen to supplement the viewing experience), her audience learns that Marilyn is hoping to become an editor for a nonprofit publication or to pursue a career in photojournalism. She explains that this is her first digital portfolio and notes that all of the photographs throughout the ePortfolio are her own.

Marilyn carefully constructs each of the six main content pages by identifying the course outcome, spotlighting her selected texts, and providing images of her texts. Through this repetition, the ePortfolio exhibits a visual unity desirable in a print composition and required for one on the screen. Marilyn also accompanies each page with a thoughtful "mini-reflection" that helps explain what the audience is (and should be) seeing and learning from her project. For her "Objective One: Explore & Learn" page (Figure 8.8), for example, Marilyn selected her annotations from a class reading as her text to demonstrate that she had in fact fulfilled Course Objective 1: "You have *explored* and *learned* theories of composing-designing and the rhetorical principles that guide the composing and designing of texts for different environments (in print and new [digital] media)." The center slideshow rotates through several images of her annotations; she also includes a PDF of the original text. And in her mini-reflection, she writes: "At the time of my reading it, I was just beginning to learn and gain an understanding of rhetoric and the theories of composing that it inferred. Some of my annotations now seem silly to me because I have a more refined understanding of the theories and principles of rhetoric, but that's exactly why I believe this text meets objective one's implications."

In explaining to students how to create a portfolio generally, Doug Eyman reminds us, in *What Every Student Should Know About . . . Creating a Portfolio*, "Selection requires reflection: you should be conscious of the decisions you

Figure 8.8   Marilyn's ePortfolio

make about what to include in each portfolio you construct, and you should be able to write about why you selected each component and what function it serves within the portfolio" (2007, pp. 10–11). Marilyn takes his cue: she demonstrates her understanding of the role of selection and reflection in the ePortfolio genre. She gives her audience an inside view into her experience by providing an authentic glimpse of her compositions, and in the case of the readings uses the annotation example to show how she has developed as a compositional thinker. By admitting that her annotations appear "silly" to her in retrospect, Marilyn shows that she has revisited her work and thought critically about how this text has shaped her understanding of the course objectives. She articulates her conscious decision-making process in her mini-reflection, explaining her rationale for selection and justifying its function within her ePortfolio.

Marilyn effectively executes reflection, choosing to strategically integrate it throughout her ePortfolio with her use of mini-reflections. Instead of introducing her ePortfolio with a reflective letter or concluding with a comprehensive reflection, Marilyn provides a complementary reflective piece for each page that focuses on that particular objective and text (see Figure 8.9 for an example of a mini-reflection). This move emphasizes the role reflection had in shaping her understanding of the three components: the individual selected texts; the ePortfolio in its entirety; and, in effect, the course as a whole. Reflection is a constant presence across her ePortfolio. As a result, her audience has

Figure 8.9   Marilyn's reflection-in-presentation on the mini-project

For this mini-project, three classmates and I were asked to scope out different types of texts in our classroom building, and then choose a bulletin board to redesign and repurpose. We decided to choose the best-looking board in order to attempt to make it look even better. The original Digital Studio board was interesting and eye-catching, and appealed to the digital culture of FSU students, but the board still had many flaws. The board's information seemed to gather around one corner of the board, leaving most of it blank and unused, therefore, we decided to make the most of the bulletin board's space. We created our project digitally, with me being the primary designer. I created it on Microsoft PowerPoint and then exported it into PDF and JPEG images. Both are available here. This was our first crack at repurposing, and I believe it prepared us to learn about remediation later on. For more information on this assignment, click on the "Assignment" button on the right. For a look at the entire project, click on the "WEPO Blog Post" button. And for more information on the Digital Studio at FSU, click on the "Digital Studio FSU" button.

Marilyn

the opportunity to follow Marilyn's reasoning, engaging with each page in a way that Marilyn orchestrates. She uses reflection as a means of knowledge making—as a way to make sense of her learning experience for both herself *and* her audience. In addition, she uses the mini-reflections to articulate for her audience the connections she wants them to recognize between the course goals and the selected text(s).

Not least, and in addition to successfully satisfying the goals of the project, Marilyn manages to effectively situate herself within an online network, creating her own intranet of related documents and links as a node inside the web. Her ePortfolio functions as a node, connecting and linking to other online venues and texts, and Marilyn is aware of how her ePortfolio will function as a text on the Internet, which she conceives as a hub for her audience that connects them not only to the internal components of her ePortfolio but also to other, external website venues. She offers several external links, including one to her own photojournalism blog (see Figures 8.10 and 8.11), one to her Flickr account, and one to FSU's Digital Studio website; she also links to three of her group members' ePortfolios. Here, we see that Marilyn recognizes the

Figure 8.10   Marilyn's blog, connected to her ePortfolio

The Expectant Wanderer

HOME   ABOUT   REFLECTION

Reflection

This blog is written by a student, who in all honesty, knew barely anything about what the field of photojournalism consisted of. That was my challenge. I wanted to run a blog on something I didn't know much about so it would challenge me to really research what I was writing. It's why I called the blog "The Expectant Wanderer", I knew I would like photojournalism, I was expectant, but I still did not know what would lie ahead. I chose to focus on photojournalism because I am extremely interested in photography, and I knew it would be a great way to become acquainted with the field.

Search

[Search]

Follow Blog
Join 210 other followers

[Follow]

Tweets:

Figure 8.11   Marilyn's mini-reflection-in-presentation explaining her blog

For this objective, I chose to showcase both Journal 3 from the WEPO class blog, and Project 2—my Photojournalism blog, "The Expectant Wanderer." Journal 3 is a good fit for this objective because I believe I wrote with and against Faigley's "Material Literacy and Visual Design" by critically exploring his point of view on communication, and clearly expressing my findings. I believe that my blog, as a text, ties in well with this objective because I was given the freedom to write with and against a style of my choosing and had the opportunity to gain feedback not only from my classmates, but from a larger audience on the Internet. Each blog post on The Expectant Wanderer was well researched, I put a lot of time into writing each one, and connected with my own voice through discussing my interest—photography—through a blog. Because this was a public blog, the audience was anyone and everyone, not only my classmates, who were interested in photojournalism and photography. I believe I gained a lot of positive experience and skill from running that blog.

Marilyn

affordances of both the Wix software and the Internet itself, and she demonstrates that she understands how to respond strategically to the ePortfolio genre and locate it so that its material circulates within the classroom, on the class blog, and on the web.

Marilyn's ePortfolio showcases her audience in multiple ways as she reflectively guides us toward an understanding of her experience. In part, she was able to achieve this outcome because she responded to the prompt in both expected and unpredictable ways: in the latter, especially, making evident how audience awareness shaped her approach. Given the content of Marilyn's mini-reflections, it's clear that she has developed an awareness of an audience beyond the teacher—an audience not familiar with her, the course, or even the major. She took the time to explain who she was, what she was doing, why she was creating this project, and what the major premises of the EWM major and WEPO course are. Marilyn recognizes that the online platform can make her compositions available to others both through the ePortfolio links posted on the class blog and through search engine results. Unlike in an "ordinary" class, then, in WEPO and through the online portfolio, a student can access an audience beyond the teacher. Marilyn's small reflections-in-presentation also demonstrate how audience functions as a source of invention for her. Marilyn constructs each of her mini-reflections based on the familiarity she assumes her audience has with her, the course, and the major, and this is evident from the in-depth detail with which she describes her meaning-making experiences—detail about which her teacher and peers would have already been aware. The content of her mini-reflections was directly influenced by her presupposed audience; these reflection-in-presentations functioned as guideposts for her audience, and this approach, no doubt, was a result of the way in which she chose to incorporate reflection into her ePortfolio.

THINKING LIKE A FUTURE COMPOSITIONIST: LEARNING ABOUT AND APPEALING TO AN AUDIENCE OF THE FUTURE

The third ePortfolio model that we consider asks the student to imagine a writing future and a prospective employer. A social pedagogical approach thus underpins the portfolio design in that a specific kind of real-world audience other than the teacher is directly addressed. Geared toward a high-stakes audience of potential future employers, this version asks students to create a portfolio wherein they strategically collect and archive different materials that together present them as credible and qualified job candidates for a particular profession. Toward that end, students drew from and utilized many of the rhetorical terms we considered and enacted throughout the semester.

They also used their visual composing skills—drawing on principles of visual design, such as proximity (placing like elements with other like elements on the screen) and contrast (using contrast as both a conceptual and navigational signal)—to create a set of texts that functioned together as a unified portfolio. As in the case of the prior two models of ePortfolios, students with minimal web design experience were encouraged to use "what you see is what you get" (WYSIWYG) webpage builders such as Wix.com and Weebly.com, but they also had the option of creating their portfolios using other platforms (e.g., blogging software, Adobe Dreamweaver, Nvu). In addition, two kinds of peer review were built into the curriculum. First, to help students understand what a professional ePortfolio might look like, they were asked to review a set of professional portfolios and report on the class blog what they had found, responding to explicit questions, such as "What conventions, in terms of design and content, did you see across a set of professional portfolios?" and "What professions are you considering pursuing postgraduation and what are the requirements of those professions?" Second, students brought their drafted ePortfolios to class for a workshop day. And finally, in addition to completing their portfolios, students were required to write a reflection-in-presentation to the teacher, in this case articulating and explaining the rhetorical choices they made in the construction of their portfolios.

Casey's ePortfolio

We share Casey's portfolio for two reasons. First, it was one of the better portfolios in the sense of its being more complete; and second, Casey, despite creating an adequate initial portfolio, realized that as her skills developed, she could improve her portfolio to represent the type of expert she aspired to be, thus demonstrating that she was *thinking like* an expert—as she was in the process of becoming one. And more generally, Casey's ePortfolio illustrates the potential and the challenge in the threefold portfolio focus of career, future, and employer.

Casey was a sophomore who, like many of her peers, wasn't entirely sure what she wanted to do professionally postgraduation. In her reflection-in-presentation, she said she wanted to target internships and/or jobs that would combine her two passions: writing and the outdoors. We can see her affinity for the latter manifesting itself in both the overarching design of her portfolio and the writing that accompanies her opening page. In deciding on the design of her portfolio, Casey browsed many of the templates available on both Wix.com and Weebly.com before settling on what she termed an appropriate nature-themed template from Weebly. On her opening portfolio page,

Casey made a concerted effort to address her potential future employers and to outline her interests by providing a condensed biography addressing her academic aspirations, living history, and appreciation of both the outdoors and writing. Casey also included a picture of herself in the woods, which not only underscored her connection to nature but also humanized her portfolio by connecting an actual person to it. To be sure, Casey's brief biographical sketch helps capture and sustain her audience's attention, a task not all of her peers were able to manage effectively (see Figures 8.12 and 8.13).

In addition, Casey makes deliberate attempts to address her audience in the other pages of her professional portfolio. For instance, in her "Some of

Figure 8.12   Casey's biographical sketch

My name is Casey Dunphy and I am a sophomore at Florida State University. I am double majoring in English: Editing, Writing, and Media and Sports Management; in addition to my double major, I am also minoring in Recreation and Leisure Management. It is an interesting combination of studies, but I believe that there were many experiences in life that lead me to peruse this study path and I am thankful for all of the opportunities I have had that lead me in this direction.

Figure 8.13   Casey's ePortfolio

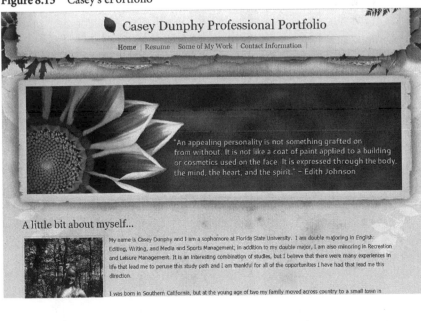

My Work" page, Casey inserted a synopsis for each sample text she included in order to provide her audience with necessary context that in turn might motivate them to read her work. In including these synopses, Casey was thinking rhetorically: that is, she realized she needed to couch her texts within specific rhetorical situations, ones equipped with a specific audience and purpose. However, in reflecting on this page in her process memo, Casey described it as the section of her portfolio she "was least proud of." According-ing to her memo, she intends to rearrange her collection of sample texts, categorizing them more effectively—for instance, by genre—rather than almost randomly, as is the case currently. As important, she plans to include additional texts, some more germane to her potential profession and some created outside of school. As she explains in her process memo, this will high-light her initiative as well as her dedication to writing. Perhaps most impor-tant, particularly given the focus of this portfolio model, Casey, in reflecting on her process as a whole, started to see the larger, rhetorical implications for not only what work she included but also how she contextualized and categorized that work.

Overall, Casey's professional portfolio is not as robust or as detailed as it could be, but such shortcomings are, in part at least, symptomatic of being in the early stages of the job hunt. In other words, as was the case for many students, these professional portfolios felt like works in progress, like pol-ished starting points. That said, in reading across Casey's and other students' reflections-in-presentation, we can see the role that reflection plays in pre-paring students to revise and improve their portfolios, especially professional ones that can continue to evolve and that have salience outside the classroom. Completing this assignment gave Casey a better understanding of the impor-tance of web design, the portfolio as a professional text, and the intricacies involved in creating a credible professional portfolio.

OUR OWN REFLECTIONS

The suggested syllabus for all sections of WEPO, as outlined earlier, includes the portfolio, but other than a "portfolio reflection"—which presumably was included in the portfolio's compositional processes of "collection, selec-tion, and reflection"—the syllabus does not speak to reflection, especially not to reflection as a mode of theorizing. As indicated in our discussion here, however, our version of WEPO constructs both the ePortfolio and reflection as ongoing and cumulative practices, based in reflection-in-action and in reflection-in-presentation and in a portfolio that is integrated into the course. Our pedagogies are designed to provide scaffolded, reiterative opportunities for students to think like experts: like scholars inquiring into new composing practices inflected by a medium or into the power of known and unknown audiences on the web to shape discourse, or like faculty considering issues of representation and identity. In sum, we see WEPO as a portfolio course located in social pedagogies, emphasizing three dimensions of composing linked to audience expressed through the portfolio: (a) the portfolio as a site for theory and practice of composing in three spaces, (b) the portfolio as node on a network with multiple audiences, and (c) the portfolio as a planning and enacting space for a future compositional self.

Moreover, in each of these portfolio models, the students bring together academic and personal interests: Valentina in pursuing the relationship of medium to meaning, Marilyn through independently blogging about photo-journalism and bringing that visual thinking to her collaborative composition in WEPO, and Casey in visually and verbally connecting writing and the outdoors. All of these students, who are novices acting as emerging experts, use reflection and the construction of a course portfolio as practices to locate and inform their learning, much as composition researchers Nancy Sommers and Laura Saltz (2004) suggest:

> A major conclusion of our study is that students who initially accept their status as novices and allow their passions to guide them make the greatest gains in writing development. As novices who care deeply about their subjects, these students have a reason to learn the methodologies of their chosen disciplines, encouraged to believe that following their own interests is important to their success as students. And as they become more comfortable with these methodologies, they begin to see how disciplinary inquiry can help them build their own fields of expertise. (p. 145)

WEPO is a site for beginning such disciplinary inquiry.

We also believe there are several practices that account for the success of these students, and we recommend them to others interested in designing a similar approach:

- *Reflection is designed into the course as a regular, normal, and sustained intellectual activity.* Too often, reflection is an add-on or afterthought, but we know that deep reflection calls for time; opportunity; and, often in the case of students, prompts. Too often, reflection isn't well defined: unless we explicitly specify its role, reflection can range from description of a process to evaluation of courses. In our versions of WEPO and based on recent research, however, we define *reflection* as an intellectual practice: to explain, to synthesize, to talk back to course material, and to theorize. Identifying reflection as intellectual and including it as a regular practice in a course are the first steps in implementing a course design like ours.

- *The portfolio is likewise an integral part of the course, so much so that the course itself becomes a portfolio course.* One of the issues with ePortfolios, as the name suggests, is technology, and students can think they are more adept at composing with technology than they in fact are, especially if they are trying to work with unfamiliar technology at the end of the term, when they often are experiencing so many other demands on their time. Beginning early in the term and pointing students to a variety of software packages provide students with different levels of proficiency the same opportunity to participate fully. Beginning early and continuing through the term allows students to experiment—indeed, to play—with technology before they need to have enough control to complete their portfolio. But an even better reason to begin the portfolio early, to embed it into the course, is to ensure that students *use* it, in Hughes's terms, as a site for *documenting learning as it occurs*—as a space to think, over time, as students encounter and consider new ideas; as they remix, or integrate, new learning with prior knowledge; and as they think about what they want to share in their final portfolio with a larger audience and why. Beginning early also means that students can use the ePortfolio as an archival space to house all their artifacts. Thus, students have their materials on hand when they make selections for the culminating portfolio.

- *We encourage students to include work samples, or artifacts, from outside the course inside their ePortfolios.* We know that students' learning occurs inside courses and outside them as well. We thus encourage students to include in their ePortfolios artifacts—where appropriate—from multiple sites. Valentina includes the poster she made for her photography club, for example, and Marilyn her photojournalism blog. The key, of course, is that students need to explain *why* they have included such artifacts; in doing so, they explicate connections across different sites of learning and theorize their understandings using the full range of materials available (and known only) to them. In addition, in explaining such inclusions, they exercise an authority congruent with their evidenced claims.

- *We build in multiple opportunities for peer interaction, collaboration, and review.* We understand learning as social and reflection likewise, so we build in multiple sites and occasions for reflective interaction:

in class as students review professional ePortfolios and imagine a future; in the electronic space of a blog as they revisit their theories of composition; in class as they review each other's portfolios. Often, occasions are designed to help create the rhythm of the course; thus, for example, blogging weekly becomes not only a class assignment, but a regular habit of engaging with others about the material of the class.

At the same time, we have several questions that we continue to consider.

- *How do the varieties of reflection work together?* Despite our own focus on reflection as a theorizing practice, we understand that there are many varieties of reflection: accounts of process, self-assessment generally, and self-assessment in terms of outcomes, to name three. Alternatively, we could mean accounting for learning, synthesis, or exploration. Often, we mean making connections—between prior and new knowledge, between what we don't know and what we need to know. Is it possible to be more precise with our definitions? Is it possible to know which kind of reflection to invite at a given moment? Is it possible to interlayer those for what we might call a full reflective capacity?
- *Do or should we assess reflection?* We know of efforts to assess reflection, especially in medical education (e.g., Wald, Borkan, Taylor, Anthony, & Reis, 2012), but until we are more precise about our expected outcomes and their efficacy, we are unwilling to create a scoring guide, and even were we more sure in this regard, we're not certain we would want to assess it via a rubric. We know of efforts to do so, especially in preprofessional educational settings (e.g., medicine, education), but we would need two issues to be resolved before we would adopt such an approach ourselves. The first of these is what we think of as the ineffability of reflection, its tentative and thoughtful quality; it's not that such a quality and nature cannot be described, but evaluating it seems to link it too closely to what are now-common negative student experiences with rubrics, at least at our institution, under the No Child Left Behind testing regime. The second concern is likewise linked to effect and perception: enacting a rubric-based approach seems to reduce reflection to a formalized practice subject and a fairly mechanical assessment that is at odds with the kind of foundational academic and personal accounts we saw here in all three models of portfolios.
- *The reflection we include here was almost always written: what about reflection in other modalities?* In fact, we have examples of student reflection in video, and while length may be a factor in successful

writing, it is not so in video. In our experience, a long video makes for a talking head rather than reflective analysis. Which leads us to ask: What are the conventions of a video reflection or an audio reflection?

- We see WEPO as both a social and a signature pedagogy, and we are encouraged by the students' work with theory. *At the same time, we're not yet sure of how much theory to include and at which moments.* Because WEPO is a composing class, we include considerable theory about the multimedia aspects of composing, using, for example, Bolter and Grusin's (2000) model of remediation as a framework: students read about and use the framework for their own composing. Likewise, we have incorporated portfolio theory into the course, borrowing from Doug Eyman (2007; as noted earlier) and from Yancey (1996). Interestingly, we did not incorporate theory on reflection, and in retrospect, this seems a glaring omission. Perhaps in spite of our sense of intentionality, we took reflection—in terms of a rationale for it or a set of practices—for granted; perhaps we were so focused on redesigning WEPO as a portfolio course that we overlooked reflection; perhaps we believed students who had told us they already knew about reflection. But a social pedagogy, as we have described and enacted it, requires that the theory of the practice be made available to students, and this is a change we are in the process of making. As to options, we think Yancey's *Reflection in the Writing Classroom* (1998), in combination with sections of *How People Learn* (Bransford et al., 2000), provides a possible starting point.

- *How can we strengthen the future composer portfolio model?* We are still working on the portfolio model of the future compositionists, our third model presented here. We like how it stretches students; in some ways, what students learn occurs in the Vygotskian gap between what they can currently *accomplish and what they will need to accomplish in the not so distant future*—and indeed, it may require such a gap. At the same time, we would like students to have more success with the model. What they have produced thus far is useful in terms of providing practice, but less helpful in terms of identifying work they might continue to revise, or creating a visual that could be refined and carried forward, or designing a portfolio structure they could employ later. In the future, these are areas we'll address more fully, and probably earlier in the term.

- *We believe that we need more scaffolding, both for design and for theory: how much and where might it occur in the course?* Design needs to be more heavily stressed, not just for aesthetic appeal but also for the rhetorical force those decisions carry; Casey includes a photo of herself, but it's an informal photo rather than one showing an emerging professional. Likewise, even with the considerable reiteration we've provided, we think we need more, especially for students' own theorizing of composition. Having students compose a provisional composition theory that we read and comment on, around midterm, would help all students reach a greater depth in their thinking.

Based on our experience as illustrated here, we have a proposition to offer: that WEPO is a prototypical site for a signature social pedagogy. In part, it provides such a site because of its roots in rhetoric, which has at its center attention to audience. In part, it provides such a site because the question at the heart of WEPO—How do we compose?—is one that offers a genuine question that scholars continue to pursue; that in practice all writers are answering; and, equally as important, that WEPO students in their portfolios theorize, demonstrate, and reflect upon. In our curriculum, we've provided a framework for taking up the question, through attention to composing processes keyed to print, screen, and networks, which together provide a means of focusing on both historical and contemporary writing practices, contextualized theoretically, and on the relationships among them. The curricular invitation to students, then, is authentic: help us understand how this new world of composing works, how your own reflections can help all of us learn, and how an ePortfolio as a new genre might be constructed and shared. And critical to answering such questions, as we see in the three portfolios included here, are social spaces themselves, in the classroom, on class blogs, and on the web. Our signature pedagogy for WEPO is a distinctly social one.

Such pedagogies also invite us as teachers to develop our own social pedagogy, one where we learn separately and together how to design pedagogy, observe it systematically, share our progress, and refine what we do—all in the hope that we can do it better. It's a truism, of course, that in U.S. higher education, we are shifting from a sage-on-the-stage model of teaching to one more student centered, but critical to this educational transformation is examining the *effects* of our curricula and our pedagogy on our students. Not insignificantly, an ePortfolio shows much: our interaction with students, their in-depth understandings, and their links to other classes and other learning experiences. Through the ePortfolio, we can literally see student learning, and as our students have demonstrated, there is much to celebrate—their willingness to take risks, to talk back, to create an ePortfolio that is both personal and academic, and to imagine a self-in-process. At the same time and as our study of ePortfolios also demonstrates, we still have much to learn.

REFERENCES

Bass, R., & Elmendorf, H. (n.d.). *Designing for difficulty: Social pedagogies as a framework for course design*. Retrieved from https://commons.georgetown.edu/blogs/bassr /social-pedagogies/.

Bolter, J. D., & Grusin, R. (2000). *Remediation*. Boston: MIT Press.

Bransford, J. D., Pellegrino, J. W., & Donovan, M. S. (Eds.). (2000). *How people learn: Brain, mind, experience, and school* (expanded ed.). Washington, DC: National Academies Press.

Edgerton, R., Hutchings, P., & Quinlan, K. (1991). *The teaching portfolio: Capturing scholarship in teaching*. Washington, DC: American Association for Higher Education.

Eyman, D. (2007). *What every student should know about . . . creating a portfolio*. New York: Longman.

Gurung, R., Chick, N., & Haynie, A. (Eds.). (2008). *Exploring signature pedagogies: Approaches to teaching disciplinary habits of mind*. Sterling, VA: Stylus.

Hughes, J. (2009). Becoming ePortfolio learners and teachers. In D. Cambridge, B. Cambridge, & K. B. Yancey (Eds.), *Electronic portfolios 2.0*. (pp. 51–59). Sterling, VA: Stylus.

Penny Light, T., Sproule, B., & Lithgow, K. (2009). Connecting contexts and competencies. In D. Cambridge, B. Cambridge, & K. B. Yancey (Eds.), *Electronic portfolios 2.0*. (pp. 69–81). Sterling, VA: Stylus.

Schön, D. (1984). *The reflective practitioner: How professionals think in action*. New York: Basic Books.

Sommers, J. (1988). Behind the paper: Using the student-teacher memo. *College Composition and Communication, 39*(1), 77–80.

Sommers, N., & Saltz, L. (2004). The novice as expert: Writing the freshman year. *College Composition and Communication, 56*(1), 124–149.

Wald, H., Borkan, J. M., Taylor, J. S., Anthony, D., & Reis, S. P. (2012). Fostering and evaluating reflective capacity in medical education: Developing the REFLECT rubric for assessing reflective writing. *Academic Medicine, 87*, 41–50.

Yancey, K. B. (1996). Portfolio, electronic, and the links between. *Computers and Composition, 13*(2), 129–133.

Yancey, K. B. (1998). *Reflection in the writing classroom*. Logan, UT: Utah State University Press.

Yancey, K. B. (2004a). Made not only in words: Composition in a new key. *College Composition and Communication, 56*(2), 297–328.

Yancey, K. B. (2004b). Postmodernism, palimpsest, and portfolios: Theoretical issues in the representation of student work. *College Composition and Communication, 55*(4), 738–761.

Yancey, K. B. (2009). The impulse to compose and the age of composition. *Research in the Teaching of English, 43*, 316–338.

Yancey, K. B., Robertson, L., & Taczak, K. (Forthcoming). *Writing across contexts: Transfer, composition, and sites of writing*. Logan, UT: Utah State University Press.

Contributors

EDITORS

Matthew Kaplan is managing director of the Center for Research on Learning and Teaching (CRLT) at the University of Michigan, where he runs the day-to-day operations of the Center and collaborates with CRLT's professional staff to meet the needs of the university's instructional community. He has published on the academic hiring process, instructional technology, and the use of interactive theater for faculty development. He is coeditor of *Advancing the Culture of Teaching on Campus, The Scholarship of Multicultural Learning,* and two volumes of *To Improve the Academy,* and he has served on the Core Committee of the Professional and Organizational Development Network in Higher Education (POD).

Danielle LaVaque-Manty has a PhD in political science and an MFA in creative writing. She was a lecturer at the University of Michigan's Sweetland Center for Writing for five years, teaching courses in first-year writing, quantitative analysis and writing in the social sciences, and writing pedagogy. She is coeditor, with Abigail Stewart and Janet Malley, of *Transforming Science and Engineering: Advancing Academic Women.* Her book reviews have appeared in *Nature, Social Science Quarterly,* and *The Antioch Review,* and her short fiction in *Northwest Review* and *Glimmer Train.* She is currently a freelance academic editor and writing consultant.

Deborah Meizlish is assistant director at the Center for Research on Learning and Teaching (CRLT) at the University of Michigan. She consults with administrators, faculty, and TAs on course and curricular issues, including assessment; plans university-wide programs on teaching, learning, and academic leadership; and conducts seminars on a wide variety of pedagogical topics. Deborah coordinates CRLT's faculty grants competitions and codirects the LSA Teaching Academy. Her research and writing focus on the scholarship of teaching and learning, academic hiring, preparing future faculty developers, and academic integrity. She has a PhD in political science from the University of Michigan.

Naomi Silver is associate director of the Sweetland Center for Writing at the University of Michigan, where she also has a faculty appointment teaching courses in writing and writing pedagogy. Her research focuses on writing across the curriculum and writing in the disciplines, electronic portfolios, multimodal writing, and multiliteracy centers. She also codirects the Sweetland Digital Rhetoric Collaborative.

CONTRIBUTORS

Jeffrey L. Bernstein is a professor of political science at Eastern Michigan University. He is coeditor and contributing author of *Citizenship Across the Curriculum* (Indiana University Press, 2010). His work has appeared in journals such as the *Journal of Political Science Education, Political Research Quarterly, To Improve the Academy*, and the *Journal of the Scholarship of Teaching and Learning*, as well as in numerous edited volumes. He previously served as a faculty development fellow at Eastern Michigan University, and is a board member of the International Society for the Scholarship of Teaching and Learning.

Steven Beyerlein is a professor of mechanical engineering at the University of Idaho, where he coordinates the interdisciplinary capstone design program and is engaged in a variety of program assessment activities. These efforts, along with those of a team of colleagues, were recently recognized by the National Academy of Engineering as an exemplar of real-world engineering education. His research interests include catalytic ignition systems, student-centered learning pedagogies, and interactive learning systems.

Ahrash N. Bissell is a project manager for the Monterey Institute for Technology and Education (MITE), a consultant on innovation in education and science for several projects and foundations, and a board member for a number of organizations, including Peer 2 Peer University. His work encompasses educational research and technology, with a special focus on STEM disciplines, critical thinking and "deeper learning," open educational resources (OER), and data-sharing. Prior positions include executive director of ccLearn at Creative Commons, assistant director of the Academic Resource Center and research associate in biology at Duke University, and instructor at several universities.

Dr. Bissell has a PhD in biology (evolutionary genetics) from the University of Oregon and a BS in biology from the University of California, San Diego.

Patricia Brackin is a professor in mechanical engineering at the Rose-Hulman Institute of Technology. Her BS and MS are from the University of Tennessee, and her PhD is from the Georgia Institute of Technology. Her area of expertise is design methodology. She has significant industrial experience and is a licensed professional engineer. She has been active with the Capstone Design Conference for the past five years. In addition, she serves as an ABET program evaluator and is a current member of the Engineering Accreditation Commission of ABET. She has taught design courses at the freshman, sophomore, junior, and senior levels over the past thirty years.

Amanda J. Curtin-Soydan is assistant director of the Academic Resource Center at Duke University (Duke's undergraduate learning center). As a higher education learning specialist, Amanda works with students struggling in undergraduate science courses, and she helped develop the Science Advancement through Group Engagement (SAGE) program for high potential but academically less-well-prepared science students at Duke University. She also lectures in the biology department and conducts research in fossil and extant mammalian bone microstructure. Amanda received her BS Honors in palaeontology and MS in zoology from the University of Stellenbosch in South Africa. She received her PhD in biological sciences from Drexel University. Her research interests include bone microstructure and skeletal growth patterns, microevolution, functional morphology, and ecological physiology, as well as science education and the scholarship of teaching and learning.

Jane Danielewicz is an associate professor of English and the Hiskey Distinguished Professor in Research and Undergraduate Teaching at the University of North Carolina, Chapel Hill. She directs the first-year writing program, a genre-based writing-in-the-disciplines program that involves students in undergraduate research. Her research areas include genre studies, writing curriculum, innovative pedagogy, and an emphasis on life-writing, particularly memoir.

Denny Davis is an emeritus professor of chemical and bioengineering at Washington State University (WSU). He has led a number of National Science Foundation funded projects focused on creation and testing of instructional materials and assessments for engineering design and professional skills. For six years he directed WSU's Engineering Education Research Center, a catalyst for scholarly engineering education research. He is the recipient of numerous teaching awards and was named a Fellow of the American Society for Engineering Education (ASEE) in 2002.

E. Margaret Evans is an associate research scientist at the Center for Human Growth and Development and a lecturer in the department of psychology at the University of Michigan. Her PhD in developmental psychology focused on factors that influence the emergence of scientific and religious concepts in children and adults from diverse communities. Her subsequent work, funded by the Spencer Foundation, the National Academy of Education, and the National Science Foundation (NSF), has built on this foundation. Most recently, she has integrated these studies into research projects and exhibit development for five different exhibits on evolution and related topics, funded by NSF and the National Institutes of Health. In this work, she and her colleagues have developed informal learning experiences for children and students of all ages.

Leigh Graziano is a PhD student in rhetoric and composition at Florida State University. She has taught courses in the first-year composition program and the editing, writing, and media major. Leigh has delivered conference presentations at both the Conference on College Composition and Communication and the Rhetoric Society of America. Her dissertation research focuses on bringing the currently unclassified phenomena of vernacular memorials into the rhetorical canon in order to broaden our understanding of twenty-first-century rhetorical praxis.

Elizabeth Ashley Hall is a PhD candidate at the University of North Carolina, where she has been trained in rhetoric and composition, digital rhetoric, pedagogy, curriculum design, and writing program administration. Ashley is a cofounder of the *People, Ideas, and Things (PIT) Journal*.

M. Javed Khan is professor and head of the Department of Aerospace Science Engineering at Tuskegee University. He received his doctorate from Texas A&M, his MS from the U.S. Air Force Institute of Technology and his BE from the PAF College of Aeronautical Engineering in Pakistan. His experience spans academics and industry. His disciplinary research includes aircraft design, configuration aerodynamics, and vortex-dominated flows. He is actively involved in engineering education and has received several grants and contracts from the National Science Foundation, NASA, and the Army for improving K–12 math and science education, incorporating innovative learning modules into undergraduate education and improving the visualization skills of soldiers.

Mika LaVaque-Manty is an Arthur F. Thurnau Professor and an associate professor of political science and philosophy at the University of Michigan. His most recent book, *The Playing Fields of Eton* (2009), explores controversies about equality and excellence in modern meritocracy from the eighteenth century to the present. His work increasingly combines questions from political theory–for example, what practices and institutions foster autonomy–with scholarship on teaching and learning. He is a member of the University of Michigan's Learning Analytics Task Force.

Rory Lee is a PhD candidate in rhetoric and composition at Florida State University and a teaching assistant in the first-year composition program and the editing, writing, and media undergraduate English major. He also has served as the director of the English department's Digital Studios and has presented at several conferences, including the Conference on College Composition and Communication, and Computers and Composition. Rory is currently working on his dissertation, which explores the role of multimodality within undergraduate majors in writing and rhetoric.

Paul R. Leiffer is a professor in the School of Engineering and Engineering Technology at LeTourneau University, where he has taught since 1979. He is currently chair of the Department of Engineering. He received his BSEE from the State University of New York at Buffalo and his MS and PhD degrees from Drexel University. Prior to joining the faculty at LeTourneau, he was involved in cardiac cell research at the University of Kansas Medical Center. He has worked with engineering senior teams for over ten years and has collaborated with the IDEALS capstone assessment project since 2006. His professional interests include biomedical signal processing, engineering education, and engineering ethics.

Paula P. Lemons is an assistant professor in the Department of Biochemistry and Molecular Biology at the University of Georgia. Her research focuses on discovering how undergraduates solve problems and the processes by which faculty change their teaching practices. Her long-term goal is to help transform undergraduate biology courses into learning communities where students actively engage in problem solving, coached and guided by reflective teachers. Paula obtained her PhD in biochemistry from the University of Kentucky and served as a postdoctoral scholar at Duke University.

Marsha C. Lovett is director of the Eberly Center for Teaching Excellence and a teaching professor in the Department of Psychology, both at Carnegie

Mellon University. At the Eberly Center, she applies theoretical and empirical principles from cognitive psychology to help instructors improve their teaching. In her research, Dr. Lovett studies learning, memory, and problem solving. She has published more than fifty research articles on learning and instruction. Dr. Lovett has also developed several innovative educational technologies to promote student learning and metacognition, including StatTutor and the Learning Dashboard.

Jay McCormack is an assistant professor in the mechanical engineering department at the University of Idaho, where he is an instructor for the college's interdisciplinary capstone design course. Dr. McCormack received his PhD in mechanical engineering from Carnegie Mellon University in 2003. Prior to joining the University of Idaho, he cofounded a company that created computational tools for printed circuit board design. His areas of research include engineering education, computational design, and increasing the accessibility of design and fabrication tools for a broad audience.

Jennifer O'Malley is a PhD student in rhetoric and composition at Florida State University, where she has taught courses in the first-year composition program and the editing, writing, and media undergraduate English major. She has served as the assistant to the director of the First-Year Composition Program and the editorial assistant for the journal *College Composition and Communication*. She has presented at several conferences, including the International Writing across the Curriculum conference. Jennifer's dissertation research focuses on the social turn in composition studies and the effect of curriculum on students' understanding and enactment of the social turn in their writing.

Julie A. Reynolds is associate director of Undergraduate Studies and an assistant professor of the practice in the biology department at Duke University. Her research focuses primarily on writing-to-learn pedagogies across the STEM disciplines and on pedagogies of engagement that promote learning for diverse student populations. She is an Atlantic Coast Conference Teaching Scholar, a facilitator for the American Society for Microbiology's Biology Scholars Program, and vice president for Education and Human Resources for the Ecological Society of America.

Michael Trevisan is a professor of educational psychology and interim dean for the College of Education at Washington State University. For the past eighteen years he has collaborated with Dr. Denny Davis on the development and assessment of professional skills in undergraduate engineering education. The work was supported by several grants from the National Science Foundation and resulted in numerous conference presentations, proceedings, and journal articles. Dr. Trevisan is associate director for the Learning & Performance Research Center at Washington State University. He has published widely in the fields of measurement, assessment, and evaluation.

Jennifer Ware is a Mellon postdoctoral fellow in the Institute for the Arts and Humanities at the University of North Carolina at Chapel Hill. She is a technical editor for *Enculturation: A Journal for Writing, Rhetoric, and Culture*. Her research interests include digital media, multimedia production, new media assessment, and changes in networks due to the introduction of new technologies. Ware has worked for Landmark Communications/The Virginian-Pilot newspaper as an online video advertising director/producer and for a CBS affiliate as a broadcast journalist.

Ralph Williams is an Arthur F. Thurnau Professor Emeritus in the Department of English Language and Literature at the University of Michigan. He specializes in Medieval and Renaissance literature, Shakespeare, literary theory, comparative literature, and Biblical studies. He has taught such wide-ranging courses as The Bible in English, the literature of Chaucer to Frederick Douglass, and the works of Primo Levi and the Memory of Auschwitz. Dr. Williams was instrumental in creating and developing the Royal Shakespeare Company (RSC) Residency program at the University of Michigan. He continues to work closely with the University Musical Society to further the activities of the RSC Residency.

Mary C. Wright is director of assessment and associate research scientist at the Center for Research on Learning and Teaching (CRLT) at the University of Michigan (U-M). She works with U-M's faculty and academic units on assessment of student learning, evaluation of educational initiatives, and the scholarship of teaching and learning. Her research interests include teaching cultures, graduate student professional development, undergraduate retention in the sciences, and qualitative research and evaluation methods. Her book, *Always at Odds?: Creating Alignment Between Faculty and Administrative Values*, was published in 2008 by SUNY Press. Mary has served as an external evaluator for several National Science Foundation grants and is a member of the Core Committee of the Professional and Organizational Development (POD)

Network in Higher Education. She earned an AB in sociology from Princeton University, an MA and PhD in sociology from the University of Michigan, and an MA in higher education from the Center for the Study of Higher and Post-secondary Education at U-M.

Kathleen Blake Yancey is a Kellogg W. Hunt Professor of English and Distinguished Research Professor at Florida State University, where she directs the graduate program in Rhetoric and Composition Studies. She has served in several national leadership roles—as president of the National Council of Teachers of English and Chair of the Conference on College Composition and as cofounder and director of the Inter/National Coalition for Electronic Portfolio Research, which has brought together over 60 institutions world-wide to document the reflective learning that takes place inside and around electronic portfolios. She is the author, editor, or coeditor of over 75 chapters and refereed articles and eleven books, among them *Portfolios in the Writing Classroom* (1992), *Assessing Writing Across the Curriculum* (1997), *Electronic Portfolios* (2001), *Teaching Literature as Reflective Practice* (2004), *Delivering College Composition* (2006), and *Electronic Portfolios 2.0.* (2009).

Index

Cooperative Learning in Higher Education

Across the Disciplines, Across the Academy

Edited by Barbara Millis

Research has identified cooperative learning as one of the ten High Impact Practices that improve student learning.

If you've been interested in cooperative learning, but wondered how it would work in your discipline, this book provides the necessary theory, and a wide range of concrete examples.

The chapters showcase cooperative learning in action, at the same time introducing the reader to major principles such as individual accountability, positive interdependence, heterogeneous teams, group processing, and social or leadership skills.

Blended Learning

Across the Disciplines, Across the Academy

Edited by Francine S. Glazer

Foreword by James Rhem

This is a practical introduction to blended learning, presenting examples of implementation across a broad spectrum of disciplines. For faculty unfamiliar with this mode of teaching, it illustrates how to address the core challenge of blended learning—to link the activities in each medium so that they reinforce each other to create a single, unified, course—and offers models they can adapt.

Sty/us

22883 Quicksilver Drive

Sterling, VA 20166-2102   Subscribe to our e-mail alerts: www.Styluspub.com

Also in the New Pedagogies and Practices for Teaching in Higher Education series:

Series Editor: James Rhem, executive editor of the premier higher education newsletter, *The National Teaching & Learning Forum*

Each volume of the series presents a specific pedagogy. The editors and contributors introduce the reader to the underlying theory and methodology, provide specific guidance in applying the pedagogy, and offer case studies of practice across a several disciplines, usually across the domains of the sciences, humanities, and social studies, and, if appropriate, professional studies.

Team Teaching
Across the Disciplines, Across the Academy
Edited by Kathryn M. Plank

For those considering adopting team teaching, or interested in reviewing their own practice, this book offers an overview of this pedagogy, its challenges and rewards, and a rich range of examples in which teachers present and reflect upon their approaches.

This book provides insight into the impact of team teaching on student learning and on faculty development. It also addresses the challenges, both pedagogical and administrative, that need to be addressed for team teaching to be effective.

Just-in-Time Teaching
Across the Disciplines, Across the Academy
Edited by Scott Simkins and Mark H. Maier

"*Just-in-Time Teaching* commendably promotes the pedagogical procedure that bears its name. The book is an excellent resource for professors who are serious pursuers of improving students' learning... The text is adeptly compiled and skillfully written."—*Teaching Theology and Religion*

"I found the ideas presented by the authors intriguing, and I'm already thinking about how I'm going to make use of them myself."— *EDC Resource Review*

Just-in-Time Teaching (JiTT) is a pedagogical approach that requires students to answer questions related to an upcoming class a few hours beforehand, using an online course management system. While the phrase "just in time" may evoke shades of slap-dash work and cut corners, JiTT pedagogy is just the opposite. It helps students to view learning as a process that takes time, introspection, and persistence.